Doubts and Decisions
for Living

VOLUME II
The Sanctity of Human Spirit

(Enhanced Edition)

List of Books by This Author
(As of June 20, 2020)[*]

Non-fiction

The Nature of Love and Relationships 2011, **2016**
Doubts and Decisions for Living:
  Volume I: The Foundation of Human Thoughts **2014**
  Volume II: The Sanctity of Human Spirit **2014**
  Volume III: The Structure of Human Life **2014**
Relationship Facts, Trends, and Choices **2016**
The Mysteries of Life, Love, and Happiness **2016**
Relationship Needs, Framework, and Models **2016**
Gender Qualities, Quirks, and Quarrels **2016**
Marriage and Divorce Hardships **2016**
Being Better Beings **2020**

Fiction

Persian Moons 2007, **2016**
Midnight Gate-opener 2011, **2016**
My Lousy Life Stories **2014**
Persian Suns **2021 (Planned)**

---

[*] 12 older books are Enhanced Editions and printed in 2020. They were resubmitted to the Library and Archives Canada Cataloguing as well. If a book's 'print date' on the copyright page is older, the newest version is available at Amazon and bookstores.

Doubts and Decisions
for Living

VOLUME II
The Sanctity of Human Spirit

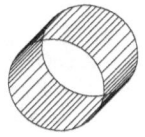

Tom Omidi, Ph.D.

Copyright © 2014 by Tom Omidi
Copyright © 2020 by Tom Omidi

All rights reserved. No part of this book may be reproduced, translated, or transmitted in any form or by any means—graphic, electronic or mechanical, including photocopying, recording, taping or information storage or retrieval systems—without the prior written permission of the publisher or author.

Omidi, Tom, 1945-, author
Doubts and decisions for living / Tom Omidi, Ph.D.

Contents: Volume I. The foundation of human thoughts
Volume II. The sanctity of human spirit
Volume III. The structure of human life.

ISBN 978-1-988351-11-7 (v. 1 : pbk.).
ISBN 978-1-988351-12-4 (v. 2 : pbk.).
ISBN 978-1-988351-13-1 (v. 3 : pbk.).

1. Conduct of life. I. Title.
II. Title: Foundation of human thoughts.
III. Title: Sanctity of human spirit.
IV. Title: Structure of human life.

Old Edition at
Library and Archives Canada Cataloguing in Publication
BJ1581.2.O45 2014   170'.44   C2014-903378-8

Cover page design by Tom Omidi

Published by Eros Books,
Vancouver, British Columbia
Canada

erosbooks2020.@gmail.com

Enhanced and Printed in 2020

For my children

"And you…!?
"When will you begin that
 long journey into yourself?"
                    Rumi

Table of Contents

	Page
Author's Note	1
A Heads-up for the Youths	5
Introduction	8

PART I: Psychology and Spirituality

Chapter One: The Scope of Human Needs	17
Recognizing Our Unconscious Needs	21
Boosting Our Spirits	22
The Spiritual Sensations of Self-actualizers	24
The Unity of Psychology and Spirituality	29
The Main Personal Dilemmas	31
Preparing Our Minds and Attitudes	33
Chapter Two: Quest for the Truth	37
Human Logic's Reliability	40
Logic, Reality, Divinity	45
The Awareness Intersection	50
Facing the Reality	53
Our Main Struggles	56

PART II: Science and Divinity

Chapter Three: The Role and Goal of Spirituality	63
The Role of Religion	65
The Role of Science	66
The Role of Spirituality	67
The Role of a Divine Personal Life Philosophy	68
The Purposes of Spirituality	69
Shortfalls of the Present Spirituality Approach	71
Chapter Four: Spirituality and Philosophy	79
The Plausible Truth	85
The Truth about the Universe	86
The Truth about Our Personal Lives	87
The Truth about Humanity	88

Table of Contents (Cont.)

	Page

PART III: Potentialities and Dilemmas

Chapter Five: The Spirit in Human Potentialities 101
    The Makeup of Our Potentialities 103
    The Functions of Our Potentialities 105
    The Collective Treasures of Human Potentialities .. 107
Chapter Six: Career (Genetic) Potentialities 109
    The Reality of Job Markets 111
    The Implications of Unfulfilling Professions 112
Chapter Seven: Divine (Organic) Potentialities 117
    'Self' Dilemmas 121
    Who Cares 'Who We Are?' 123
    What Are We Here for, Really? 127
    Self-assessment Challenge 134
    Selflessness Attributes 139
    Selflessness Structure 141
    The Final Judgment 141
Chapter Eight: Humans' Insights and Foresights 145
    Potentialities and Opportunities 145
    Potentialities and Confidence 147
    Potentialities and Fairness 150
    Potentialities and Interests 153
    Potentialities and Perseverance 154

PART IV: Limitations and Victories

Chapter Nine: Living Limitations 157
    Social and Economic Limitations 157
    Natural Limitations (Physical and Mental) 161
    Personality Limitations 163
    Self-imposed Limitations 164
    Timing Limitations 166
    The Ultimate Limitation 169

Table of Contents (Cont.)

	Page
Chapter Ten: Personal Beliefs and Choices	175
Abstract Experiences	178
Real Experiences	185
Life's Miracles	193
The Ultimate Victory	197

PART V: Commonsense and Self-awareness

Chapter Eleven: The Conflicting Roles of Our Doubts	203
The Nature and Level of Our Doubts	206
The Scope and Effects of Our Doubts	207
Our Doubts about Human Nature	211
Managing Our Doubts and Decisions	215
The Benefit of a Doubt	223
Chapter Twelve: Commonsense's Role	225
Developing a 'Cultured' Commonsense	228
The Value of Out Thoughts	231
Life's Major Dilemmas and Decisions	235
Chapter Thirteen: Knowing (about) Ourselves	239
Spirituality	241
Potentiality	244
Individualism (Integrity, Compassion)	248
Relationships	252
Contributions	258
Growth	260
Social Responsibilities	263
The Integral 'Self'	265
'Self' and Fate	265

PART VI: Doubts and Decisions

Chapter Fourteen: Positives Doubts (Vibes)	273
1. Social Doubts	275
2. Personal Doubts	279
The Special Case of Self-doubt	283
3. Interpersonal Doubts	285

Table of Contents (Cont.)

	Page
Chapter Fourteen: Positives Doubts (Cont.)	
4. Supernatural Doubts	288
5. Spiritual Doubts	293
Doubts' Natural Fusion	296
Chapter Fifteen: Negative Doubts (Vibes)	297
Our Doubts' Ultimate Wisdom	299
Boosting Our Decisions' Quality	308
A Chance for Personal Salvation	310
Chapter Sixteen: Decisions plus Destiny	315
Decision-making Options	318
Decision-making Factors	322
Decision-making Conditions	326
Decision-making Elements	327
Decision-making Criteria	332
Another Heads-up for the Youths	334
Epilogue	335
Appendix A: Humans' Egological Conditions	339
Appendix B: Logic Aversion Drive	340
Appendix C: Humans in the Universe	345

List of Tables and Diagrams

Table 3.1: The Main Characteristics and Purposes of Spirituality	69
Table 4.1: Basic Guidelines for Building Spirituality	97
Diagram 7.1: Selflessness Structure and Attributes	141
Diagram 11.1: Level, Nature, and Type of Doubts	207
Diagram 11.2: Domain of Intelligence and Thoughts	220
Diagram A.1: Humans' Egological Conditions	339
Table B.1: Decision Inaccuracy Ratings	344
Diagram C.1: Humans' Inner Connections	346
Diagram C.2: Humans' Outer connections with the Universe	347
Diagram C.3: Humans' Outer connections with Society	348

Author's Note

Something extraordinary seems to have happened in the last few decades to make most parents too concerned about, and attached to, their kids, much beyond the customary levels in the previous generations. For one thing, the rivalry among families to give their kids the best of everything has put most parents on edge, as they strive to indulge their kids and be the best parents they can be, to the point of often appearing too liberal and submissive. The rising social chaos and complexity is another factor that makes us anxious and more protective of our kids. We hope to give them enough confidence and guidance to handle life's inevitable pains and disappointments most graciously. Parents of my generation were not so concerned and attached to their kids and they did not show their love and worries adequately, if at all. Maybe they were too relaxed, but their approach seemed more practical, natural, and in line with humans' inherent need to find their own ways of living. We learned much faster to become self-sufficient and get ready for life's hardships. But now, things have changed and we have been drawn into this overly liberal, yet protective, mentality towards our kids. Still, we do not get the right results, while we also keep wondering whether we are fulfilling our duties. We are not sure whether our approach is appropriate and our guidance is helpful to them. Nobody is quite sure about this matter anymore! Actually, the outcome so far indicates that the youths have been too spoiled for their own good. They have indeed become more confused about the purpose of life. Instead of learning humility, which is the seed for exploring our spirituality and identity, the youths are encouraged to maximize their individuality, happiness, confidence, and success through aggression, arrogance, greed, competition, and sexuality. They are driven by fashion, fantasy, and superficiality. They do not learn much about humans' innate limitations and potentialities, or about humans' spirit that must be raised only through self-realization, not self-gratification. In this superficial environment, it is doubtful that anybody can grow a moral mentality or any sense of spirituality to lift his/her spirit.

Our intention to guide our kids also fails due to our deformed perceptions of success and happiness. We not only keep defining them erroneously and push them on our kids, too, but also feel entitled to them automatically despite our shoddy lifestyles. Thus, while we doubt the meaning and means of capturing success and happiness subconsciously, both parents and society are ruining the youths' chance to recognize life's realities as well. The youths grow high expectations for all kinds of privileges and happiness, which they believe results from their shallow pleasures without building pious minds. Thus, they get confused and overwhelmed when they encounter daily turmoil. They have no clue or patience regarding the huge amount of efforts and sacrifices needed just to maintain a simple life, never mind attaining that elusive happiness that only a few people with grasp of 'self' might achieve.

We like to develop our kids' mentalities, wisdom, spirits, and lifestyles by explaining the rules and values of the prevalent life structure. Yet, parents and societies' guidance cannot depict life's realities, since we have not even fixed our personal convictions, have no realistic notion of spirituality, and fail to see the vanity of our modern lifestyles. We cannot help our kids when personal and socioeconomic defects have crippled our own lives. Without revamping our mentalities and values substantially according to a more compassionate vision of the world and society, we cannot get a proper sense of our spirits or help our children build theirs amidst the chaos we have inherited and forced to accept as the best option for living.

Naturally, learning about ourselves and grasping the daunting risks of our present values is hard for most of us. Yet, gaining this basic level of wisdom is the only way to build both our own and our kids' spirits. We must find our sense of spirituality outside the prevalent lifestyles without recourse to religious teachings, away from the positive thinking propagandas that mislead us, and by avoiding our own personal prejudices, which are usually the most limiting factor for helping our kids.

Exploring human spirit and hoping to boost it naturally in ourselves or our children is surely a daunting task. For one thing, our genetics, rearing experiences, and personality defects hinder a person's capacity to explore his/her divine potentialities, embrace spirituality, and feel the essence of his/her being. Moreover, the unrelenting social pressures on us, especially the youths, make the objective of independent thinking and soul-searching almost impossible. We are all too attracted to the rewards and promises of modern life and crave social acceptance desperately. Thus, we hardly find time or motivation to attend to the deeper aspects of our being, i.e., spirit and 'self,' that are ambiguous dimensions of humans, anyway, and quite an abstract topic.

For enriching my kids' lives, I *strived* to provide them with a rather calm and comfortable environment, all the privileges that other kids enjoy in modern societies, and a presumably liberal, open communication channel. My goal was to help them build strong, independent minds to grasp the hassles and beauties of life realistically, away from the debilitating notions of the illusive world engulfing us all. By learning about various obstacles and traps of our prominent life structure, I hoped they would be ready to face life's hardships positively, make the right decisions, and succeed in pursuing a simple lifestyle with the least amount of frustration and setbacks. They needed a basic, solid foundation of thoughts and a reliable knowledgebase about the structure of life, but also the right beliefs, personality, and outlook to withstand disappointments and proceed confidently with optimism, despite all the pervasive clues about the social chaos surrounding us. I wanted to tell them about the power and sanctity of their spirits. However, it all proved a very tough chore.

Discussing spirituality with our kids in a sensible format—maybe as a divine, hidden personal potentiality and the conduit for freeing our spirits—is difficult for everybody. In particular, unreligious parents like me, with no sacred stories to support our beliefs, face a bigger challenge discussing some vague notions of spirituality to invoke our kids' spirits. On the one hand, religious families have a better chance to inject their faith in their kids' heads and naively believe they have satisfied their kids' spiritual needs, too. On the other hand, unreligious people usually have a better chance of finding their own spirituality and reviving their spirits more honestly and naturally.

Thus, this volume of *Doubts and Decisions for living* outlines the task of building our spirits and spirituality by firming up our personal beliefs, identities, and positivism. Ultimately, only our private sense of spirituality can help us restore our frigid identities and strengthen our spirits without recourse to religions or some crude positive thinking mottos. This requires self-analysis and self-cleansing, while resisting all social temptations and wicked personalities that always attempt to manipulate our souls. After all, we must honour the sanctity of our spirit that is overwhelmed by all the superficialities and egoism within and around us.

This trilogy also stresses on the importance of making many major life decisions and choosing a practical path of life. Sadly, achieving satisfactory results and finding peace have become too difficult, especially for the youths that must handle more natural and social mayhem every generation, while the whole civilization has lost its way. Still, this and other volumes of this trilogy might help in making the cumbersome task of existence a bit easier if one takes the time to test some of the points raised in these books.

Happy reading
Tom Omidi, Ph.D.
Vancouver, 2014

A Heads-up for the Youths

Every generation must make finer and timelier decisions just to survive financially and emotionally. Sadly, they would face more doubts and challenges, including a harder time to communicate with their parents or among themselves as friends and marriage partners. Worst of all, they would not have the right mindsets and decision criteria to make their major life decisions properly. Yet, they should make those crucial decisions when they lack enough wisdom, patience, and guidance, but a lot of bad influence. Thus, their fluid decisions often derail the course of their lives. They spend many years at universities and colleges, and then end up following unrelated careers they do not enjoy for the rest of their lives. They make their marriage decisions based on crude values that society endorses, nowadays. Their raw decision criteria lead to tough conditions along with confusion and depression.

The main point of this heads-up to the youths is to make them remember forever that often we get surprised by finding out, at a later stage of our lives, how perfunctory our decision, especially about love, success, and happiness, had been. After many years of pains in pursuit of wealth or love, our raw criteria of happiness and success prove too naive. How foolish a person feels when s/he reaches that sad conclusion! So many precious years of lost youth, wasted efforts, vain thoughts, and unnecessary concerns! If only I knew! What if my parents were intelligent enough to direct me at least to the books that could give me a better sense of better things in life rather than just passing on their materialistic values of so-called civilized social living? What if I had some friends, books, or other sources to learn the wisdom of thinking for myself? What if I had realized what decisions were so crucial to make timely? Quite often, we feel sad for not having enough time and energy to change many things that we now wish we could have done differently.

Depending on our decisions' outcomes, we end up living with a sense of success or failure for years. Besides our senses of guilt and regret, we blame ourselves for not assessing our life options and their consequences adequately when we had a chance. Thus, our spirits shatter, while our doubts about existence become more complex and confusing. Sometimes, we can change the course of our lives when we are in our mid-life or old ages to pursue a more authentic lifestyle and find some peace. Yet, the problem is that at those ages we are usually trapped in binding circumstances caused by our earlier decisions. Escaping those traps will be hard, and it will take a longer time to fathom, and adjust to, a new life path. Our decision-making options deplete fast as we age.

Sometimes, we seek refuge in others to escape our depressing lives or get advice for making decisions; we may even resort to a stranger or fortune-teller if we are desperate. Some of us are ultra conservative and fear the risks of every decision. And, of course, sometimes, merely our deep emotional turmoil numb or distort our decision-making ability, e.g., during love related situations. Our fear to decide or act is usually due to our inexperience or bad experiences. However, it mostly shows that we have not built a proper foundation for thinking and setting our beliefs. We have not chosen a proper life path and decision criteria.

Nevertheless, we are responsible for our decisions' outcomes, since blaming people, external factors, and destiny is futile. One way to ensure we fulfil our responsibility is to enter into a clear, conscious contract with ourselves regarding every major decision after projecting its expected rewards and risks and remembering that the 'future self' would find us accountable for the decisions made today and condemn our negligence or naïveté harshly.

Despite his aversion to give advice—just to avoid annoying people or embarrassing himself—, thirty basic points or words of wisdom *(the author's precious two cents!)* are also outlined in the Epilogue of Volume I mainly for the youths' benefits.

Introduction

Each volume of this trilogy is largely about one of the three main functions of humans, i.e., thinking, feeling, and doing. Our dire, lifelong doubts and decisions arise from our thoughts, sentiments and actions, too. Volume I focuses on the 'thinking' function mostly by studying humans' philosophical dilemmas and our motives and means for building the foundation of our thoughts. Volume III explains the 'doing' function, as we traverse within a preordained structure of life hesitantly. We try to cope with the peculiarities of socioeconomic environment by doing the right things and making the best decisions.

This book (Volume II) explores the 'feeling' function mostly by reviewing the role and vigour of our spirits for guiding our authentic urges, accessing our sacred senses, and finding peace and happiness. Our spirits also provide the energy and insight to soothe our erratic thoughts and stressful encounters. If we let our spirit sink, life's daily setbacks make us feel lonely and helpless. Building and maintaining our spirits is quite onerous, however, nowadays, for many reasons raised in this volume. It is becoming harder every day to stay positive and keep our hopes high when we should live in such diseased, confusing societies and deal with hypocritical and egocentric individuals regularly.

Nevertheless, grasping the realm of our spirit and learning how to empower it through a personally defined spirituality is the only way to bear life's hardships and maybe even build a rather peaceful existence. As another natural wonder of the universe, fortunately, our urge for spirituality is very deep within us like a conduit for appeasing our spirits. Of course, attaining this private sense of divinity is a personal challenge, which neither religions nor scholars can explain to us or help us attain. We should set out to grasp it on our own in a hard way. Then, we can draw on this natural source of inner strength and intuition readily to establish our personal beliefs, build our identity, and keep our spirit intact. Otherwise, we would just stagger along with the cocky crowd without knowing who we are and what we are living for.

Regardless of the possibility of God's existence and the tiny chance for afterlife, human spirit is a plausible reality. Our spirits manifest regularly during our selfless rituals, and sometimes the sensation becomes heavenly during self-actualization experiences and moments of awakening. Almost everybody is familiar with this sacred feature of being, which might also be our main point of distinction from animals. Without our divine spirits guiding and empowering us, we soon perish under the pressures of life's hardships and self-inflicted pains. Yet, nurturing and keeping our spirits high is a tough mission, too, considering the heartbreaks and pains of living in allegedly modern societies. Our encounters with people, including friends and family, as well as social rules and hypocrisies, drain our spirits and we never get a chance to find a relative sense of freedom, let alone a notion of spirituality and connection to the real world. The high stress and confusion that our educational systems, work environments, marriages, and family relationships cause us are reviewed in Volume III of this trilogy. We feel entrapped with no chance to build our identities and appreciate the power and sanctity of our spirits. We simply plough on through a superficial life structure rather aimlessly and become more arrogant, demanding, and shallow.

Meanwhile, we cannot avoid many questions boggling our minds, such as, "Can humans ever develop a healthy mentality and a more natural lifestyle to nurture their spirits and earn the wisdom for living more peacefully? Will we ever give ourselves a chance to explore the real world and understand the truth about existence, which might be somewhat more meaningful than what we have fathomed so far after millenniums of thinking, fighting, and pains? Will we ever tame our Egos and neediness in order to explore and find our 'self'?" Can we ever conceive and apply socioeconomic and political mechanisms that can help us in the long run? Sadly, the history and new trends in human mentality give a resounding answer 'no' to the above questions. We are just too naïve and absorbed in our illusions to learn anything from our debilitating experiences and social havoc that is getting more out of hand every day.

The effects of keeping the mass on the globe in dark through religions and politics have brought us to this abyss and no way out of this mess seems to exist, while the rich and elites are in charge of educating and exploiting the population. The confused mass is also guilty for its tenacity to stay ignorant in their shallow shells with their religious beliefs and self-gratifying social values. Their random resistance or whining is answered with hostility, yet many people cannot give up even when their intentions are misrepresented, ridiculed, or dismissed. They are too spirited to lose hope, though. After all, waiting for humanity's demise feels absurd, although this fate seems inevitable more every day.

For now, however, no viable option for human salvation seem to exist, while we try to cope with the status quo and wait for that final blow in our faces to grasp the irrationality of our lifestyles and mentalities. We do not have the courage and motivation to change ourselves and resist the alluring symbols of modern life, while our illusions about pleasure and freedom are merely raising our confusions and burdens of living. How can we humans do this to ourselves? Why are we so stupid?

Ironically, exploring our spirits and spirituality is a natural urge, mostly as a direct by-product of self-awareness. The more we learn about our inner nature as a human, the more our sense of spirituality emerges naturally and the freer our spirits become.

Basic self-awareness and spiritualism are on the same continuum, although reaching enlightenment needs determination, sacrifice, and patience to go thru a long process of learning and exploring. Still, it would be an easier task for people with curiosity about life and 'self' than it is for religious fanatics with set mentalities and reluctance to look for the truth independently. Brainwashing kids' minds with religious tales would only restrict their chances for self-awareness and self-ridden spirituality. The youths, especially, need guidance to think independently and find their own inherent potentialities, including divinity, gradually, the same way they learn about all other facts based on their instincts, research, logic, and intelligence.

Then again, who has the responsibility and means of warning the youths of the repercussions of doomed social norms mixed with business tactics to keep people's spirits high artificially with shoddy slogans about positive thinking or living in the now? Who would teach them that society's attempt to spread positivism only makes people more confused and anxious? And that these slogans and philosophies are mostly for washing people's minds for economic purposes. Many of the positive thinking mottos in the recent era, in fact, harm us when they often do not match our personalities or the overall workings of human psyche. They hurt us, as we fail to fulfil those illusive dreams that positive thinking and modern living promises. Our illusions merely distract us from learning and facing the growing harsh realities of life in the 21st century head on. Instead, we only hide behind an immense veil of desires, get flustered, and nag regularly when our fantasies, even if fulfilled, do not bring us the happiness and authentic positivity that only our liberated spirits can offer naturally.

The brief discussions of spirituality in this volume reflect its importance for boosting our beliefs and spirits, and for satiating our curiosity about existence. However, spirituality is also crucial for developing the foundation of our thoughts and gauging the validity of our lifestyles. Sadly, the present state of spirituality and the approach it has taken so far cannot help the public much.

Its existing dire shortfalls are explained in Chapter Three. Thus, if a reader is interested to know the author's notion of spirituality in advance, s/he may read Chapter Three first. Yet, besides general suggestions, this book does not get into the details of building our spirituality, which is a mission to explore mostly personally.

An inherent link also exists between our spirit and psyche, but it should be fortified thru spirituality by gauging our urges and needs' authenticity and revamping our deluded mentalities about life and 'self'. We must come to terms with our neglected, pained spirits somehow by growing a personal sense of spirituality and feeling our link to the universe. This self-awareness would also help us gauge our beliefs, curiosities, and doubts about the matter of existence per se. We build a rather positive attitude about life and people, despite all the injustice and cruelties out there, and we become better and humbler human beings. Accordingly, our notion of spirituality develops naturally and independently, which feels authentic and sensible. At the same time, our invigorated spirituality bolsters both our psyches and spirits to redefine and enrich our lives, as explained in the following chapters.

Many spiritualists' ideologies sound quite attractive and they might be even useful for curbing people's need for feeling and expressing divinity. However, we require a more natural mode of spirituality to help us grasp 'who we are,' and reach a relative sense of peace and freedom within our chaotic socioeconomic environment. In fact, a progressive type of spirituality, based on intelligence and scepticism, would probably be the best way to defeat the global gullibility that religions and rulers of the world have injected in the public's minds. Especially, some spiritualists' certitude and persistence about the absolute truthfulness of their ideologies hinder the task of exploring spirituality and ruin even the basic effects of their words and efforts. In all, it is imprudent to get carried away by some illogical claims and certitude about the existence of God or another life form for humans beyond their earthly being. Some hollow spirituality claims should not delude us again now, like what religions have done for centuries.

Besides the theoretical explorations about spirituality in this book, the author's interpretations, based on personal experiences and feelings (as presented in Chapter Ten), are included only as examples and insights for building his foundation of thoughts. In the end, the spirituality topics and quotes in this book are only philosophical conjectures and nothing more.

Book's Structure

Part I addresses the psychological and spirituality dimensions of humans and their links. Chapter One explains how satisfying our varied needs can empower our spirits and senses of spirituality, or merely disrupt even our basic touch with our psyches and spirits. Chapter Two discusses our quests for the truth and strengthening our spirits. Conversely, our spirits drive our quests for the truth mostly thru spiritualism. This natural drive in humans for finding the truth and the 'self' by itself proves the existence of spirit.

Part II delves into topics of science and divinity in hopes of finding a rationale for our spirituality choices and the means of developing it methodically gradually. Chapter Three reviews the role and goal of spirituality and explains the need for discovering our own private sense of divinity independently outside religions and social influences. Chapter Four explains spirituality as a main pillar for both human identity and the foundation of our thoughts. After all, our search for the truth—mainly for managing our lives —requires both a solid foundation of thoughts and a strong spirit to withstand the pressures of living.

Part III discusses human potentialities and dilemmas in order to develop both our careers and spirits. We can use our divine potentialities to understand our personal and social limitations and expand our self-awareness. Chapter Five explores the nature and purpose of our potentialities. Chapter Six reviews our career related potentialities for making a living, though at the high risk of dampening our spirits and divine urges in the process. Chapter Seven discusses the role of our potentialities for pursuing our interests, building our confidence, and facing social unfairness.

Chapter Eight discusses humans' insights and foresights in line with their potentialities.

Part IV explains personal and social limitations and ultimate victories despite incessant setbacks and disappointments. Chapter Nine explores the nature of life's limitations as well as social and self-imposed limitations as obstacles for using our potentialities and building our spirits. Chapter Ten explains how our beliefs, faith, and compassion evolve and boost our spirits, which would in turn reinforce our willpower, faith, and beliefs. Some of the author's important life experiences leading to his spiritual beliefs are also discussed in this chapter.

Part V reviews commonsense and self-awareness as the main tools for managing our doubts and decisions effectively, and for keeping our spirits intact. Chapter Eleven studies the conflicting roles of our positive and negative doubts. Chapter Twelve studies our commonsense. Chapter Thirteen describes the mission of learning *who we are* by exploring the seven elements of 'self.'

Part VI tackles life's major decisions and doubts for building our outlooks on life and finding happiness. Chapters Fourteen and Fifteen explain our positive and negative doubts in some length respectively. Chapter Sixteen explains the factors, conditions, elements, and criteria for making our major life decisions.

Appendices A, B, and C at the end of the book provide some rather technical theories as well as a summary of crucial concepts discussed in this book about the role and position of humans in the universe and society.

The quotes from esteemed scholars in this book are merely for reflecting worthy viewpoints on related topics without any prejudice. They are plausible opinions stated liberally in public domains regarding such philosophical topics, thus have become relevant for general review purposes. Although the author does not necessarily agree or disagree with them, they are precious points that interested readers are encouraged to check in those books for further detail and reflection.

PART I
Psychology and Spirituality

CHAPTER ONE
The Scope of Human Needs

We have three types of needs: Physical, psychological, spiritual. The physical type is comprised of tangible, basic needs that are evident since birth as our means of survival and bodily growth. These needs are intuitive and usually fulfilled as a matter of habit. They stay in our conscious mind and impose strong impulses, e.g., hunger, for satisfying them. We recognize the signal and know how to deal with it, e.g., we know that it is time to find food and eat it. Our physical needs' direct impulses keep us aware of our deficiencies. Moreover, we have been taught largely how to recognize and satisfy these primary needs.

The psychological needs, on the other hand, are hardly clear to us like the basic needs, and they are too complex to pinpoint and study. No direct, simple, or automatic signals or stimuli warn us about many of our psychological needs or deficiencies. They are mostly our subconscious needs and we are at best only aware of them indirectly and subtly. Some of them, like loneliness, are felt rather readily. Even then, we feel helpless to handle them or deliberately neglect satisfying them. Sometimes, we do not know how to fulfil those needs, and often satisfying a psychological need requires an outside source beyond our means. For example, 'belonging or love' is a strong psychological need that a person can fulfil only through another individual or group. Grasping and fulfilling most of our pressing psychological needs become quite cumbersome, compared with our basic physical needs. Thus, they cause deep personal deprivations, insecurities, defects, and stress.

Our psychological needs are genetic or the influence of our rearing environment. The mere existence of these needs affects the psychological imbalance of almost all people at some degree. But as society and relationships get more complex so rapidly, the intensity of psychological needs are rising fast and the nature of their development in each person is getting harder to diagnose and cure. For example, the need for love develops in different intensities and formats depending upon individuals' experiences since childhood. Furthermore, our misleading cultural and social teachings cause added stress, deeper illusions, and psychological deprivations, e.g., when people keep seeking love obsessively as a tangible commodity that everybody can uncover and acquire. We imagine that our need for love can be fulfilled as naturally as we are taught to satisfy our basic needs. Our family and culture merely teach us to depend vastly on the illusions of love, power, pleasure, and similar symbols of happiness.

Abraham Maslow has offered a model of personal needs tree. At the bottom of this tree are basic needs like food and shelter. As these needs are satisfied, one moves up to the next levels such as belongingness, social, and status until one reaches the highest level of need in this hierarchy (tree), which is self-actualization. A higher need on the tree emerges, mostly subconsciously, as soon as the lower ones are satisfied. This model suggests that humans would never be satisfied until they satisfy their highest level of needs, i.e., self-actualization and spiritualism.

In line with Maslow's model, our needs become more of the psychological nature as soon as we go past the very basic needs. Our need for compassion, love, belongingness, recognition, and self-actualization are all highly complex and psychological. Thus, they have a great potential for causing our sense of insecurity, suffering, and confusion, because satisfying these higher needs is very difficult and often depends on other people's view of us. We often feel helpless and at the mercy of outsiders to satisfy our psychological needs. While not evident in our daily lives, we feel the impact of our psychological deficiencies, sometimes even without being able to link our anxiety directly to any particular need. The most prevalent symptom regarding our psychological need deficiency emerges in the form of loneliness or restlessness, even when many loving family members and friends surround us. When such signals emerge, we attempt to at least understand the psychological need behind it, although satisfying it properly usually proves very difficult. Often, we ignore the source of our unrest, not understand or misinterpret it, respond to it incorrectly, or feel helpless to do something about it.

Every day, more scientific proofs emerge about the import of psychological health for keeping our sanity and heightening our mental capability, for sustaining our physical health and growth, and for building our spirits. The crucial point, however, is that we should learn regarding our varied psychological needs mostly for coming to terms with them, instead of becoming more needy or expecting to satisfy them all the time. We should learn to expect the chance of not satisfying some (or often most) of these needs, e.g., love, all our lives and still cope with such deprivations rather constructively.

We all know about the body-mind connection and the value of psychological health. Some scholars put even a higher stress on the relationship between physical and psychological health to the extent they believe that the cure for terminal diseases like cancer might be found more readily in psychological treatment instead of conventional therapies.

In *The Ageless Body, Timeless Mind,* Harmony Books, New York, 1993, Deepak Chopra M.D. states the following:

"The biochemistry of the body is a product of awareness. One of the greatest limitations of the old paradigm was the assumption that a person's awareness doesn't play a role in explaining what is happening in his body. Yet healing cannot be understood

unless the person's beliefs, assumptions, expectations, and self-image are also understood. Although the image of the body as a mindless machine continues to dominate mainstream Western medicine, there is unquestionable evidence to the contrary. Death rates from cancer and heart diseases are probably higher among people in psychological distress, and lower among people who have a strong sense of purpose and well-being." Ibid., page 20.

And in another book, Deepak Chopra says:

"If I have a patient who is afraid, I can grasp his hand reassuringly and he will feel better; this happens even under anaesthesia. You can grasp the patient's hand at a difficult moment in surgery and see the monitors for blood pressure and heartbeat register the calming effect. The heart and the brain, it seems, are connected much deeper than where molecules are. One sees the truth of this whenever a baby is cradled in its mother's arms. Within a few minutes, the two of them will be breathing together, even if the baby is asleep, and their heartbeat will start to synchronize (they will not match beat for beat, since the child's heart rate is faster than the mother's). This body-mind connection is invisible, but who would call it unreal? It has been passed on silently from generation to generation. Perhaps it still wraps us all in a bond of sympathy. Out of separate beings, trapped in their own concerns, it helps to mould one human race." Quantum Healing, Deepak Chopra, M.D., Bantam Book 1989, page 132.

Our psychological needs pinpoint and stir the intrinsic means of strengthening the body-mind connection and heightening our awareness. Thus, grasping and dealing with our inner needs is essential for creating a sensitive and effective connection between our body and mind. But again, the trick is to accept initially that we should face up to our psychological needs more often than we can expect to satisfy them permanently and fully. For achieving this kind of progressive mentality, which demands some type of graceful resignation, we should realize our 'self.' Regardless of our psychological deprivations that we can never resolve, such as love or recognition, we can still try to climb the 'personal needs tree' and approach self-actualization as the ultimate personal need and achievement.† At this stage, one gains high awareness and body-mind connection, which is the boundary of spirituality. At the same time, though, one recognizes, and learns to live with, the chance of never fulfilling even some of the lower personal needs, especially psychological ones. Thus, another purpose of learning about 'self' is to become less needy and cope with the big chance (and deprivations) of never finding love, recognition, fame, etc. This is an essential requirement for building our spirits.

Recognizing Our Unconscious Needs

We refer to 'spirituality' as a special state of transcendence. In fact, though, **spirituality is a high need that drives and reflects humans' psychological growth and aspirations.** At this sacred point, self-awareness and body-mind connection cease being an unconscious matter in the form of an idea. Rather, they manifest as a conscious affair and a way of life. Referring to Maslow's research, we can conclude that, at the highest level of the needs tree, i.e., self-actualization, the psychological needs approach and intermingle with people's spiritual needs, most likely without them even recognizing it. While most of our psychological needs are felt at subconscious level (often as familiar needs), some of our psychological and most of our spiritual needs have gradually submerged deeper and deeper to the unconscious level for the majority of us (unconscious needs). Handling our subconscious needs (e.g., love and belonging) is already a tough task, although we at least recognize them and somehow know how to go about satisfying them. Accordingly, we might appreciate the difficultly of dealing with our unconscious needs that we can hardly even recognize. At the same time, the 'needs tree theory' indicates that,

---

† This theory somewhat refutes Maslow's theory that one moves up the 'Need Hierarchy' tree only after satisfying the lower ones.

as we grow, we finally realize that none of the other needs in the middle range (e.g., love, status, recognition) are as essential as we had thought, nor are they even authentic needs once we finally mature enough to look only for self-actualization and spirituality. All our efforts and pains for satisfying our middle range needs feel so unnecessary and vain.

On the contrary, our inability to recognize and attend to our unconscious needs (e.g., self-actualization and spirituality) causes constant surges of negative reactions and conditions in our lives, including anxiety, frustration, psychological dysfunctions, and family/social conflicts. Our hidden potentialities strive to surface when we receive various signals in the form of strong inner urges, aspirations, and restlessness. We feel a need to explore our potentialities, which seem to reside in our unconscious as some precious, unexplored resources. They are available for satisfying our higher needs, including spirituality. In all, learning about our unconscious needs protects us against, or relieves us from, daily psychological deprivations and dysfunctions. It also provides the opportunity to access our hidden potentialities. It helps us grasp the futility of worrying about our middle-range needs and causing ourselves so much pain for nothing. In the process, we also gain new insights about the real world that is ordinarily hidden from us. We learn about the world of illusions that has misguided us all along. To achieve these objectives, our main challenge is to bring our highest psychological deprivations, including spirituality, from unconscious into our conscious mind and transform our insights into a deep drive for self-awareness and body-mind assimilation.

Boosting Our Spirits

Courage, confidence, happiness, and optimism spring from a well-groomed spirit. In itself, a high spirit reflects the soundness of our choices and actions as well as our psychological strengths. Therefore, we have the power and responsibility to heighten our spirit by choosing a simple lifestyle in sync with humans' natural needs. Otherwise, it stifles under the pressures of our superficial needs and crooked lifestyles. For example, we naively believe that pleasures and extravagance can lift our spirits, whereas they actually dampen it by making us more needy and phony every day. Most people realize these basic facts and the importance of keeping their spirits fresh and free. Yet, we forget that nurturing our spirits needs perpetual attention, care, wisdom, and sacrifice. Although a divine dimension of humans, our spirit deteriorates very fast if we neglect it. It should be constantly monitored and empowered with our inspiring thoughts and deeds, while eluding people's casual or intentional efforts to kill our spirits is an even harder task.

Our spirit also has the mandate of making us a 'self'-fulfilling being. Satisfying our sacred needs, such as self-actualization and spirituality is a strong urge driven by our spirit subconsciously. Yet, seldom anybody gets a chance to fulfil these essential needs, since we are hypnotized by social norms and follow the crowd for defining and managing our lives. We struggle a lifetime out of greed or for mere survival, financially and emotionally, mostly because we feel trapped or do not know any better way of living. Even worse, we often cherish our mentalities and lifestyles that satiate only our neediness, arrogance, and sexuality. All along, our only goal is to find that illusive happiness that our fantasies and narcissistic ambitions are supposed to bring.

In all, the rising social pressures for blind compliance and our pleasure-seeking mentality prevent us from pondering our deeper needs that can fuel our spirits. We are too mesmerized by our illusions to see the real world or even the sporadic clues about it. We are unwilling to accept that for attaining even a relative peace of mind, we should grasp the real purposes of living, revamp our needy mentality, and follow a simple lifestyle through a peaceful, slow process of self-awareness. No other way for salvation exists. Only through this long learning exercise, we might discover our inherent limitations and potentialities, which would provide big opportunities for self-fulfilment and happiness. Clearly, creating the right mentality and circumstances for exploring our innate traits and potentialities is hard. Self-actualization is one method for doing that. Yet, before setting sail for that long destination towards enlightenment, a more taxing task is to defeat (or at least acknowledge) our superficial habits and needs, and evade the illusions we have come to cherish in the perceived world. Chris Hedges comment regarding the world of illusions is interesting:

"A culture that cannot distinguish between reality and illusion dies. And we are dying now. We will either wake from our state of induced childishness, one where trivia and gossip pass for news and information, one where our goal is not justice but an elusive and unattainable happiness, to confront stark limitations before us, or we will continue our headlong retreat into fantasy. Those who cling to fantasy in times of despair and turmoil inevitably turn to demagogues and charlatans to entertain and reassure them. And these demagogues, as they have throughout history, lead the crowd, blinded and amused, toward despotism." Chris Hedges, Empire of Illusion, Alfred A. Knopf, Canada, 2009, back flop.

The Spiritual Sensations of Self-actualizers

Maslow describes the attitude and feelings of self-actualizers who were the subjects of his research in great depth. He discusses the spirituality realm that a self-actualizer reaches during his 'peak experiences'. From his findings, it appears that these individuals are not merely satisfying their psychological needs, but rather transcending to a new height that is usually witnessed by, and ascribed to, spiritual persons and moods. They overcome their Egos, become self-reliant, and find an extremely high level of consciousness and contentment from the basic things they do. They reach out and touch their spirits. These descriptions indicate that a self-actualizing person senses and explores his spirituality needs even when s/he is merely driven by his/her psychological needs (i.e. recognition and self-actualization). Maslow's findings and theories are excellent examples of the relationship between humans' hidden potentialities and spirituality dimension. Many other scholars have reached similar conclusions during their own scientific research. These findings substantially affirm that some intrinsic aspects of our psyches bring us to the threshold of our spirituality. Some of Maslow's findings in terms of the feelings and characteristics of self-actualization (peak) experiences are quoted in the next couple of pages.

"It is true that human beings strive perpetually toward ultimate humanness, which itself may be anyway a different kind of Becoming and growing. It's as if we were doomed forever to try to arrive at a state to which we could never attain. Fortunately we now know this not to be true, or at least it is not the only truth. There is another truth which integrates with it. We are again and again rewarded for good Becoming by transient states of absolute Being, by peak-experiences. Achieving basic-need gratification gives us many peak-experiences, each of which are absolute delights, perfect in themselves, and needing no more than themselves to validate life. This is like rejecting the notion that a Heaven lies some place beyond the end of the path of life. Heaven, so to speak, lies waiting for us through life, ready to step into for a time and to enjoy before we have to come back to our ordinary life of striving. And once we have been in it, we can remember it forever, and feed ourselves on this memory and be sustained in time of stress." Toward a Psychology of Being, Abraham Maslow, Van Norstrand Reinhold, 1968, page 154.

The following findings by Maslow about his subjects' divine feelings during these peak experiences are especially interesting:

"In some reports, particularly of the mystic experience or the religious experience or the philosophical experience, the whole of the world is seen as unity, as a single rich live entity. In other of the peak experiences, most particularly the love experience

and aesthetic experience, one small part of the world is perceived as if it were for the moment all of the world. In both cases the perception is of unity." Ibid., page 88.

"...the experience or the object tends to be seen as a whole, as a complete unit, detached from relations, from possible usefulness, from expediency, and from purpose." Ibid., page 74.

"...the percept is exclusively and fully attended to. This may be called "total attention". What I am trying to describe here is very much akin to fascination or complete absorption. In such attention the figure becomes <u>all</u> figure and the ground, in effect disappears, or at least is not importantly perceived. It is as if the figure were isolated for the time being from all else, as if the world were forgotten, as if the percept had become for the moment the whole being." Ibid., page 74.

"...perception can be relatively ego-transcending, self-forgetful, egoless. It can be unmotivated, impersonal, desireless, unselfish, not needing, detached. It can be object-centred rather than ego-centred. That is to say, that the perceptual experience can be organized around the subject as a centering point rather than being based upon the ego." Ibid., page 79.

"In all the common peak experiences which I have studied, there is a very characteristics disorientation in time and space. It would be accurate to say that in these moments the person is outside of time and space subjectively. In the creative furor, the poet or artist becomes oblivious of his surroundings, and of the passage of time. It is impossible for him when he wakes up to judge how much time has passed. Frequently he has to shake his head as if emerging from a daze to rediscover where he is. But more than this is the frequent report, especially by lovers, of the complete loss of extension in time. Not only does time pass in their ecstasies with a frightening rapidity so that a day may pass as if it were a minute but also a minute so intensely lived may feel like a day or a year." Ibid., page 80.

"At the higher levels of human maturation, many dichotomies, polarities, and conflicts are fused, transcended or resolved.

Self-actualizing people are simultaneously selfish and unselfish, Dionysian and Apollonian, individual and social, rational and irrational, fused with others and detached from others, and so on." Ibid., page 91.

"The person at the peak is godlike not only in senses that I have touched upon already but in certain other ways as well, particularly in the complete, loving, uncondemning, compassionate and perhaps amused acceptance of the world and of the person, however bad he may look at more normal moments." Ibid., page 92.

"...as the essential Being of the world is perceived by the person, so also does he concurrently come closer to his own Being (to his own perfection, of being more perfectly himself)." Ibid., page 95.

The above characteristics of peak experiences of self-actualizers demonstrate that spirituality needs are in fact a continuum of the psychological needs and very much interconnected. We strive to deal with our psychological needs to maintain our mental health and strengthen our body-mind connection. As a main step, we build our convictions, ethics, spirits, and certain plans to control our psychological defects and needs. However, it is interesting to also note that, while we habitually associate the knowledge of psychology with our mental defects and neediness, in reality, our psyche is the root of purity and tranquility when it is cleansed and groomed properly. We can approach the spirituality continuum of our psyches once we curb our personal hang-ups and move on beyond our futile middle-range needs and greed that agitate and taint our psyches in our customary living.

We have accepted various psychological theories and we practice them as a body of scientific knowledge with expected benefits and effects. We have come to believe in psychology as a valid scientific approach to deal with one's psyche and to treat the sick with special and sometimes drastic measures. We find these treatments necessary and effective. However, humans' psychic power in terms of spirituality has not yet been given adequate attention. Our scepticism towards spirituality stems from the fact that all such ideas have come from gurus, prophets, old cultures, and ordinary people who have not offered a scientific proof and methodology for their claims. Even assertions by scholars with educational credentials and Ph.D.s remain mostly speculative and unsubstantiated by scientific evidence. Nevertheless, while full proof in all respects is still lacking, it seems that the link between psychology and spirituality is becoming more established and better validated in our minds. Because of our presumptions about the value of the Western science in psychology, we are now more flexible in accepting spirituality ideas as plausible realities.

Moreover, with the reduction of faith in religions, partly due to these organizations' rising disrepute, along with controversial practices of all religions, people's spirituality needs should, and appear to have, become more active at a different level with a new perspective. Now, people are trying to find it themselves, which is the right way, compared with the traditional blind faith and dependence on others, such as clergies, explaining it to them. It is the right way because spirituality starts with an inward search to find one's self and then reach a higher level of consciousness to see beyond the realm of physical life. It is quite plausible that we intuitively seek spirituality now by referring to psychological knowledge that can help us learn about ourselves. Carl Jung has reached the conclusion that:

"The public desire for more psychological knowledge is largely due to the suffering which results from the disuse of religion and from the lack of spiritual guidance." Psychology and the East, First published in 1978 by Art Paperback, page 125.

Nowadays, in fact, we look for psychological knowledge to penetrate our inner self and satisfy our innate need for spirituality. Let us hope our self-realized personal spirituality and proactive compassion would replace our need for religions soon.

The Unity of Psychology and Spirituality

The link between psychology and spirituality is obvious, with the individual's 'psyche' being the main denominator to study and heal. In spirituality, though, the psyche steps into the supernatural domain to seek a more fundamental remedy through a divine connection with the universe. In such an instance, the psyche supposedly becomes the same as, or joins, individuals' spirits for the purpose of self-therapy and containing the perils of humans' wicked nature. Other disciplines, such as biology and physics, are also finding some common denominators with spirituality and psychology, which makes future research and theories intriguing, maybe even providing a background for understanding our souls.

Humans have always felt their need for spirituality intuitively. However, we have never developed and benefited spirituality effectively, while we have relied on religions and superstitions to satiate this need. Thus, our present spirituality modes have little potential for building our spirits and perhaps even giving us a higher wisdom beyond our illusive perceptions of the universe.

Nowadays, some evidences in the scientific world also affirm the importance of spirituality to soothe our souls for physical and mental health. The Western world seems willing now to give a benefit of the doubt to the teachings and thoughts of the Eastern philosophy, such as the Buddhism and the notions of karma and yoga. Now, modern psychologists, physicists, and philosophers are offering ideologies akin to ancient Eastern philosophies. The fields of medicine, psychology, philosophy, physics, and many other disciplines are getting more integrated and coming to terms with the ideas that were considered illogical and whimsical a few decades ago. For example, Gary Zukov's scientific conclusions and thoughts as well as Deepak Chopra's assertions in the field of medicine appear to suggest the convergence of scientific notions into some kind of reconcilable observations regarding spirituality. Some of their remarks have been quoted in several places in this book, including the following quotes from Gary Zukov:

> *"According to quantum mechanics there is no such thing as objectivity. We cannot eliminate ourselves from the picture. We are part of the nature, and when we study the nature there is no way around the fact that nature is studying itself. Physics has become a branch of psychology, or perhaps the other way round."* The Dancing Wu Li Masters, Gary Zukov, Morrow 1979, 1st Edition, page 31.
>
> *"If the new physics has led us anywhere, it is back to ourselves, which, of course, is the only place that we could go."* Ibid., page 114.

Without judging the validity of these assertions, the point here is scientists' zeal to link psychology and spirituality by scientific facts. Surely, still a long way is ahead before these speculations find practical meanings and applications. Still, we are moving into a new frontier where spirituality research and notions could become more objective, instead of mere speculations.

Spiritual senses and supernatural ideas have always bemused and overwhelmed us at a personal level rather regularly, although spirituality and our need for it is not well explored and grasped. Our main goal now is to redefine the meaning of spirituality and isolate it from superstitions and traditional rituals, as well as the dogmatic presentations of spirituality by some scientists or gurus. We must remain sceptical, with an open mind, about the validity of so many subjective interpretations regarding supernatural and spirituality, nowadays. If not careful, the new approach could easily contaminate the foundation of our thoughts in a different way and damage our spirits even more. The only thing we can say rather conclusively is about the unity of human psyche and spirit, and the high value of studying psychology and spirituality somewhat together. It seems that our psychological and spiritual needs coincide and our ability to satiate these needs collectively would boost our spirits and maximize our wellbeing. We are born with them and we need to satisfy them in order to survive physically and mentally.

The Main Personal Dilemmas

Our psychological and spiritual urges make us think regularly, mostly subconsciously and unconsciously, in order to refine our beliefs, maintain a peaceful life, and raise our spirits. In particular, the following five dilemmas (objectives) occupy our minds often:

A. Know (about) ourselves. Our thoughts and actions reflect our grasp of who we think we are and how aware we are of our quirks. We like to establish our identity as a worthy human and gain a spiritual wisdom through **self-awareness**. This topic will be covered in Chapter Thirteen.

B. Reconcile facts and myths of life. We like to know why we are conditioned to believe in certain facts and myths. Our minds attempt to understand the authenticity of *presumed* facts of life in relation to myths, while reconciling them remains a tense, lifetime challenge. This topic is explored in Chapters Four and Five of Volume I.

C. Find the secret of happiness. We like to know if a lasting happiness is possible and how a personal *formula* of happiness may be developed. We like to explore the traits of a hypothetical role model and find how s/he behaves and defines happiness. Accordingly, this would be a definition of a desired self. This subject is discussed in detail in Part III of Volume I.

D. Establish a philosophy of life. With a grasp of the above objectives (A-C), we would like to establish an overall picture of a presumed lifestyle (life philosophy) that can contain, nurture, and direct an ideal personality for a peaceful existence. This life philosophy can also help us grasp external factors that affect us, including society, family, spiritualism, etc. It would help us judge the strength of prevalent socioeconomic environment objectively. Overall, a personal philosophy of life would lead us in our daily routines in line with our wisdom about self and the universe. This topic is covered in Part IV and Chapter Two of Volume I.

E. Use the formula of happiness and life philosophy (our 'wisdom') to make our major life decisions. This is for keeping ourselves alert about major life decisions and actions that direct our lives and for being *somewhat* prepared to handle significant life issues effectively. This is how we apply our foundation of thoughts and our free spirit to guide us in the journey of life. This topic is covered partially in Part VI in this volume as a general framework and then expanded in Volume III.

We wrestle with the above five main life objectives (dilemmas) routinely without realizing the process or distinguishing them as fundamental principles that influence our daily lives and spirits. In our subconscious, however, these objectives (and their related dilemmas) are passively linked and vainly pursued for survival and finding salvation. Thus, making an effort to learn the nature of these dilemmas has some value for us. Especially, objective A, knowing (about) ourselves, as discussed in Chapter Thirteen, is important for both making major life decisions and boosting our spirits. Self-awareness is also useful for addressing the ongoing stressful routine in our minds to gauge and manage life's traps and tricky variables.

If only we become interested to learn about ourselves, we might realize the nature of our higher needs beyond the basic needs of food and shelter. We might learn about, and fulfil, our psychological and spiritual needs, remember our living purposes, and boost our psyche and spirit. Then, we would honour only our authentic needs that can enhance our effectiveness in our daily routines and thoughts and boost our chances for self-actualization, selfless love, and lasting inner happiness. Meanwhile, many of our superficial needs could be gradually abolished from our lives. Thus, trying to resolve the first dilemma per se, i.e., learning about ourselves, thru self-awareness, can prepare us to face life with more resilience and patience. Self-awareness (objective A) and the other four objectives listed above are addressed in depth throughout this trilogy as noted for each of these five objectives.

Then again, only few of us find adequate incentive, interest, time, motivation, or desire to pursue a strenuous self-awareness regimen with humility to resolve these five personal dilemmas (objectives). We need the right mindset to ponder, understand, and satisfy our psychological and spirituality needs in serious and sincere manner. Without a proper mindset and attitude even our most obvious, potent potentialities would not come to fruit and we cannot even fulfil our self-actualization need, let alone attain a full sense of spiritualism.

Preparing Our Minds and Attitude

Attending to our psychological and spirituality needs requires courage and motivation to resist the status quo and the social (life-conditioning) rules containing us. We need strong faith and conviction to explore our deepest feelings and unconscious mind for a preliminary level of self-awareness, which might then turn into an *awareness motion*. Every day a higher level of motivation and satisfaction would fuel the energy required to move ahead and keep pace with the expansion of our mind and spirit. Reading the books of ancient gurus and philosophers can help us build the required momentum for gradual development of a deep personal belief, although this self-awareness routine is only for expanding our brains outside so many juvenile, old-fashioned suggestions about spiritualism. This approach for preparing our minds is also different from positive thinking techniques that assume people can grow their enthusiasm and motivation levels automatically, with just a simple desire, to get over life obstacles and personal limitations and achieve what they wish.

Positive thinking techniques advocated these days allegedly motivate and enable a person address his/her suppressed needs by taking riskier actions in order to find success and happiness. S/he is expected to change his/her mindset fast, while still functioning smoothly within his/her normal routines. Yet, the implementation of our good intentions is usually hindered by human limitations, life's persistent erratic challenges, and every individual's unique psychological characteristics.

Only if a person can build a highly refined, flexible mindset, s/he might implement and benefit from some positive-thinking techniques. Preaching any type of positive thinking and making people believe that it is easy to change quickly and painlessly are futile, misleading attempts. Actually, those efforts often result in further frustration and setbacks when people fail to fulfil such high expectations (mainly quick fixes) from their psyches. For example, videos and books on diets and workouts, or exercise machines, try to motivate people to change their lifestyles and get major results fast, but they are mostly marketing gimmicks. After spending their money and raising their hopes for quick results, most people realize that they do not have the right mindset to pursue a rigid and demanding workout program. This leads to further damage of personal self-image. Overall, positive thinking principles become practical only to the extent they realistically fit all the factors related to human nature, socioeconomic realities, and each person's unique personality and potentialities.

Although positive thinking is meant to be an internal (mental) process to induce motivation, it is treated more like an external stimulus—a quick fix. It is meant to force us believe in ourselves or 'reconsider' our rooted feelings and views of our abilities. It attempts to achieve all these goals without recognizing our deep dysfunctional traits that override all our positive thinking efforts. We get excited suddenly and pursue something for a while, and then lose our motivation and stamina. For changing our mindsets, we should become fundamentally convinced of our needs and plans first through gradual self-awareness and by developing a deep conviction about our objectives and mission for a realistic goal—and positive thinking per se could never achieve this.

Contrary to explicit or implied suggestions by some experts about humans' ability to revamp their attitude and personality fast, people's unique mindsets and life conditions at any specific time and age depend on their genetics and life experience, and thus cannot be modified rapidly. People's unique life conditions and intelligence limit their abilities to change fast and maintain a new mindset. Becoming a positive thinker and benefiting from any technique to improve self-image requires an internal stimulus for developing a tremendous level of motivation merely to grasp and manipulate our existing mindset and life conditions. Thus, the first level of any positive thinking must emphasize on finding the right inner stimuli that can motivate a particular individual. A strong, sustainable personal incentive is required based on each person's level of authentic needs and aspirations. This goal can be achieved only personally through gradual self-awareness and mental adjustments. Only if these prerequisites are fulfilled, and only if s/he still finds it necessary to pursue whatever his/her new challenges are, s/he might utilize his/her newly gained wisdom and motivation towards the next and final goals. S/he would then also learn many techniques (including positive thinking) that are expected to help him/her.

Overall, mindset calibration is a long process that should be implemented successfully over time before we can apply any techniques to recondition our means of thinking, behaving, and feeling. Never a technique can influence a person's mind to learn and reverse its operation quickly and painlessly, and not before deep personal beliefs and mindset allow the use of a technique like positive thinking. With this guideline, one might ask, 'Then, what would be the learning value of any book and particularly this one?' The answer is that discussions in this book are only for raising self-awareness, while introducing the concepts, means, and techniques of achieving it. It is intended to provide only the stimulus that people need to ponder and manipulate their own mindsets for whatever purposes. Only personal conviction and perseverance, and mostly due to an authentic need deeply felt by an individual, can lead to success.

We can never be a positive thinker if we are not inherently a positive doer by the conviction of our inner urges, or if we are not highly trained to recondition our convictions when necessary.

Our thoughts and deeds are reinforced from the same source, i.e., our habits and conditioning forces registered in our brains. Thus, we cannot turn into a positive thinker or doer if our mind is not properly recalibrated and prepared to be one such person with a high capacity to control his/her emotions as well. Many years of reconditioning (self-awareness) might reset one's mentality to become a natural positive thinker and doer, but never as a result of reading a book or attending a few seminars. A *real* positive thinking attribute might grow only through a long, rigid process of learning and mindset transformation, which demands a great deal of patience, motivation, and hard work to develop humility and self-awareness.

Accordingly, delving into the questions of, 'Who we are and what we are here for,' can be a good scheme for stirring the initial motivation within ourselves. This initiative would soon generate the inner power required to perceive our life's dilemmas properly and resolve most or all of them gradually, while we boost our spirits along the way as well. As our self-awareness heightens, we build up self-commitment and energy to develop a sensible personal life philosophy and introduce fundamental changes in our mentalities and lifestyles.

CHAPTER TWO
Quest for the Truth

Humans' lasting quest for the truth is for finding a lasting sense of triumph and peace. However, 'TRUTH' is a broad, existential myth that confuses our brains a lifetime. We wish to unravel the meaning of life as we strive for success or salvation at least. Yet, all our good intentions and efforts reveal nothing regarding this mysterious truth.

Chapter Four particularly discusses our search for the truths about, i) the universe, ii) our personal lives, and iii) humanity in some lengths for drawing a general picture of humans' mental state and burdens in the early decades of the 21st century. Besides our curiosity about these existential truths, we also wrestle with too many facts about the nature and goals of our confusing social affairs. For example, a haunting truth is our loss of trust in our social systems, people, and human nature overall, yet feel obliged to comply with social norms helplessly. Another odd truth is that we trust people less every day, yet still raise our expectations from one another and life. Meanwhile, we have big difficulty accepting this unsettling reality (the rising social mistrust), as if too eager to discover a better nature and higher morality for humans!

Most of us admit that our present lifestyles cause too much disappointments and hardships, though some tentative success and gratifications give us enough hope to keep on ploughing. Then, we often ponder a big dilemma—a philosophical doubt: Would humans' idiotic struggles ever lead to a *meaningful or soothing* sense of victory? When? How? Intuitively, we expect some form of social stability, a sensible value, or a reward for our vast efforts to figure out and live this perplexing life. Are we only dreaming? Are we ever going to be able to get out of the mess humans have created under the names of freedom and civilization?

Besides our crusade to justify our existence and build a certain lifestyle based on a thoughtful life philosophy, a cruder dilemma is whether we must accept all these 'hardships.' Is not there really a way out of this depressing existence other than suicide perhaps? Not only the existence itself, but also the agony of defining and maintaining it often feels absurd and humiliating. Why should we try so hard for everything, even for a simple subsistence? Are our Ego-ridden sufferings and greed-driven worries warranted in the big scheme of things—when humanity is facing its demise?

We hope our pains and experiences have some educational value at least. Yet, erratic events and personal priorities restrict the value of our experiences for future purposes or decisions. In addition, without a sensible life philosophy to justify our efforts every single day, any personal experiences remain just random events with little significance or practical application. Thus, does this mean we are doomed, as seldom any of us knows the reasons for his/her hardships? Hardly anybody has a realistic, authentic purpose for living in this chaotic perceived world. Nowadays, we hardly get the chance or motivation to even invent some real life objectives. We just imitate the mainstream, cherish our shallow interests and desires, and strive to cope with external forces (i.e., socioeconomic facts and interpersonal issues). That seems to be the best way we humans will ever learn to live! We have proven quite incapable of using our brains to live easier.

Overall, social limitations and humans' rooted idiosyncrasies, such as insecurity and egoism, prevent us from thinking outside the box for a better means of living. We are conditioned to accept hard labour automatically as a duty for existence with a chance for some random pleasures. 'No pain, no gain,' is a big motto. But are we really serving ourselves with our set crude mentalities and lifestyles, especially since most of our experiences usually end up dampening our spirits? Do some sporadic pleasures really make up for all our pains and incessant disappointments? Do we have any other option for living? Or, should we conclude that we just have to struggle because we are born as humans and bound to live in our substandard societies with our crooked nature? Just because God wants us to suffer? Or only because we are stupid? These chronic questions become more painful and relevant every year in line with the growing social chaos, life complexities, and people's inability to relate effectively.

Naturally, we like to stay positive, lift our spirits any way we can—usually by engaging in silly pleasures—and move forward. We have no other choice. We want to fight off negativism and lethargy that build up gradually during our routine struggles for victory, which by itself remains indefinite and intangible in our heads. We resort to positive thinking and motivation enhancing techniques to boost our moods and performance for another day or week. We strive to achieve certain rudimentary goals. We also hope that our rooted, dysfunctional habits, inner conflicts, and fears would eventually suffocate underneath our phony optimism, flimsy pleasures, and gaudy pretences—so that we suffer less.

Alas, even our optimism and pleasures cannot help as long as our formed mentalities and social distractions sabotage our sacred inner quest for the truth. Many obstacles, such as the mirage of happiness, hinder our ability to face the reality, too, as explained in the coming pages. We simply cannot handle *the truth* about the sad state of our social structure even when its harsh symptoms hit us like an avalanche. Accordingly, our struggles and experiences only feed our habits and strengthen our coping mentalities. This universal mayhem cannot be remedied in the near future, either, until a miracle happens and, 1) a large majority of people learn to think rather independently with less attachment to social norms, and, 2) society understands humanity compassionately, instead of manipulating and brainwashing the public for economic goals. It is hard to imagine that these two ideals would ever materialize.

Nonetheless, not knowing the purpose of our lifelong hopes and struggles remains a torturous mystery until we rather satisfy our personal quest for the truth at some level. This sacred mission is etched in our subconscious and we cannot avoid pondering it at least occasionally. We feel obliged intuitively to resolve our inner conflicts about life's realities somehow and to anticipate at least a small chance for triumph at the end!

Human Logic's Reliability

Another major truth we like to unravel is the validity of our logic. This becomes particularly crucial because following a spiritual path of life with higher consciousness for attaining wisdom and enlightenment does not sound logical to us. As practical, rational people, we remain sceptical about these intangible concepts, as they cannot be explained by scientific proofs or at least plausible theories. Yet, many philosophers and spiritualists argue that not all concepts, e.g., inner self, can (or need) be explained by science in the way it is developed today. The intricacies of the universe are too complex to be explained by any human logic and science. For example, the concept of infinity and the idea of the universe expanding indefinitely are beyond our brains' ability to visualize or comprehend. For one thing, we cannot grasp the idea that some event or object has no ending. Second, we simply imagine that if something is expanding beyond its limits, it must be doing so into another space that should have already existed. However, this seemingly logical perception does not apply to the universe and so we remain baffled. In fact, another theory existed until recently about the universe stopping to expand eventually and starting to contract instead. This theory is even harder to absorb, since the whole world will return to 'nothingness,' as it had been prior to the Big Bang. All the space would be gone too! Then, the newer science proclaims that the universe will actually expand forever. What does 'forever' mean? No one can fathom. Nonetheless, human logic is willing to adopt these findings as notions worth contemplating—to build a scientific foundation—as plausible hypotheses for more analysis and speculation at least. Therefore, the question is how much trust we should have in our logic and science, even when they fail to make sense, i.e., the universe's endless expansion into nonexistent space. At the personal level, in particular, it seems we trust our logic too much naively. We have become arrogant and stubborn about our ideas, because we imagine we have reached definite conclusions according to our alleged superb logic. It is a major irony indeed to rely on human logic even slightly to unravel the truths about existence and the universe. What Ego! The infancy of human logic is even more apparent considering the absurdity of ideas and faiths that almost all humans have embraced about god, afterlife, etc.

On the other hand, in spite of its severe limitations, humans' collective logic and science have been following a systematic and proven track. A continuous development of ideas has turned into workable theories, tools, and machinery that have accomplished specific purposes. The progress of science has been cumulative, disciplined, and methodical (all limited to certain laws and rules we have created in our perceived world, of course). Furthermore, these scientific principles have been examined within the natural settings of the universe and have proven to comply rather nicely with some of the specific laws of nature. Travel in the space and landing spaceships on other planets or on the moon, breaking the nucleus of atom and extracting huge levels of energy, discoveries at the bottom of the oceans where no light has ever reached, the amazing technology of computers and cybernetics, and the vast amount of medical and other scientific knowledge that we have accumulated, especially in the last 50-60 years, seem consistent with the basic laws of nature. It is easy to show that the logic we have been using to explain events and phenomena, to visualize new notions and theories, and to set newer scientific objectives, are working nicely in line with the general laws of the universe, all subject to human brains' limited capacity, of course. Since we use less than 5-10% of our brains, we can hope that eventually humans can explain more facts about the universe and life. Our brains, logic, and scientific knowledge are still at a primitive stage, yet it appears that we have followed some form of logical process and a scientific foundation; we are not dreaming logic, although our personal logic often becomes dreamlike.

At the same time, we must remain alert regarding a possible bottleneck. That is, human brain and logic appear reliable and viable only to the extent they fit nicely with the natural laws of the universe, e.g., building an airplane to defy gravity, finding a cure for a disease, etc. Human logic is not driven by a mysterious, inherent power within us, but it is merely a tool for making an inference according to past experiences and specific methods to verify what is out there. Even at this level—for making plausible inferences—our logic has not yet helped answer the majority of questions and phenomena that the universe challenges us with. Our intuition and intelligence are inherent, but human logic is manmade partly based on our intuition and intelligence. Overall, outside its application to natural laws for scientific purposes, we have no other criteria for measuring the meaning and power of human logic for deciphering other complex features of human existence and thoughts. Even for applying our logic to scientific research, we must usually go through a long process of trials and errors, and experimentation of random ideas (e.g., for finding a cure for cancer), until finally someone stumbles upon a solution. Therefore, at best, we are fitting our logic to the requirements of science to prove natural laws. Again, this means that human logic is not an inherent and reliable tool, but merely a dynamic means of organizing our thoughts and activities in line with our wisdom. We do not even accept human *intuition* as a logical process or tool, *just because we want to stay logical!* Meanwhile, everybody seems to have his/her own crooked logic, thus often incapable of agreeing even on simple principles during their daily lives.

Accordingly, scientific discoveries have been based on a rather random generation of ideas driven merely by human logic and also tested within the scope of human logic in compliance with the natural laws of the universe. Therefore, both science and human logic find their limited validity only according to their capacities to explain or control a natural phenomenon or work in harmony within certain previously tested parameters. Beyond this small scope, neither science nor human logic has an independent capacity to guide or enlighten us within the *Real World's* context, especially considering their inherent high interdependency.

Our logic is incapable of speculating, let alone resolving, the dilemma of, 'Who created the creator,' since we cannot develop even a basic hypothesis for this quandary, never mind inventing a method to test it scientifically in a natural setting. Of course, the simple dilemma of 'who or what created the universe?' stands behind all these fundamental questions that challenge our logic. Our logic has been able to explain the process of creation at a much smaller scale, however, such as the creation of an embryo or a cell. If human logic has helped to explain these rather smaller phenomena, can it possibly work eventually to explain the bigger picture, such as the universe, and reveal more about the real world? It seems very doubtful at this point.

Nonetheless, both our logic and science remain limited now by human intelligence, which is presently functional mostly within our perceived world, and only for speculating about some of the simpler natural laws. Ironically, our logic and science also offer plausible notions about the existence of an unparalleled real world beyond our convoluted perceptions of reality. For now, however, they are inadvertently and inconsistently applied mostly in the perceived world to answer only our basic questions.

To avoid making the topic of human logic complex at this point, further discussions are included in Appendices A and B at the end of the book. Overall, humans' logic and knowledge about our world can be summarized as follows:

1. Many unexplained questions remain about the universe and our role in the journey we call life.
2. Humans' present logic and science cannot provide the right answers, at least not for many millenniums.
3. Human logic and science cannot either prove or refute the existence of supernatural and spiritual phenomena.
4. Some evidences, or at least claims, suggest the existence of supernatural and spiritual phenomena.
5. We have all felt some kind of special energy within ourselves and experienced unexplainable connections that we call luck, intuition, coincidence, telepathy, etc.
6. Most of us at least entertain, mostly subconsciously, the high chance of a real world existing beyond the perceived world that seems easier to sense, relate to, and love.
7. We have come to assume that human being is a super being with special connections to *the creator*, only on the grounds that we have used our brains more effectively and created more things. The fact that we think, have logic, and master some form of science, is assumed to make us different from other animals. Humans' unique abilities and spiritual urges are undeniable, yet there is no evidence that humans must be given any preference over other species in terms of divinity and their connection to the supernatural. Well, we have had prophets and spiritual leaders who have made us feel special. However, why we should be considered special within the kingdom of the creator of the universe is not clear. Other animals have instincts, some ability to use logic and think, too, though their mental development is in its primitive stage. Perhaps they also have, or will have, a spirituality dimension, which we do not know about. Just wait a few million years! Even some plants are deemed to have a mysterious type of intelligence and possibly consciousness.
8. Humans' existence is most likely a minuscule, purposeless, by-product of the creation and not a celestial scheme, even though we have divine potentialities and spirituality drives.

Nobody can prove otherwise. Thus, accepting unfounded prophecies about humans' immortality and priority in the universe is only a clear indication of humans' poor logic and gullibility, plus incredible pomposity.

9. Our varied curiosities, questions, intuitions, and doubts have a direct impact on our ways of thinking and making tough decisions. They affect our lives, and cause us agony and anxiety, yet we remain unable to ignore or do anything about these inner urges.
10. Our deep inner needs and conflicts persistently boggle our minds and make us feel obliged to create logic and science to resolve personal and life's uncertainties for attaining some degree of mental equilibrium and peace.
11. We realize that answers to socioeconomic problems of the 21st century cannot come easily, because human logic and commonsense are extremely deficient, especially outside the scientific applications.
12. Solution to human misery cannot be found within the context of our existing socioeconomic structures, but rather requires a new source of energy, stronger logic, and deeper thinking. For example, we would never agree amongst ourselves on the mechanisms of governing our countries or even in terms of simple issues of controlling our national debts and budget deficits, which are so desperately needed. And of course, we have a long list of socioeconomic problems. The bottomline is that our personal logic and social beliefs are not necessarily accurate and reliable, but they seem to be all we have and can rely on. Worst of all, we humans cannot even use our limited logic for our benefits.

Logic, Reality, Divinity

Let us confess that even our impression or definition of the *reality* (including the universe and Creator) could be highly flawed. Are we just inventing a fictitious real world, since our brains suggest that such a world (the universe and possibly even God) should *logically* exist? Are not we only imagining a divine world merely through our flimsy logic formed within a perceived reality world and fanciful societies driven largely by people's illusions?[‡]

Conversely, many of our scientific laws and human logic may be invalid, since we understand so little about the real world, and definitely our raw perceptions obstruct our learning process, too. Yet, we think that the universe is an inherent phenomenon that constitutes the real (divine) world. Without this belief, everything becomes just a figment of human perceptions, including the idea of creation and the creator, all the sciences, and anything that any philosopher or prophet may say about human souls and divinity. However, for now, even from within our perceived world, we can imagine the existence of a real world, based on a unique mix of personal experiences, logic, and inferences. We can attribute these testable physical phenomena, and the *sound* logic behind them, to a fundamental world of realities beyond our meagre perceptions. That is, for now, we are merely hanging in bewilderment within a realm shared by both real and perceived realities.

Ironically, we are hoping and struggling to cross over from our perceived world to the real world with the use of our logic! We often believe that both levels of creations—the creation of the whole universe and the creation of a cell or embryo—are parallel fundamentals of the real world. Thus, we conclude that our logic and science are viable tools for explaining other fine questions in time, if and when our brains develop enough capacity to ask the right questions, which are testable in a natural setting.

In all, we like to believe that a world of real realities resides in the universe beyond our perceptions. We cannot deny its *real* existence outside of humans' thoughts, logic, and perceived link to it. This world of real realities would have existed according to the same laws and phenomena regardless of our knowledge or

---

[‡] Some scientific notions regarding our innate disability to use our logic can be found in this author's book, *Being Better Beings*.

perception of it, or even our existence. We can make this simple assertion, since we can safely assume that we are only *perceiving* the whole concept of existence and the universe. This is a raw assumption; but our logic insists that it is a reasonable one. We believe it is rational, even though the theories of quantum physics suggest that we, as observers of events, influence their outcomes.

Now let us go one step further and declare (in a rather circular argument) that everything other than human perceptions belongs to the real world. This includes all the things, animals and plants, and even our *accidental* pure thoughts (intuitions) outside our perceptions. The only thing that keeps us humans away from the real world is our diverted perceptions of this world. How strange! What a discovery! However, despite its ironical simplicity, it is interesting how the complex issues of duality of the worlds that we belong to can be a notion understandable even by our naïve commonsense. Our perceptions have become so dominant that a new world has been created—the world of perceived realities that includes such weird notions, including our religious beliefs, about the real world, too. Thus, the good news is that we may get a sense of the world of real realities as soon as we doubt the validity of our perceptions in the world of perceived realities. No special efforts, pain, or meditation are required—at least not at the entry level—if only we can get rid of our idiotic perceptions. Although it is not easy to rid ourselves from the deeply imprinted notions of the perceived world, we can see the entrance to the real world once we stand at the awareness intersection. MAYBE!

By definition, the perceived world is only a manifestation of our minds. Thus, we may begin to distinguish the authenticity of values and concepts only through awareness and by retraining our brains. In that sense, the strengths and clarity of our minds determine how effectively we can separate a perceived reality from a real one. Nevertheless, the power to distinguish the two levels of realities must come from, and flourish within, our minds and logic eventually, despite the influence of the initial (existing) misperceptions registered in our brains and logic.

In a few millenniums, humans might learn to distinguish the signals they receive from inner and outer sources as perceived or real. Then, they can apply some of the real ones in their everyday life to fortify their connection with the universe and the world of real realities. Some humans might grasp the real world better thru their REAL thoughts, which would grow only when they are largely free of their corny perceptions, attachments, and religions. Even then, that privileged group can still only speculate about their grasp of the real world. In the end, merely how we think and see objects make them perceived or real. Only how we humans connect to the universe puts us in the perceived or real realms for our limited grasp and purposes. Still, embracing this basic notion is important for entering one of the wisdom paths towards the boundaries of the real world. This might be a viable mechanism for testing and refurbishing human logic, too.

An even simpler idea can be generated from this discussion. We can suggest that humans' mind grasps outside information and values at two levels, perception and comprehension. At the perception level, we grasp the information superficially at its face value, or based on an existing criterion applied by a stimuli, logic, and usual conditioning—e.g., values reflected in social norms. A simple example is when one is asked to listen to a piece of music. The music is heard and perceived to satiate one's taste or not. A classical, country, or exotic music of foreign lands may feel odd to people not exposed to those kinds of rhythms. The response would be, 'Yes, I like it,' or 'No I do not like it.' The music is evaluated merely against some prejudiced and perceived notions. It is merely another act of *perception* without any special attempt to comprehend it. At a comprehension level, though, we feel, and mentally connect, to each individual note of the music and grasp the message it is communicating without making a reference in our minds (if we can) to any other music we have heard before. Few people can achieve this level of consciousness, though.

In fact, without an initial interest, we are unwilling to focus, anyway. For reaching the 'comprehension' level about our deeds and judgments, and for delving into our thoughts about a special issue, we must mainly get detached, perhaps through some form of meditation, from our existing mental prejudices. Attaining this rather divine state of mind sounds illogical and impossible for most people, though. Yet only at this level of consciousness, we can envisage and follow the path towards the real world. At this high degree of self-awareness and mental synthesis, we learn to run all aspects of our lives rather harmoniously. We can bring our minds to this 'comprehension' level in order to understand the meaning of many concepts and communications satiating our lives. Only with this type of enlightenment, our logic might find some form of intrinsic value for reflection and focusing as well.

For now, the validity of our logic and science beyond our raw perceptions is debateable from different angles. Yet, the goal here is just to reflect our erratic tendency to trust or doubt the validity of logic and science. This very fanciful mindset is equally at play when we set our beliefs and make our choices. We are not easily persuaded to engage (and believe) in a philosophical notion or abstract sensation that appears illogical to us, opposes the existing scientific knowledge, or defies our personal beliefs.

In all, we must haggle with our dilemmas about human logic, science, and realities and find reasonable criteria for building our personal faith and purposes to run our lives. For sure, we cannot, and should not, discard our urge to explore exotic ideas that have been called supernatural, spiritual, or myths despite our cynicism. We should assume that, with an open mind, we always have a chance of finding other life paths that can never become obvious to a rigid mind, even if all kinds of evidences were in front of the person. Thus, it seems that we could (should) never trust our logic fully. Our erratic logic cannot be useful or make enough sense, e.g., for grasping God and supernatural, when in fact our intuition or imagination goads us to believe in myths or some other reality beyond the perceived world.

On the other hand, we cannot second-guess the validity of everything, (not even the perceived facts) that we have been able to prove by using our logic and science, on the grounds that they might be only our perceptions and not real. Human logic and knowledge have evolved rather purposefully and systematically over millenniums, although they remain extremely limited due to the frailty of human brain (including our perceptions). We cannot refute the validity of events and things that happen to us in the perceived world on the grounds (or allusion) that everything we do and see in this world is only a dream or an illusion. It sounds illogical to believe that we may be awakened from this dream to enter the real world—e.g., to go to heaven. The basic logic tells us that any attempt to create an illusion out of an unknown or exotic phenomenon, by using the analogy of an existing event, is most likely a fallacy and leads to other forms of illusions. For instance, expecting a swift awakening out of our present state of ignorance, similar to waking up from a dream, would not be of much help for explaining our relationship to the real world and who we are. A divine awakening happens gradually according to a persistent regimen of learning, feeling, and practising.

In the final analysis, it seems more plausible (and logical too, perhaps) to assume that human logic and science would never be able to explain so many phenomena and questions regarding the universe, Creation, humanity, our relationships, etc. Yet, sadly, we still do not wish to acknowledge our ignorance and use this awareness to at least stop judging everything and everyone so fast adamantly. We do not wish to admit our mistakes, not even in those cases where our crooked actions and selfish beliefs seem unexplainable even by humans' crude logic, science, or theories.

The Awareness Intersection

Thus, the truth about human logic remains another enigmatic concept for the near future and we might as well remember this crucial fact when our dogmatism besieges our lives. So, how can we make good choices? How can we avoid life's traps somewhat to mitigate our sufferings? Can we overcome our inner conflicts and mental pressures a little at least? If yes, how? While no fix formula exists, we each find a plausible path for inner peace at last if we start the *long journey into ourselves* (as Rumi puts it) towards the boundaries of the *mystical* real world. Surely, this long process evolves gradually as we feel a genuine urge to do an honest self-assessment to find our identity, the right reasons for living, and the purpose of our struggles. We meditate and gauge our thoughts, feelings, and experiences freely and objectively—beyond the prevalent social criteria—to become more aware of our deeds and events around us. We grow our faiths and spirits to find inner peace and serenity. Soon, a basic sense of contentment signals our approach towards the awareness intersection.

On the other hand, many of us reach this intersection by fluke, most likely after a big shock, a major setback, or losing patience with common lifestyles and existence. We feel tired of relying on deceitful people and systems to entertain our superficial identity. Therefore, we sometimes arrive at this intersection by chance after having exhausted all living options and doing a lifetime of damage to ourselves and others.

Sometimes, the most common experiences of one's life, such as a family predicament, near death experience, or issues of social interest or concern, such as ecology, evoke the self-questioning process. A sense of emptiness (of the self) also drives us to look for more substance in our lives. After losing so many years of our precious lives and ignoring the sacred energy within us, we might at last arrive at the awareness intersection and notice the variety of paths that we can pursue in our quest for the truth and a contact with the real reality world. This may be the point where, for the first time, we get a notion about the person that 'we could be,' instead of what we have been ignorantly or quite idiotically.

At this saturation point, we are no longer happy despite all our pleasures and power. Our struggles to accumulate more wealth in a world of perceived realities suddenly feel so futile and infantile. Thus, we start to think deeper, which might trigger a process of self-questioning and possible awakening. Then, we see and sense the subtle *truths* that had never occurred to us or even considered worthy of discussion at a younger age. Accordingly, the process of self-questioning and awakening evolves.

Sometimes, simple questions erupt mysteriously and we get an urge to explore the depth of our mentality within the context of humanity with simple thoughts like, 'Why do people kill each other?', 'Who or what created the universe and why?', etc. These basic thoughts might also raise our curiosity to explore the truth about ourselves, including our *perceived* and *real* roles in life and society. Within this frame of mind, we gradually see the bizarre deceptions behind most perceived realities or at least get a chance for contemplation and new visions. We abhor the mainstream's influence on shaping our characters, and thus begin to reassess our zeal for social values and rewards of compliance.

Many other factors, including our inner conflicts, might also goad us to convert and evolve dramatically and hastily. It begins often with a sense of loneliness and withdrawal, which is the only venue for deep thoughts and questions. A person might become physically lonely or not, which could be a contributing factor or not. Yet, what matters is that his mind has drifted away from the mainstream and questions the validity and value of his regular thoughts that had kept his brain constantly busy, e.g., the thoughts of workload, promotion, family needs, etc. Now, he can relax his mind and let some fundamental thoughts get a chance to spill out of his subconscious. Sometimes, because of loneliness, emotional pressures, or the lack of gratifying experiences, a person suddenly arrives at the question of, 'Why am I doing these things?' and 'Whom am I doing them for, after all?' And, of course, the direct derivative of these questions is, 'Who am I, anyway?', and 'What is the purpose of my life?'

Many other basic questions occupy our minds during this mental explorations, too, like, 'Why must I die?', 'What have I achieved?', 'Is this really all living supposed to be?', 'Is there anything else I could do to relieve my lifetime anxieties for a chance of becoming happier now?', 'Why life feels so vain and shallow, and why did not I realize how quickly it goes by?', and lots of similar questions.

At the end, all these reflections might lead to a deeper grasp of our needs and identity, after discarding our juvenile obsessions, thoughts, and feelings that we have pampered all along to build a phony personality and life. It becomes clear that those thoughts and feelings have been only delusions and deceiving distractions. They have not brought us closer to our souls and self. Now, we feel an urge to transcend the world of appearances into the sphere of real realities where the real *I* is anxious to be born—*a real birth due to a fuller consciousness.*

Facing the Reality

At middle-age usually, suddenly the meaning and implications of death shift to a higher level of consciousness and *existence* feels more tangible than before. Most of us reach this point when we get older and feel restless, lonely, and lost, thus sense the reality of our mortality better and realize the vanity of our attachments. The questions of, 'Who am I and what the purpose of my life is' feel more relevant and urgent. Now, we remember! We realize our being and need for salvation if very soon we are not going to exist! Our perceived reality of 'death' turns into a real reality for existence after being buried in our subconscious so many years to elude this painful fact. A conscious knowledge of death awakens the shallow individual that has been to meet the real self that exits within him. We might even decide to write our will, too, at last. Many people who have had near death experience (NDE) have been suddenly awakened by a similar mysterious urge. In all, a person may be driven into a self-questioning mindset for many reasons. However, it usually happens after we have tasted the futility of the perceived world's norms, principles, and pleasures.

Thus, we arrive at last. And when we arrive, we do not know what to do except the basic withdrawal and isolation from the perceived reality and people who have kept us a prisoner in their world. Our parents, teachers, friends, or anybody else never took us to this intersection when we were young and had not gone through a lifetime of misery, mistakes, disappointments, and maybe some futile experimentation. Where we go from here is a personal choice. At this stage, we stand at the sacred awareness intersection with several paths branching from it. We pause with awe, study each path, and learn about not only its destination and demands, but also our personal power and objectives to follow that particular path—the obstacles, rejections, isolations, hazards, loneliness, and inevitable disappointments—all for a possible salvation. At this point, we start to delve into certain fundamental thoughts, similar to the discussions in this trilogy, for months and years, before we possibly grasp and adopt a more viable path of life than we have been chasing so far. We must not choose a path hastily again before years of contemplation and self-awareness.

Several paths offer lifestyles and a reality we can *practically* embrace and manage, which would be a mix of values from both the perceived and real reality worlds. Most of us can follow only a path that stands somewhere between these two extremes after we gauge our options, courage, strengths, and stamina. The path towards ultimate divinity is the hardest one to conquer, but if we ever do, we may even approach the SUMMIT. However, it is usually wiser to choose an easier path that feels like a practical destination for us. We can always experiment along the way to learn about our final destination by advancing from an easier path to a finer one with more demands on our time and thoughts.[§]

Some of us might have had a sudden glimpse of this insightful awareness intersection and perhaps paused a few days when we had been younger and touched by some thought-provoking ideas or books. However, most likely we had soon been distracted by the forces of the perceived world when they had quickly engulfed our minds and feelings. The ideal situation would have been to

---

[§] An elaborate discussion of 'Awakening Stages,' the Eros Dimension, is provided in Volume I of this trilogy.

arrive at this intersection by choice (not by accident) at younger ages perhaps as part of some kind of initiation ritual. The ideal would have been that our parents had had the wisdom to know, believe, and teach us at least a notion of the 'real world,' rather then merely reinforcing the teachings and beliefs of the perceived world including religions. We wonder, 'What are older people really good for then, nowadays!?'

Anyway, the first and most important stage is to make sure we have arrived at *the intersection*. It means we have decided to give ourselves a chance to face reality, abandon our superficial personality, and embrace our true 'self' through a long process of self-therapy. We are ready to change ourselves and challenge the values and rules that we have accepted and lived by so obediently all along. We realize our weaknesses, helplessness, and lack of integrity. We believe we deserve better and finding tranquility is a realistic destination, while lasting happiness is only an illusion. We also sense a feeling of rejuvenation, control, freshness, and inner power. Then, if we are lucky and appreciate what has been achieved, we acquire a high level of steady consciousness that can make our enlightenment permanent and paramount. Our high spirits and spiritual strength at this sacred stage would guide us in choosing the right path. Otherwise, we must keep experimenting until we find the right one eventually according to the level of independence we desire and can handle without the normal deep attachment to society and people. We do not wish to wait forever to decide which path to choose, though. It is usually better to start slowly and build momentum on the way to the higher paths of self-awareness along with a gradual detachment from the norms of the perceived world.

At the higher levels of awareness (and fuller consciousness), our wisdom heightens enough to capture and feel the real world somewhat more clearly. The precious reality of our existence becomes apparent within the context of full-conscious activities, decisions, pains, and joys that keep happening in our lives. This personal awakening affects all other aspects of a person's life when he discovers the real reality behind every concept that had all along had a different (often-childish) implication and meaning at the perceived (reality) level. Many divine notions and feelings imprisoned in our subconscious and unconscious suddenly begin pushing up toward our conscious mind. For example, as we grasp the beauty of Nature in awe with deep awareness, we acquire a novel impression about the overall majesty of creation with all its intricacies, which we still cannot fully comprehend, but embrace at a magical level. The real reality of Nature reveals itself to us if we learn how to seek it. From a high level of consciousness, this beauty and aura manifest a splendid sense of being and sacred attachment. The limited perception of beauty by one's eyes turns into a rising grasp of 'magnificence' with mind, sentiments, and insights—a state which could never be explained by superficial interpretations in the perceived world. At such unique states of consciousness, we are awakened by a fine experience or thought and introduced to a new way of seeing things and living. These types of experiences affirm our gradual progress on the new path, if we understand and nurture them properly as divine, deepening symptoms of awakening and wisdom. This chance for gradual learning and self-realization towards enlightenment also supports the idea of one dimensionality (continuity) of the 'wisdom paths.'

Sadly, many of us do not get an opportunity to reach the awareness intersection, or we arrive too late. This is particularly depressing as it takes a long time to travel from there to a decent destination, while we suffer a lot in life for absolutely no reason. We need the inner power when external forces have the highest impact on our lives. We need our confidence and self-reliance more than ever when we are being dominated and exploited—when we are young with naïve aspirations and imaginations. Yet, we do not have the right tools and minds, because we are trained merely for living in the perceived reality world—a world made merely of fantasies and illusions. Anyway, if we happen to arrive at the awareness intersection, it is better than not arriving at all. We can still give it a try as we build our faith for a higher truth.

Our Main Struggles

In spite of our rising inner strengths and the power of our faiths and spirits, we cannot elude the mandate of existence altogether. Our endless struggle, unconsciously or knowingly, relates to our inner quarrels to attain a *psychological equilibrium*. Mainly, we strive to grasp and align the truths boiling inside every intelligent human (the real realities) with this perceived world's realities, which we have learned or conditioned ourselves to adopt. The struggle is to grasp, and live with, the contradictions between 'what we have become' and 'what we could be' in our purest form when God created us, free from societal influence and rules. After all, it is hard to believe God intended to create such sad, pathetic, and thoughtless humans, if we prefer to believe in God! Generally, we try not to think about these contradictions. We keep rationalizing who we are and what we do—so idiotically too often—in order to reduce our pains. We deny or subdue our inner quest for the truth or its value. As intelligent beings, we know that hunger, crime, destruction of environment, genocide, racism, drugs, wars, and all the other manmade evils of this world are not the signs of a healthy life and mind, but every one of us is somehow involved in propagating these symbols of civilization and conformity, anyway, directly or indirectly. We have become part of the social and economical systems carrying these values and diseases across the borders and brains. And we have sunk in our egoistic pleasure-seeking attitudes and personalities so deeply that we can no longer even look up and see the storms of pain and thunders of anger passing above our heads ready to bring us, including the human history and culture, to our ends.

The struggle is to *communicate* with people about the path of inner satisfaction and self-questioning, especially with those we love and worry about so much. Only a small group understands these abstract concepts, or are motivated enough to explore these types of thoughts. Although we can hardly communicate at these levels, the struggle for self-questioning continues within us as a natural growing process. Every time, the process may last a few seconds, hours, or days, for most of us; or may turn into a lifetime crusade for a devoted group, such as gurus, philosophers, and humanitarians who seek the truth about existence eagerly.

The struggle is to *believe* that the questions of, 'Who am I?' and 'What the purpose of my life is?' are indeed instinctual and constitute the principal pillars of human identity and humanness. Life distractions and perceived realities (mostly fighting with sad social realities) disturb our quest for the truth and self-questioning quickly; before we find the chance to delve into the depth of the questions. The cry of children and families for food and shelter, personal weaknesses and desires, greed and pleasures, are all real obstacles to attend to our philosophical thoughts about the truth, life, and purer lifestyles.

Nonetheless, our struggles must continue to understand and *manage* our ceaseless doubts and prepare ourselves for handling major life decisions and demands, as discussed in Volume III, towards some form of social or mental victory.

The struggle is to *remember* how insignificant and vulnerable we are and that the value of life could not be simply summarized in making a living, having a family, engaging in materialistic or emotional pleasures, fighting amongst ourselves, then leaving as ignorant as we were born. There should be some purposes for our lives beyond what we have habitually defined for ourselves. For gaining an even minute sense of victory, humans must be largely free from socioeconomic manipulations, hypocrisy, physical and psychological pains, insecurities, immoralities, drugs, ignorance, arrogance, and fears that we wrestle with a lifetime. Our existing social structure and mentality could not be a definition of a real reality and humanity, simply because we can see the evidence of Nature. How could animals, plants, fields, and farms pervade so much beauty and harmony and yet the most intelligent creature on earth be so miserable, confused, unfulfilled, and destructive? How dare we ruin their harmony, too? It is hard not to wonder whether we are really the smartest species on Earth, or this is still another one of our egotistical imaginations. Even the wildness of Nature and natural disasters are at least explainable in terms of intrinsic motives or scientific phenomena. Conversely, humans' pains and disasters are mostly self-inflicted and foolish. Thus, our struggle is to realize 'why?' Why are we so naive and selfish?

The struggle is to *identity and exploit* our real potentialities in order to resolve the inner conflicts about who we are and how we feel and behave. We like to be successful, but at what price! We like to feel happy, but are looking outside ourselves to receive it from others and things!—mostly by abusing and hurting them, too. We like to be accepted and approved by members of family and society, but we betray one another and sell our souls in the process! We like to enjoy life, but work like slaves for objectives that do not mean anything to us! We like to live in peace, but do not want to let go of our egoism and self-indulgence! We like to be mentally and spiritually strong, but fight for ruling others! We need a simple life, but have made it too complex to live every single day of it! We struggle to be free, but are trapped inside our shallow mentalities and by our dependence on others and things! The list of contradictions and contrasts in our baffled mentalities never ends.

Our ongoing struggle to find even *basic contentment* usually fails, too, as we look for it within a social format not suitable (or capable) for offering it. Our habits and lifestyles support power, greed, arrogance, sexuality, and pleasure, but not peace of mind. We fail to recognize that gaining even some relative happiness depends on our ability to elude socioeconomic traps that have crippled our natural existence. Therefore, humans' struggle to find happiness would remain merely an immense, futile fantasy in this environment. However, even a harsher struggle is to accept that happiness is a myth to begin with, which has become even more elusive when we insist on finding it in our Ego-driven professions or around our crooked friends, family, and spouses.

Most of us can directly associate with these contradictions, struggles, and dilemmas. Yet, we deliberately choose to forget about them, mostly because we feel incapable or unwilling to do anything about them. We simply accept that we are extremely helpless in the scope of the social order to change anything. (But of course, we get haughtier every day and stir more social chaos, anyway.) We feel our frailty to be a nonconformist and challenge all these fixed values. Yet, we bask in the shoddy joys of artificial pleasures, sexuality, and phony appearances. Fashionable clothes, fancy automobiles, beach houses, glamorous parties, vain fame, casual sex, promotions and status, unrealistic and mushy movies, and all the rest of them are alluring. Still, wiser people who have mustered all these corny symbols of success and happiness have felt their vanity. They have realized that all this extravagance has really been a mirage and at the end, they still feel lonely and lost, in a vast desert of anxiety and ignorance. They just repeat the same old routines and habits like robots and just fool themselves with their own crooked thoughts and philosophies.

Surely, the temptations of worldly rewards for conforming and excelling in the execution of societal rules and demands are hard to resist. This is especially true when we do not know what to replace the existing social rules with and how to acquire a new wisdom to support our required mental overhaul. The discussions in this book about the magic of 'self' realization through inner peace and wisdom feel evasive and hard to grasp for those who have not tasted it. Even for those who enjoy a small dose of this spiritual state of mind, seeing beyond the first layer of ideas and feelings is impossible, thus hard to remain faithful and advance in their unorthodox reality. Simply, imagining an alternative way of existence more in line with humans' inherent needs and living purposes is hard, but most depressing is our nonchalance about the need for a better means of developing humans' mentalities and finding saner, more practical lifestyles for this lost species.

Meanwhile, our struggles—to *boost our spirits* personally the best we can and run the rest of our lives in peace—continue.

PART II
Science and Divinity

CHAPTER THREE
The Role and Goal of Spirituality

Previous discussions suggest that humans' urge for spirituality is ingrained in their deepest unconscious as a primary personal need. Actually, spirituality is so instinctual we can arrive at some basic conclusions: First, our drive for spirituality provides a plausible clue about the existence of spirit as a distinct human feature aside from his/her body and mind. Second, human spirit feels real and evolves faster when we stir our divine potentiality (spirituality) to understand 'who we are.' Third, while human urge for spirituality is responsible for finding and strengthening our spirits, the spirit within us is the force that drives our desire for spirituality. Fourth, our spirits' craving for spirituality is simply for liberating itself and us from social entrapments and artificial needs that humans impose upon their psyches. Fifth, our mental stability and peace depend on our ability to develop a personal means of spiritualism away from superstitions, religions, and afterlife dreams. Most of us would agree with these basic principles behind humans' urge for spirituality if we attempt to find it by exploring our 'self.'

Overall, spirituality is the most natural way of reaching our spirits, cleansing our minds, and connecting to the universe. It also offers a chance to build our foundation of thoughts and a simpler outlook to face our major life challenges, decisions, doubts, and limitations. In reality, however, we are killing both our spirits and chances for spirituality with our shoddy lifestyles and religions. Therefore, the chaotic world we live in. With our sullen spirits, we wander aimlessly in life and never learn how to handle its hardships or show compassion. We have no idea how to draw on our divine potentialities to boost our shattered spirits.

Volume I of this trilogy raises many unsettling questions about life and the dilemmas of living. We humans (our spirits actually) appear determined to resolve all those life mysteries like a sacred mission embedded in our psyches—as if our spirits' salvation depended on the accuracy of our answers. Obviously, the main question is about the creation of this incredibly complex universe that is quite orderly and formulaic beneath all the chaos it poses on us. We like to rely on logic and mathematics to explain this amazing phenomenon, but more vitally, to understand humans' *imaginary importance* amidst this colossal creation. To do so, we apply commonsense, philosophy, psychology, physics, theology, and other disciplines to come to terms with ourselves and find peace and happiness, too. We think too highly of our status at the centre of this grandeur, as if no amount of science and knowledge could convince us of our infinitesimal existence. Mainly, we like to satisfy our curiosity about 'who we are,' which most of us, and many scientists, believe to be inherently linked to Nature and a universal existence. We believe the essence of 'who we are,' the 'self,' our spirit, is the entity that supposedly connects us to the real world and our mysterious creator.

All humans, in the last ten thousand years at least, seem to have encountered similar questions and dilemmas according to their intelligence and teachings. In recent centuries, however, we have become even more curious and scientific about our ways of thinking and living. We have delved into detail research within a wide spectrum of subjects and disciplines. We now need more facts and proofs about the issues we discuss among ourselves and apply to our daily lives. At the same time, we have also become too romantic and philosophical about the nature of our existence and the role that a plausible form of spirituality could possibly play in answering the fundamental questions of living. The role that religions used to play for centuries to guide people is fading away gradually, too—thank god! No longer can those simplistic, untenable assertions withstand the test of science or even our rising commonsense. Thus, a new question is how a common person with average intelligence and patience can go about building his/her beliefs, foundation of thoughts, and spirit truthfully. What would be the main platform for justifying our conclusions, setting our mindsets, and choosing a proper path of life? Can we depend on religion, philosophy, science, spirituality, or a mix of them to get a relatively reliable point of view about our existence and purpose of living?

The Role of Religion

Fortunately, the role of religion is diminishing in line with the rise of people's education and intelligence in recent decades, as well as their accelerating thirst for immorality. In modern societies, in particular, only a small percentage of the population believes in religion and practices it seriously beyond their habitual gestures. This is amazing, because the percentage of people believing in God is still high. This seeming contrast is interesting in many ways. **First,** it proves that people's need for divinity is so intrinsic that almost everybody senses and seeks it urgently. **Second,** it emphasizes the depth of people's disappointment with religions to satisfy their divinity need rather intelligently. **Third,** it shows that people are getting smart, thus no longer willing to put their faith in any shallow type of divinity, despite their extreme and urgent need for a means of reaching their gods. **Fourth,** it reveals that people can somehow feel and attempt to contact their gods outside the religions, though not everybody is quite certain about the method of doing it. **Fifth,** although science can answer many questions about the creation and the origin of the universe, people still need an intimate way of connecting with a creator beyond the narrow connectivity that the scientific world offers and everybody accepts as facts, too. **Sixth,** people seek a more practical, reliable, intelligent, and honest means of fulfilling their spirituality urges. **Seventh,** people are failing to satisfy their instinctual sense for spirituality and building their spirits, since they are distracted by phony social values and sexuality. **Eight,** people's attempts to grasp the new spirituality ideas discussed in society feel phony and shallow, too, like all other features of modern living. **Ninth,** people still hope to satiate their niggling spiritual urges fast only by adopting some shallow concepts, instead of devoting adequate time and efforts to explore the means of spirituality personally and objectively mainly by learning about themselves.

Nevertheless, a vital (**tenth**) conclusion now is that we are all beginning to at least realize that no religion can fulfil our inherent spirituality need, nor any amount of science can disconnect us from our inner need for a symbolic god, beliefs, spiritual thoughts and feelings. *We all have a neglected spirit struggling to redeem itself through an authentic sense and means of spirituality.*

The Role of Science

The supersonic progress in science in the recent decades does not need any explanation here. The volume and depth of scientific discoveries in thousands of fields can make us all proud, although only a small fraction of us has played a significant role in all these amazing achievements. While the majority of us struggle with our life issues and pleasure-seeking endeavours, a small number of geniuses are devoting their brains and lives to the betterment of human knowledge and living condition. We owe them a heartfelt salute, although they are the ones reaching the height of elation with every one of their accomplishments and getting the ultimate rewards of existence through self-actualization. They have better means of answering many existential questions and dilemmas for themselves at least, while the rest of us struggle with our doubts and decisions forever. Many of them have somewhat found their spirits and means of spirituality, too, during their search for the truth. What are the rest of us supposed to do with our narrow minds preventing our chances for 'self'-realization?!

Yet, with all its power to enlighten us regarding our origin and organism and to help us live longer, healthier, and easier, science cannot still fulfil our quest for the truth that appears too deeply engrained in our psyches. We are still not impressed by scientific explanations. We still want a god and we still need to feed our souls. Actually, it is doubtful that science can even play a role in terms of humans' general wellbeing and easier life structure, in spite of all the new gadgets and tools that have become available to us. Certainly, more astonishing discoveries will come in the future decades if that very same science and knowledge do not bring us to the verge of idiocy and extinction. Anyhow, no matter how successful we humans (our scientists) feel about scientific discoveries, or how stupidly humans (mainly politicians) ruin our psyches and spirits with technology and profit motives, science and religions would never satiate our need for the truth we must unravel within ourselves personally. In fact, now scientists are merely exploited for manipulating humans more than they serve the pure, intrinsic needs of people, while business pressures and agendas have contaminated scientific discoveries.

The Role of Spirituality

In the recent decades, many concepts like self, truth, awakening, meditation, consciousness, enlightenment, transcendence, and reality have evolved under the heading of spirituality. Whether borrowed from ancient cultures or invented in-house, we have felt the need for a new discipline to satisfy people's rising thirst for spirituality now that religions have failed to do so. We all seek a means of connecting with a higher reality to boost our spirits, raise our hopes, and get at least some temporary relief from the superficial reality our societies have imposed upon us. Thus, we try to at least understand some of the spirituality concepts that many of us, including this author, would like to develop logically and propagate. However, this innovative approach has not borne fruit so far, but actually caused vast confusion about the purpose and process of spirituality. We are becoming familiar with the jargons and likely benefits of enlightenment, but very few of us start the journey on a path of spirituality, because its purpose and process are obscure. Meanwhile, we believe that some form of spirituality is our only chance for saving our souls and regaining our confidence about the purpose of living.

Besides inducing a sense of divinity, spirituality can help us raise our consciousness and study our spirit and 'self,' including its basic seven elements. The goal is to become 'self' conscious for living freer and easier, instead of remaining too self-conscious for being popular and loved in our superficial social environment. As stressed before, spirituality is also a vital vehicle for building our identities, the foundation of our thoughts, and a practical life philosophy. Our ultimate goal is to use at least the therapeutic property of spirituality intelligently, without getting carried away with another bunch of naïve assumptions about afterlife or the intentions of a supreme creator for His beloved humans.

The Role of a Divine Personal Life Philosophy

Eventually, all our personal knowledge, scepticism, beliefs, and needs must make sense within a **sensible divine philosophy** that validates our existence and daily struggles. We measure both our authentic and artificial needs and appreciate the ultimate goal of fulfilling our spirituality need. We grasp our general beliefs and life purposes. We strive to know 'who we are' in order to exploit the strength of 'self.' We recognize our needs, idiosyncrasies, and doubts through self-awareness by doing plenty of self-cleansing. We try to learn from some honest scholars' scattered ideas about spirituality. We expand our mindsets and learn the secrets of the universe that science keeps unravelling. We grasp the misleading role of religions in the history of humanity and their dire guilt for stifling our spirits and freedom. Then, at last, we turn all these fundamental thoughts and feelings into a dynamic life philosophy that also satiates our sense of spiritualism. We design a sensible life structure and choose a lifestyle fitted for a humble, confident, and independent person. We strive to build our mentality, future, and peace of mind on this platform, while strengthening our life philosophy with actual experiences and compassion along with our self-designed spirituality rituals towards transcendence.

The ultimate purpose of all these efforts and explorations is to maintain our sanity in this chaotic world by our inner strengths that grow in line with our life philosophy and spirituality rituals, while we follow some general principles to guide our practical contacts with normal life conditions and deteriorating societies. In the end, we might find many plausible answers and perhaps even some truth about existence to affirm the soundness of our life philosophy that is driven by a soothing sense of spirituality. This is certainly a divine ideal, yet we can envision it with our primary wisdom upon a strike of awakening.

The Purposes of Spirituality

In order to build our own personal ritual for spirituality, we must grasp the main characteristics and purposes of spirituality to elude the temptations of creating wild imaginations and expectations. Thus, some guidelines are offered in Table 3.1, while the shortfalls of present spirituality practices are listed in the next section.

Table 3.1
The Main Characteristics and Purposes of Spirituality

1. Spirituality is a personal journey and experience to explore our 'self' without going overboard and making outrageous claims about some imaginary truth and reality or practising some rituals blindly in hopes of outwardly rewards, such as a promise for a fantastic afterlife.

2. Spirituality needs discipline and long commitment for self-cleansing and raising self-awareness to find basic tranquility.
3. Spirituality requires complete knowledge of its purposes (as briefly outlined in this chapter) before one starts the journey. In particular, spirituality's main purpose is to lower social gullibility, and instead assist people raise, and rely on, their intelligence and intuition to build their beliefs independently.
4. Spirituality is not for proving the existence of a particular god or heaven. Nobody is in a position to understand or claim any fact about the deeply enigmatic aspects of the universe with certainty, especially about its creator and His intentions, even if such an incredible phenomenon exists.
5. Spirituality is built on basic beliefs with open mind, instead of blind faith or certitude. In fact, one objective of spirituality is to elude and eradicate dogmatism and fanaticism that comes with current religious practices.
6. Spirituality is for building a simple belief system in response to humans' natural urge and curiosity for divinity, but also for boosting our spirits.
7. Spirituality is for propagating compassion and comradeships among humans, too, instead of arrogance and hostility that certitude and dogmatism cause.
8. Although humans are built from same molecules and energy that the universe is, the existence of human soul, cognition, or its connection to a universal consciousness is at best just an idea. Thus, any claim beyond this crude theory is absurd. Even the basic meaning of humans' levels of consciousness is still vague and arbitrary, let alone all the crude speculations about its connection to this alleged universe's consciousness.
9. The universe does not appear to have a specific purpose for itself, let alone for human existence, which is a tiny element of this colossal system. Yet, human life can find a purpose if a person gets smart enough to set it properly for him/herself without trying to relate it to the purpose of the universe or human existence.

10. Spirituality is just one crucial dimension of human life and thoughts. It helps us build our spirits, but it should serve us only as another philosophical notion for building the overall foundation of our thoughts and pursuing a simple life. Thus, spirituality must not dominate our life philosophy and plans, because it is as speculative and instable as all other kinds of beliefs we include in the foundation of our thoughts.

In line with the above realistic purposes of spirituality, we can also remember the weaknesses of humans' present approach.

Shortfalls of Present Spirituality Approach

1. Too many gods

The first point to stress here is that the type of divinity prescribed by known religions is not included in the concept of spirituality in this book. The reason is that those religions have evolved out of naïve speculations about God and His direct words in holy books. They have advocated their own peculiar rules and rituals with certainty, as if representing different gods.

Besides religions, many new spirituality ideologies have also spread through Eastern cultures, mainly China, India, and Persia. Those spiritualists and philosophers have tried to formulate a path of transcendence in their books and lectured us with no common ground or purpose. They surely seem to have the good intention of helping us find our serenity and a path of wisdom. Yet, their ideas lack objectivity and uniformity, thus have created similar types of confusions that religions have caused for centuries.

Accordingly, now, an intelligent description and mechanism for spirituality is needed to draw people's attention and trust for self-development and divine goals. Otherwise, spirituality would never be understood and accepted as a process for addressing our spiritual needs and exploring our 'self'. It would lose its value and effect the same way religions have.

2. Goal ambiguity

Religions' basic intention has been to tame people's evil through all kinds of fears and fanciful promises. They have had very little, if any, interest in focusing merely on spiritualism as a prominent personal need. Consequently, all those religious principles and approaches have only caused more animosity and wars, instead of fulfilling people's basic need for compassion and divinity. They have caused more segregation than integration of humans' life and mentality. They have only raised people's gullibility with no intention to promote personal initiatives for exploring and grasping spirituality. No real God would destine all these atrocities on its privileged creatures if our logic about God's compassion and ultimate wisdom should withstand a test of validity.

Most ironically, these prominent spiritual entities, especially religions, have failed to offer a uniform means of reaching basic personal peace that humans seek their entire lives. Therefore, our cynicism about these traditional organizations has grown, while they try to influence and exploit our naivety forever. Meanwhile, without a uniform purpose and outlook, spirituality thoughts and rituals would remain meaningless, tenuous, and inconsistent. In order to propound a kind of true spirituality to a larger group and gather credibility, too, some form of rational notions and methods are necessary to unite humans. The question is how to organize some plausible spirituality thoughts without creating yet another big self-serving organization to exploit the naivety of people.

3. Lack of proof and credibility

Like religions, modern spirituality ideas also insist on afterlife in line with God's, or a divine entity's, intention to pity and control humans. Clearly, these new spiritualists would have a hard time drawing people's attention if they do not promise some form of human immortality at least. Thus, they make outrageous claims and offer convoluted assertions without offering any solid proof.

They also remain adamantly unconcerned about building a basic credibility for themselves, other than depending on their charisma for stirring people's emotions and building their faiths in some unseeable, unimaginable, unexplainable reality. They just want us to take their words and agree with their flawed logic as proofs and evidences. Just have faith, they say.

Deepak Chopra quotes a 'startling idea,' according to him, from the Indian source *Yoga Vasistha,* for describing the reality as,

"It is that which we cannot imagine, but from which imagination springs, It is that which is inconceivable, but from which all thinking springs."

Deepak Chopra then adds his conclusion,

"To me, this statement is so close to quantum reality that I keep wondering when my scientific friends will jump into the water—and discover that not only it is safe, it's familiar." The War of Worldviews, Deepak Chopra and Leonard Mlodinow, Harmony Books, 2011, page 291.

To most of us with sufficient intelligence, however, the *Yoga Vasistha's* quote (above) appears only like some hollow playing with words that proves nothing, nor clarifies anything regarding reality—quantum or otherwise. It only induces more scepticism and mistrust about any kind of spirituality claim that is built on similar grounds. The whole description sounds, at best, like only another abstract presentation of a made-up phenomenon beyond our comprehension. The vagueness and wordiness of a sentence is supposed to boost our faith, since it might soothe our inherent need for spirituality and immortality!—simply because it feels like a great scapegoat for our laziness to fathom spirituality on our own with some efforts and pain! This does not sound like a productive way of drawing people's attention to spirituality and enlightenment, but stirs only more confusion and apprehension. Deepak Chopra's both remarks, about the similarity of *Vasistha's* quote to quantum reality, and his astonishment about scientist not yet jumping in the water (*which is safe and familiar*) after reading the *Vasistha's* quote, cannot convince many of us, either, if not sounding rather bizarre, in fact.

Spiritualists resort to their own or other people's experiences or interpretations as a viable proof of spiritual facts, e.g., humans' consciousness as their guiding light and means of connection to a higher power beyond their normal potential. Again, expecting people to accept these examples and assertions blindly, even if the wordings of those claims were honest and clear, is a doomed expectation. The problem is not merely the lack of proof and credibility, but rather the spiritualists' pushy, irrational approach to make their points. Instead of offering some random magical experiences as evidences, in hopes of being possibly affirmed by scientific facts someday, too, spiritualists must admit the inherent limitation of human logic to grasp even simple mysteries of the universe. This would not deprive us, including spiritualists, from having a deeper appreciation of the natural (and supernatural) phenomena and the complex creation that we all share with awe as divine mysteries. In fact, humans' basic privileges of existence must be sufficient clues for us to build our sacred beliefs without needing miracles, supernatural proofs, or wordy sentences.

Even if there have been saints with miraculous connections to God, it does not mean the rest of us can reach the same level of enlightenment no matter how hard we try. However, this human limitation, due to our souls' weakness or life's routine burdens, does not mean that we should deprive ourselves from finding spirituality in a simpler way without putting our blind faith in the possibility of a mysterious reality that some gurus have felt, or the fact that they have contacted this specific god or another. Those people's experiences or words cannot offer a ground for a blind faith. Spirituality should stick to the basics, instead of trying to offer crooked, shallow proofs. There could be an intelligent, but simple, language for building our personal beliefs and philosophy about living in accord with humans' limited logic. That language and understanding would fulfil our spirituality need, too.

This section's notion about 'lack of proof and credibility' is further explained in the next chapter.

4. Abstractness

The terminologies and teachings of spirituality, such as 'self', consciousness, truth, reality, are too abstract to absorb easily or even explain to people adequately. For example, a big difference of opinion exists between scientists and spiritualists regarding the nature of consciousness. Some scientists have rather succeeded in proving that consciousness is merely a mental function, whereas spiritualists insist that human consciousness is a holy phenomenon outside the brain, as an extension of the universal consciousness. Most of us cannot even grasp this abstract interpretation about consciousness, let alone trust it. We like to know the meaning of this 'consciousness' in a tangible manner, instead of haggling with the vague notion that this word creates for us. Similar types of ambiguities in terminologies and concepts about spirituality cause us lots of frustration and become an obstacle for addressing our need for spirituality seriously. Sometimes, the emptiness of words and concepts, e.g., about consciousness, sounds surprising and worrisome in terms of both its meaning and the means of reaching that proposed level of consciousness. Worse, how can we trust those spiritualists who insist on pushing such abstract notions so emotionally and expect us accept their words and all those ambiguous concepts without having had an opportunity to explore spirituality personally in a natural, hard way?

5. Lack of a clear, uniform guidelines

If people attempt to follow a path of wisdom, especially such a long one typical for spiritual enlightenment, they must grasp the steps and expectations for doing so at the outset. They should believe that it is a reasonable and feasible process for a normal person to follow during his/her heavy daily duties and struggles for survival. In fact, spiritualists and religions have not yet created even a uniform set of guidelines to share among themselves as a basic platform for spreading the main purposes of spirituality that make sense within normal social settings. Instead, they have only offered a large variety of incongruent ideas and rituals, which people are expected to adopt robotically in hopes of attaining enlightenment or maybe qualifying for afterlife. Spiritualists seem nonchalant regarding the simple fact that without some uniform, practical guidelines humanity would only fight more even about their varied gods and goals forever, too.

Naturally, building our own spirituality beliefs and rituals, as suggested in this book, also lacks a uniform methodology and ritual that people can follow or share. Yet, personal spirituality beliefs and rituals are at least not tainted by ludicrous hopes, e.g., about afterlife, or driven by purposeless guidelines and rituals. They are only developed gradually within each person's psyche according to his/her unique level of awakening, intelligence, and sincere efforts towards well-defined goals.

6. Scepticism and apprehension in general

The present approach for spreading spirituality ideas are ignoring people's growing intelligence and their needs for at least some sensible grasp of the purpose of spirituality. Instead, spiritualists give them all kinds of unattainable hopes and promises again, almost like the way religions tried to build their cases in the past based on people's passion and gullibility. People have doubts about any kind of spirituality that its likely limited purposes are not clear and logically presented. At the same time, people's lack of wisdom or interest to question and infer their own conclusions about all these differences among God's guidelines feels bizarre.

Ironically, it is hard to imagine that all religions and cults are not sceptical and apprehensive themselves about the rationality of their differences, too, and do not realize the effects of their open or stealthy rejections of one another on the public in general.

7. Spiritualists' naïve insistence about the truth

The biggest barrier for developing a sensible spirituality discipline is that some imaginary ideas about truth, reality, consciousness, supernatural, etc. are presented to people *with certainty*. Instead of understanding and admitting to the speculative nature of their 'truth,' spiritualists insist to have the answers to human questions and dilemmas about divinity. They simply disregard the fact that nobody, not even science, can ever answer the basic questions about the creation, human existence, god, etc. Just imagine ants trying to fathom human life and thoughts and then swear with dogmatic certainty regarding the accuracy of their discovery, too! Spiritualists' mindset to insist on the certitude of their discoveries about the truth only reflects their conceit and naivety, and it also proves all the other six shortfalls numerated above.

Both the scientific and spirituality evidences are speculations within the limited parameters of human logic and intelligence. Science stands on a more solid ground due to the mathematical and methodical supports they can offer for their theories and the manner the overall design of the universe is explained by some scientific rules. However, in the final analysis, neither science nor spirituality can answer all fundamental questions and dilemmas yet—and most likely, they would never do. In this environment, spiritualists' persistence about knowing the truth sounds merely immature and perhaps even deceitful to people who are relying more on their intelligence now than passion to build their beliefs. Spiritualists' current approach merely restricts the limited use that spirituality could have for people.

Logically, no sensible spiritualist would ever insist on his/her presentation of the truth even if s/he felt strongly about his/her beliefs. S/he would only offer it as a mere plausible theory, since at the end everything we humans see and think would remain a raw perception. We can always hope those plausible views carry enough methodology and logic behind them, similar to science, so that we eventually end up with a set of spirituality principles, instead of a bunch of scattered opinions and dogmatic cults. This is the main premise and the most plausible principle. We can only perceive things—and merely based on the strength of our spirits and the validity of our foundation of thoughts.

In particular, we can never know anything about the mysteries that stand in a domain totally outside of human range of logic or perceptions. In fact, if by any unconceivable fluke someone ever reaches that divine transcendence beyond perceptions, s/he would hardly find it necessary to discuss the presumed truth that s/he has found, let alone insist on it with such prejudice and dogmatism. S/he would be transformed into a being way outside the realms and needs of humanity. Persistence and doubtlessness are in fact the signs of prejudice, which promptly ruins any semblance of truth and humility. Certitude merely reflects personal attachment, which is more a symbol of arrogance and a desire for acceptance, or hiding one's gullibility, instead of a sign of transcendence.

In all, if we like to build a reliable foundation of thoughts and include spirituality as its main building block, the first assumption must be that we humans would never find the whole truth about the nature of the universe, our limited role and importance within this superstructure, and the very miniscule possibility of afterlife. We must build our spirits and foundation of thoughts and make major life decisions within an environment akin to endless doubts about existence and a large host of other related mysteries.

Spirituality can become a good platform for building our personal life philosophy if its present shortcomings can be remedied. Even better, maybe someone could soon put together a comprehensive manual regarding a practical approach to experience and practise spirituality based on some logical principles. Meanwhile, we can try to develop and pursue a basic self-devised ritual around some sensible purposes of spirituality, like the ones suggested in Table 3.1 above. It would be useful for enhancing our self-awareness and finding relative tranquility in this chaotic world.

CHAPTER FOUR
Spirituality and Philosophy

Philosophy's main goal is to challenge our naivety, desires, ideas, and ideals, such as heaven and afterlife, and to find better means of coexistence. Philosophy also responds to humans' inherent curiosity about existence, God, creation, and other social subjects. Accordingly, our goal for mastering spirituality emerges mostly as another philosophical notion, too. Of course, humans' sacred urge for spirituality, as an innate virtue, is crucial for stirring our divine potentialities and enriching our lives. However, handling spirituality merely as a philosophical principle within the overall foundation of human thoughts would serve people and humanity better. It would also help us eradicate social gullibility, including outdated religious fanaticism, by mixing self-development and enlightenment.

Sadly, we have not still used either philosophy or spirituality properly to help people after millenniums of efforts and research. Especially it feels strange that not even scholars and spiritualists have found a common ground for their speculations. They have not succeeded to play a useful role toward the ultimate purpose of eliminating superstitions, naivety, dogmatism, and arrogance. In fact, they also attempt to prey on people's gullibility or emotional vulnerabilities often to push their shoddy ideas about spirituality.

Besides scholars' failure to relate to people in a simple, honest language, our social structure is too impotent to care even about people's gullibility, let alone fighting the sources and motives behind the rising social credulity and hardships. The spirituality shortfalls noted in the previous chapter shows the incompetence of governments and scholars' approach to help people with their spirituality needs in a natural, honest way. At best, some scholars are offering many tentative ideas about spirituality, too, with no ultimate and uniform purpose in mind. Sometimes, even they intend to abuse people's deprived emotions now with different words for similar crooked objectives and outcomes that religions had. Anyway, the point is that humanity in general has failed to build any useful foundation of thoughts and means of fulfilling our spirituality needs according to humans' limited science and logic for a productive marriage of social life and divinity.

The success of science lies in the use of methodology, design, conceptualization, experimentation, validation in line with natural laws, and many other factors. A main principle for its success, however, is its rational scepticism even about its latest findings, as someone always re-examines and challenges older theories. They develop vaster knowledge and more details in this process, simply because science encourages scepticism, experimentation, and updates. Spiritualists could also follow the same approach to achieve tangible results and help humanity. Instead, they insist on forcing certain ideas with certitude and expect people to form their faiths around those crude ideas, too. They push for extreme, i.e., building faith, rather than focusing on the task of helping us build just a platform for pondering intelligent beliefs on our own. Their practice, to insist on the truth and answers for irresolvable mysteries, abuses people's emotional vulnerabilities. It wastes so much energy and time, while sabotaging our chances of building some practical beliefs towards a healthier life structure.

We need spirituality more than ever now to cope with life's pains and to replace the outmoded religious practices. Yet, it will take a long time before an intelligent and reliable spiritual method and purpose is available for our use. Meanwhile, our best option is to build our own mode of spirituality according to the list of facts outlined in Table 3.1 on pages 69-71. That would be the best way for now to use some spirituality notions actively, along with philosophy and a solid foundation of thoughts to boost our spirits.

Nevertheless, the goal of spirituality is to build an atmosphere, and people's incentives, for personal reflections, so that they can grow their beliefs according to their own levels of self-awareness and senses of spirituality. Accordingly, this chapter suggests a platform for developing our philosophical spirituality personally, while we could also hope that a sensible spirituality regimen is envisioned eventually to guide humanity for coexistence.

Most importantly, though, this chapter's objective has been to stress on the dangers of pursuing the present spirituality methods and ideas. We must know the risks of any form of spirituality outside a plausible philosophical format, and the danger of not changing our traditional views of spiritualism and religions. The big question is whether the current social mentality can give the public an honest and realistic view of the truth about the universe and human life. Unfortunately, many clues, including a review of arguments among scientists and spiritualists, reveal the urgency for new spirituality principles in a philosophical framework to engage people in a sensible manner. Just to offer some examples, the following quotes by Deepak Chopra and Leonard Mlodinow depict the narrow approach of spiritualists these days without any plausible support by either philosophical or scientific principles. Then, we also wonder about the foundation and purposes of these perceptions and prophecies!

"I equate the future of belief with the future of God."

"Since God is intimately tied into who we are and what life means, there is no separate future for God and for the individual. You and I will make decisions that determine if God has a viable tomorrow." The War of Worldviews Deepak Chopra and Leonard Mlodinow, Harmony Books, 2011, page 260.

These statements are perplexing and vague for most of us, as it is hard to believe that *the future of God* (as stressed in the above quotes) would ever have anything to do with the strength of our beliefs, how learned we become about God's nature and wisdom, or how much faith we have in Him. Are not we talking about the same mighty God, by the way, who is supposedly responsible for the creation of everything, including our existence and thoughts? How could God's future, such a grand creator of all things and humans, reside in the hands (actually, beliefs and imaginations) of His minute creatures? Or, are we talking about the God that is just a figment of our imaginations to begin with? Deepak Chopra is also making a big assumption that, 'God is intimately tied into who we are and what life means,' which again is not a plausible concept or base for building a case, anyway. What is he thinking?

In all, it is best that neither scientists nor spiritualists insist on their viewpoints about the nature of God, though scientists do it much less frequently due to their rigid research processes and the need for plausible proofs and applications of their theories. The arguments between scientists and spiritualists are often the result of one or both sides' persistence on certitude and the truthfulness of their thoughts. For example, Leonard Mlodinow says,

"The issue that separates Deepak and me is not whether the universe has design, but whether something designed it, and whether it was designed for a purpose. Creationists and adherents of "intelligent design" believe, as Deepak does, that the intricacies of living creatures could not be the result of natural law." Ibid., page 108

At least scientists admit the undeniable depth of the mystery regarding the universe even after their vast scientific discoveries, as Leonard says,

"Why nature follows laws is a mystery. Why the specific laws we have observed exist is also a mystery. But what is clear is that the laws of nature are sufficient to enable us to show how life

arose without the necessity of there being any immortal hand or eye executing the design." Ibid., page 108

In all, science takes a more compromising position along with their continuous research and scepticism, but also by admitting to the mystical nature of the universe along with the humans' need for spirituality, while also appreciating life per se. Leonard says,

"I would be dishonest to dispute it when Deepak says science sees human beings as 'isolated specks in the cosmos, accidental outcroppings of mind in a mindless creation.' There is much in humanity to be thankful for, but to deny that we are isolated specks in the cosmos is to avoid the truth rather than embracing it. Deepak said it takes courage to see ourselves as he suggests we should, but he paints a rosy picture, one that, as in the quote above, he likes to contrast with the worldview of science. What takes real bravery is to embrace the reality we actually observe, without regard to whether it is a bleak or a rosy picture. To grow old, to see friends die and planes crash, and to experience love and loss without the comforting illusion of a living, thinking universe imbued with a divine essence takes courage.

"At the same time. I do choose a less bleak outlook. To me, though humans might be isolated specks with accidental outcroppings of mind, what is important is that we do have the capacity to experience art and beauty and joy." Ibid., pages 240-241.

"Understanding my essence doesn't diminish my appreciation for the gift of being alive; it makes me appreciate it even more. That's not a scientific principle. It's just the way I feel." Ibid., page 133.

That is the way any intelligent person would normally feel—according to a *conditional* truth in line with everything we have fathomed so far regarding the universe and ourselves, while also appreciating the mysteries surrounding the grandeur we happen to be only some specks within it.

Surely, scientists also feel the beauty, passion, compassion, and joy that we all feel. They seem eager to include some form of spirituality within their logical minds, too. Despite his opposition to the methods and certitude of present spirituality, Leonard says,

"A scientific and spiritual life can exist side by side." Ibid., page 236.

This is, of course, an ideal possibility and necessity, and in fact not too difficult to achieve, either. The only requirement is to stop being so arrogant and persistent about views that are at best tentative hypotheses and cannot provide an intelligent answer to human dilemmas. All we need is some honesty and modesty in our views, as we try so hard to unravel the mysterious truth about our existence. We should offer spirituality only as another source of primary thoughts useful for building our beliefs, but never for proving our faiths and getting more dogmatic. We desperately need honest thoughts, beliefs, and feelings based on our personal wisdoms, but not blind faith and fanaticism.

Science alone cannot solve many mysteries around us, either. Only a mix of philosophy and spirituality can fill this gap with plausible models and arguments, without showing prejudice and persistence, while welcoming scepticism. We need an intelligent method and description of spirituality to satiate humans' urge for divinity and to replace the controversial ideologies propagated by too many religions and spiritualists for so long. Spiritualists have so far failed to see and accept these basic points. They have no platform for their arguments and models other than persistence and resorting to humans' gullibility and sentimentality. They are not serious in building human intelligence and revoking the need for religions altogether.

The foundation of human thoughts includes both spirituality and philosophy for helping us build productive mindsets, run our routines, and fulfil our authentic needs, including divinity and self-actualization. Yet, our wisdom is still infected by perceived facts and myths as well as religious and spiritualists' dogmatic certitude. Clearly, 'certitude' only stops our thinking ability and objectivity. It only diminishes the validity of our arguments and the purpose of enlightenment. The same is true for human logic that is now tainted by our perceptions and dogmatism, so remains unreliable for building philosophical and spiritual notions.

Flexibility and open-mindedness are essential principles for mental growth, but some doubtfulness must always complement our ideologies, including the foundation of human thoughts and spirituality, away from human dogmatism, gullibility, emotions, ego, and crooked logic. After all, that is the only way to look for the plausible truth!

The Plausible Truth

We all search for a more meaningful life and a purpose for living, as our experiences and ambitions seldom feel fulfilling enough. Intuitively, we believe that a more viable truth must exist behind this complex universe and all this chaos we call life. We realize that our narrow logic and huge Egos hinder our perceptions of the world. Therefore, we seek a higher truth within some realm of divinity, which actually feels like an inherent aspect of our being.

The purpose of spirituality is to help us grasp this plausible truth in hopes of bringing tranquility into our lives and spreading the seeds of a harmonious life structure. Yet, we are discouraged and disheartened by the manner our search for this elusive truth remains sporadic and unproductive. Our search and wonderment have caused us only more confusion and reduced our chance of ever grasping anything tangible about this fine truth. On the other hand, we remain obsessed to discover at least the fundamentals of this mysterious truth and its likely connection to a divine reality. To make our job a bit simpler, we can review the question about the plausible truth at three levels as follows:

1. The truth about the universe
2. The truth about our personal lives
3. The truth about humanity

The Truth about the Universe

Science, spirituality, and philosophy can help us speculate on the origin and destiny of the universe, as well as humans' inherent connection to this enigmatic scheme. Yet, we should finally get serious and admit we can never unravel such intricate mysteries. Scientists and philosophers appear wiser to accept this basic fact, while they also continue with their research and contemplation for further insights. Only spiritualists and religions still persist on knowing the truth, which they also insist lies in people's blind faith in certain ideologies they put forward with no valid support and value. Surely, their crude persistence and certitude about their knowledge of the truth merely reflect humans' dire gullibility or self-serving agendas. Sadly, this mentality hinders the chance of preparing people's minds for even an elementary perception of the truth. At the end, we all suffer individually and collectively as long as our societies promote gullibility and exploitation.

For building our personal beliefs about the universe and the humans' role within it, nowadays, we merely have two options: (1) Blindly accept the shallow claims of religions or spiritualists to build our faiths and feed our gullibility. (2) Use some degree of intelligence to admit, once and for all, that no evidence indicates the possibility of human logic ever (or at least for many more millenniums) reaching a capacity to grasp and explain even a preliminary truth about the universe. It would not matter how much science and clues we muster and how much spirituality and philosophy we adopt for building our belief systems, the ultimate truth about the universe is beyond humans' grasp. Now it is up to us to decide which of the above two options we like to choose for developing our life philosophies. We may entertain the possibility of learning the grand truth regarding the universe and creation in more detail *someday*, but we must accept that knowing this truth with even a small degree of certainty is only a sign of our huge immaturity and stubbornness. We can go even one step further and include some plausible notions about this truth (about the universe) in our beliefs, as long as we remain doubtful about our viewpoints and interpretations. Only when we lose our doubts about our own or other people's ideologies and insist on their truthfulness with certainty, we emerge as absolute fools.

The Truth about Our Personal Lives

We have *some* power to understand the truth about our personal lives, too, and deal with it in some effective manner according to our priorities and intelligence. A main purpose of this trilogy is to help us grasp the truth about our lives and choices rather easier. Yet, our psychological defects, passion, gullibility, vulnerability, needs, and social pressures make our job of handling this crucial truth quite difficult. Our illusions, as symptoms of living in the perceived world, hinder our abilities to see the truth and find our identities and integrity.

The most fundamental truth about our personal lives relates to humans' permanent fear of loneliness compared with their drive for individualism and independence, as both personal and social properties in the new era. A good portion of our sufferings in life relates to our growing doubts and indecisions about what is good for us, e.g., choosing the privileges of living independently rather alone or the likely joys of building a family if it happens to work.

A major, inherent connotation of the words individualism and independence is the person's ability to *stand alone*, which implies both the divinity and necessity of loneliness as one of humans' precious attributes. If we accept this implication of individualism and independence, along with their allusions for *standing alone* and *loneliness* stances, we can draw four big conclusions: First, we humans have not appreciated and benefited the privileges of solitude yet. Second, we have failed to imagine, and benefit from divine moments and experiences that solitude offers, which we may even share in our relationships to enjoy one another beyond our shallow, short experiences of love and lust. Third, we have not grasped individualism and independence, yet cherish, and brag about, a demented interpretation of them personally and socially. Fourth, what can we say regarding the depth and meaning of our individualism if we cannot be independent, stand alone on our feet, and withstand loneliness with grace, if not actually enjoy it?

Individuality, as a dimension of 'self' discussed in Chapter Thirteen (page 248), imposes some stoic ideals that clash with humans' inherent dread of loneliness. Yet, loneliness could give us an opportunity to explore our 'self' and discover divinity much better than we can do in our confusing modern relationships.

Overall, the main plausible truth about our personal lives is our ability to define a path of life within a simple philosophy based on some fundamental thoughts for leading a purposeful, peaceful, and honest existence. Our life decisions and quality improve all along by boosting our self-awareness, while we also try to learn the truth about humanity

The Truth about Humanity

The truth regarding humanity plays even a more significant and direct role for humans' welfare than finding the truth about the universe. Yet, we care, and learn, a lot more about the universe than humanity, as if humans are programmed to self-destruct by applying their brains to trivia and illusions than finding solutions for a dying humanity. Although our curiosity about the universe is vital for satisfying our spirituality need, the survival of human race in itself depends on how deeply and urgently we interpret and tackle the truth about humanity. Furthermore, while the truth about the universe remains forever hidden from us, gauging the truth about humanity is much easier to figure out if we become sincere and objective about a few dozen clear facts about society and human nature. This trilogy, including the scholars' opinions quoted in it, has been mostly for drawing a rather reliable picture of the fast deteriorating state of humanity. We can all notice the hardships we have brought upon ourselves and the way we have ruined our planet with our greed and arrogance, yet have gotten less tangible results from all that knowledge, efforts, and egotism. George Carlin's view of the state of humanity in the 21st century is quite to the point:

"The paradox of our time in history is that we have taller buildings but shorter tempers, wider freeways, but narrower viewpoints. We spend more, but have less, we buy more, but enjoy less. We have bigger houses and smaller families, more conveniences, but less time. We have more degrees but less sense, more knowledge, but less judgment, more experts, yet more problems, more medicine, but less wellness.

We drink too much, smoke too much, spend too recklessly, laugh too little, drive too fast, get too angry, stay up too late, get up too tired, read too little, watch TV too much, and pray too seldom.

We have multiplied our possessions, but reduced our values. We talk too much, love too seldom, and hate too often.

We've learned how to make a living, but not a life. We've added years to life not life to years. We've been all the way to the moon and back, but have trouble crossing the street to meet a new neighbour. We conquered outer space but not inner space. We've done larger things, but not better things.

We've cleaned up the air, but polluted the soul. We've conquered the atom, but not our prejudice. We write more, but learn less. We plan more, but accomplish less. We've learned to rush, but not to wait. We build more computers to hold more information, to produce more copies than ever, but we communicate less and less.

These are the times of fast foods and slow digestion, big men and small character, steep profits and shallow relationships. These are the days of two incomes but more divorce, fancier houses, but broken homes. These are days of quick trips, disposable diapers, throwaway morality, one night stands, overweight bodies, and pills that do everything from cheer, to quiet, to kill. It is a time when there is much in the showroom window and nothing in the stockroom. A time when technology can bring this let-

ter to you, and a time when you can choose either to share this insight, or to just hit delete..." Online communication by ingenious **George Carlin.**

We know a lot about the truth of humanity and we can do something about it, too, if we ever happen to become smarter beings, set our priorities straight, and see the looming demise of humans. Spiritualists blame this sad state of affair on science for its soulless approach to the truth (about life and the universe) and scientists blame it on spiritualists for their triumphant spread of gullibility and unfounded ideologies. Regardless of all these raw arguments, the ultimate truth about humanity indicates that it is at the verge of total collapse and we do not have a solution for our looming demise, nor do we seem to care. Some religions and fanatics actually look forward to, and some even strive to force, the end of humanity in hopes of reaching the judgment day faster and going to heaven. Do we really need any further proof about the depth of human gullibility?

The sad fact is that the technologies that science offer and the ideologies that spiritualist and philosophers propagate are only tools at our disposal for proper interpretation and application of reality. It is all a matter of human intelligence and goodwill as to how we apply those tools for people's welfare. When we abuse technology to destroy one another, it reveals humans' wicked nature and not science's mistakes in its calculations and theories about the laws of nature. It is our own fault when we use science for evil purposes, not the science itself. We should also blame our naivety for the prevalent social chaos when we become fanatics and put our faiths in crude ideologies of religions or spiritualism. Our looming demise is not the fault of science and not even the fault of simple-minded or phony spiritualists. Merely our own persistence to stay naïve spreads gullibility and allows another group of humans exploit us and the situation so casually. It is our own lack of conscience and growing greed that goad us promote many unfounded ideas to become famous and sell more books. Then again, humans' vile nature also seems irreparable!

A few other quotes from Chris Hedges show the scope of our naivety and the depth of human tragedy in early 21st century. The one on page 24 applies to these discussions as well.

"We are a culture that has been denied, or has passively given up, the linguistic and intellectual tools to cope with complexity, to separate illusion from reality. We have traded the printed word for the gleaming image. Public rhetoric is designed to be comprehensible to a ten-year-old child or an adult with a sixth-grade reading level. Most of us speak at this level, are entertained and think at this level. We have transformed our culture into a vast replica pf Pinocchio's Pleasure Island. Where boys are lured with the promise of no school and endless fun. They were all, however, turned into donkeys—a symbol, in Italian culture, of ignorance and stupidity." **Empire of Illusion,** Chris Hedges, Alfred A. Knopf, Canada, 2009, page 44.

"The America we celebrate is an illusion. America, the country of my birth, the country that formed and shaped me, the country of my father, and his father's father, ..., is so diminished as to be unrecognizable. I do not know if this America will return, even as I pray and work and strive for its return.

Our nation has been hijacked by oligarchs, corporations, and a narrow, selfish, political, and economic elite, a small and privileged group that governs, and often steals, on behalf of moneyed interests. This elite, in the name of patriotism and democracy, in the name of all the values that were once part of the American system and defined Protestant work ethics, has systematically destroyed our manufacturing sector, looted the treasury, corrupted our democracy, and trashed the financial system." Ibid., page 142.

"America has become a façade. It has become the greatest illusion in a culture of illusions. It represents a power and a demo-

cratic ethic it does not possess. It seeks to perpetuate prosperity by borrowing trillions of dollars it can never repay.

The corporate power that holds the government hostage has appropriated for itself the potent symbols, language, and patriotic traditions of the state. It purports to defend freedom, which it defines as the free market, and liberty, which it defines as the liberty to exploit. It sold us on the illusion that the free market was the natural outgrowth of democracy and a force of nature, at lest until the house of cards collapsed and these corporations needed to fleece the taxpayers to survive. Making that process even more insidious, the real sources of power remain hidden. Those who run our largest corporations are largely anonymous to the mass of the citizens." Ibid., page 143.

"We have been steadily impoverished by our own power elites—legally, economically, spiritually, and politically. And unless we radically reverse this tide, unless we wrest the state away from corporate hands, we will be dragged down by the dark and turbulent undertow of globalization. In this world there are only asters and serfs. We are entering an era in which works may become serfs, no longer able to earn a living wage to sustain themselves or their families, whether in sweatshops in China or in the industrial wasteland of Ohio." Ibid., page 144.

"We embrace the dangerous delusion that we are on a providential mission to save the rest of the world from itself, to impose our virtues—which we see as superior to all other virtues—on others, and that we have a right to do this by force." Ibid., page 145.

In all, in terms of the ultimate truth about humanity, we have almost all the facts, as noted above, especially regarding the truth about humans' inherent impurity, which is expanding fast due to extreme social corruption, greed, gullibility, egotism, illusions, and fake ideologies, including spirituality. This murky, ultimate truth is destroying us and our planet.

Part II: Science and Divinity

Luckily, deep down, we rather feel these gloomy truths about humanity and our personal lives, but remain incapable of facing and reconciling them with our authentic needs individually and collectively. Instead, we humans quarrel among ourselves about some bizarre beliefs and realities in imaginary realms beyond our comprehension. We prefer to feed our illusions and gullibility or fool others, instead of facing the ominous truths about the world's looming demise if we do not change our personal and social mentalities expeditiously.

The book, *The War of the Worldviews,* noted before, provides more clues about both the state of humanity and personal lives of people driven by enormously complex and often weird thought processes. Discussions in that book can be helpful for grasping the plausible truths. Reading at least the epilogue of that book would supplement the discussions in this chapter. Some crucial points raised by the authors in the book's epilogue are quoted here, starting with a comment from Leonard Mlodinow.

"When philosophizing, one can talk freely about unseen realms, invisible realities, and organizing forces that guide evolution. One can illustrate the ideas with stories and anecdotes, and argue by analogy. One can use everyday language with its pitfalls of vagueness, and terms with multiple meanings. One can pepper one's prose with satisfying terms like 'love' and 'purpose.' One can even appeal to ancient sages and texts. These arguments may seem attractive. But science answers to a higher authority—the way Nature actually works." The War of Worldviews, Deepak Chopra and Leonard Mlodinow, Harmony Books, 2011, page 297.

Leonard's summary about the role of science compared with the sloppy language that spiritualists use for describing divinity is quite understandable to many of us, especially when spiritualists keep insisting on the relevance of their assertions with certitude. At the same time, it is still plausible, as perhaps Leonard agrees too, that a real reality exists beyond the perceived reality** that we are capable of witnessing and measuring remotely according to our limited knowledge and logic. There is no harm in having this type of beliefs with adequate scepticism about the nature of those beliefs. The problem begins when some spiritualists insist on turning those ideas into blind faith.

Deepak Chopra's counterarguments are quoted below:

"I'd suggest that the war doesn't need to be fought anymore, because it's already over. Hidebound science is ready to topple, making way for a new paradigm where consciousness takes center stage." Ibid., page 300.

"If our life has meaning, it must have come from somewhere." Ibid., page 301.

These assertions, again, seem too definite and final to most of us with average intelligence, let alone in the ears of emotionally vulnerable people thirsty for any kind of easy conclusions and fanaticism. Science being toppled by *a new paradigm where consciousness takes center stage* is a major claim that is hard to swallow easily and not wonder! And in the second comment, again Deepak has already concluded that not only life has a meaning because of the mundane activities we do (what kind of meaning is that for life?), but is also assuming that this 'meaning' comes from an external source (*somewhere,* according to him) rather than being a creation of our brains based on our personal perceptions and erratic tastes, in fact. It makes absolute sense for humans with adequate intelligence to set logical purposes for their activities and lives. Yet, their urges or habits for setting purposes for their activities (for being efficient and proactive) do not prove that the universe does the same or that humans' erratic habits are a derivative of a universal purpose or direction. Any spirituality built on these types of raw assumptions is only a waste of time to discuss, let alone practise. Using humanly logic to set a meaning

---

** Real and Perceived Worlds are explained in Vol. I of this trilogy in Chapter Three.

for the universe and define its characteristics is futile, especially when those ideas come from people who insist on the certitude of their conclusions. In another example, Deepak asserts,

"When a professor of medicine smirked at the notion of the mind affecting the body, I would blurt out, 'How do you wiggle your toes? Isn't your mind sending an order to your feet?'" Ibid., page 301.

Obviously, brain's neurological system has the power to order and move all parts of the body, including our toes, not to mention helping immune systems' immense capacity to cure our bodies. This is science and proves the complexity of the brain. Yet, this type of connectivity (or human logic explaining it) does not prove the utter or spiritual aspects of the body-mind connection, which could then also be used as a ground for making other unproven claims. For example, wiggling our toes cannot aid us think better thoughts just because we like to insist on the power of body-mind connectivity! For one thing, this connectivity is not a clear and concise, two-way relationship. Wiggling our toes might at best give us weird (speculative) ideas about the extent and nature of body-mind connection. So far, the proofs offered by spiritualists in their spectacular assertions are equally speculative and flimsy— very much like the purpose of wiggling our toes. They are often just some form of nicely packaged, emotionally attractive fallacy.

Deepak Chopra, MD continues to say:

"Ordinary people aren't going to give up emotions and inspiration just because science sniffs at subjectivity. Science shouldn't be so edgy and defensive." Ibid., page 303.

"One must be decisive here: a world ruled completely by science would be hell on earth. Being wedded to rational thought is acceptable inside the lab, but once science ventures to dismantle faith, striving, love, free will, imagination, emotion, and the higher self as so many illusions cooked up in our fallible brain, a rescue effort must be mounted, and quickly." Ibid., page 303.

The above quotes also appear like some kind of effort to spread faith in some fuzzy and flimsy form of spirituality only by discrediting science. It also relies on *ordinary people* (according to Deepak) and their gullibility to propagate spirituality. Is not this approach itself the nucleus of all our problems? It sounds like making a case against science to not only cover up one's own pure subjectivity, but also invent a *novel* kind of subjectivity that strives to push absolute certitude! This weird notion and logic merely indicates either the pure naivety of some spiritualists or their ambitious agendas (maybe even similar to the exploiters of science). Some spiritualists merely laugh at the suggestibility and naivety of people, who accept any attractive idea to validate their own laziness, love, hollow sentiments, and lousy imaginations. Spiritualists' attempts to mix subjectivity, illusions, and certitude so readily are just amazing. Their ideas may have value, but, at the very least, their mode of presentation and certitude about their subjective points of view cause horrendous problems.

Analysing some spiritualists' statements in their books reveals the vanity of their approaches and the enormity of inconsistencies in their ideologies. Hiding behind words and exploiting people's emotional vulnerability and confusion would not serve humanity. We should know by now to keep subjectivity within the domain of myths and doubtfulness and leave any hint of certitude (if at all) only to cases where strict forms of objectivity are applied. Spiritualists should also realize that exploiting people's emotions and vulnerabilities has been the cause of enough religious wars and human ignorance already, now leading to the demise of the whole humanity. Following the same path of ignorance with new spirituality themes, but within the same frame of mind, would not have a better outcome.

By the way, Deepak Chopra's popularity around the world shows perfectly how easily the general population are drawn to any emotional and subjective ideologies in order to soothe their deprived and spirits and satisfy their naive minds and curiosities in our perplexing, directionless societies and philosophies.

Table 4.1
Basic Guidelines for Building Spirituality

As a first step for building a progressive and more useful kind of spirituality, spiritualists should first clarify a few hundred points before even speculating about narrower topics or fighting with science. Among those few hundred points, they must first answer to some basic questions, such as the following:

1. Do spiritualists believe in the Big Bang or not?
2. What they believe the nature of Creation is?
3. What they believe the purpose of Creation is?
4. What aspects of Creation and its purpose(s) they are certain about? On what grounds?
5. What do they think was there before that split second of the Big Bang? How can they prove, or even speculate on, it?
6. What issues they still have some doubts about?
7. What do spiritualists expect from scientists?
8. What do spiritualists want scientists to do beyond following their existing methodology?
9. Are spiritualists offering a better method for handling the known truths about human nature and the doomed destiny of humanity? Or they believe that mere faith can solve all these problems? How?
10. Can spiritualists offer a better mechanism for revamping humans' gullibility, maybe through a more intelligent means of spirituality? What are the main characteristics of such a spirituality model?

If the so-called spiritualists cannot, or refuse to, explain their positions about the above and many other fundamental questions, then what can we say about their general assertions other than attributing them to their pure ignorance, if not hypocrisy as well?

At the same time, it would be a great service to humanity if some scientists, preferably Leonard Mlodinow, too, write a few books about the kind of spirituality that might be sensible for the 21st

century, with objective scepticism about the truths and realities, to cover the following objectives:

1. Humans' need for spirituality.
2. Humans' need for science and its possible relationship with spirituality.
3. How to handle the ultimate truth about humanity.
4. How to face the ultimate truth about our personal lives and integrity with reference to both science and spiritualism.
5. Exploring our inner self.
6. Use of spirituality for soothing social stress and the burdens of living.
7. Eradicating gullibility in society.
8. Abolishing the need for naïve forms of spirituality.
9. Raising people's intelligence to find their own truths and spirituality.
10. Controlling the side effects of science on human life.

The bottomline about the 'ultimate truth' is that we will never know some (probably most) aspects of it. Yet, we have a capacity to grasp a lot about the truths that affect our wellbeing severely already, as were briefly noted in this chapter. The only condition is to become smarter and less self-serving with our ideologies and personal agendas.

Sadly, the mere ultimate truth is that 'we cannot handle the truth,' as Jack Nicholson said in the movie, *A Few Good Men*. What is the point of knowing the ultimate truths when we are unwilling or incapable of doing anything about them, such as the dire risks of current socioeconomic mechanisms on climate and humans' mere existence? We know the ultimate truth regarding the doomed future of humanity and we know how we are causing our own stress and sufferings, due to our lifestyles, mentality, and egoism, but simply do not wish to do anything about them.

What is the point of fussing and fighting over the ultimate truth when we humans are so adamant to ignore the clear truths right before our eyes? We simply cannot handle the truth. Period.

PART III
Potentialities and Dilemmas

CHAPTER FIVE
The Spirit in Human Potentialities

The enigmatic spirit that drives humans' need for spirituality (as discussed in Chapter Three), also steers their unique potentialities that transpire mainly in the form of creations and innovations. In return, our thriving potentialities and insights reveal and revitalize our neglected spirit. Chapter Seven's discussions of genetic and divine potentialities, and the quotes in Chapter One about self-actualizers' idyllic experiences, reflect this integrated connection between our potentialities and spirits.

Everybody has some talents (potentialities) and a great deal of quirks (limitations). We try to pinpoint these talents and quirks intuitively, through self-awareness, or by people's suggestions. We believe that our success and happiness in life depend on our *timely* assessment of our potentialities and limitations. We do it mostly for career planning and business decisions, but also for boosting our spirits and feeling positive. We wish to create our identity and individualism, get a chance to choose our purpose of living, and make our major life decisions rationally. All along, we sometimes also get a hunch that we can touch our 'self' and fulfil our spiritual urge through our potentialities. Thus, resolving our limitations and exploring our potentialities become crucial for not only leading a productive life, but also making our life decisions and discovering our being per se apart from our social identity.

Still, exploring our potentialities is a daunting task, because it demands initiative, learning, personal sacrifice, social adaptation, and serious decisions. It is a major challenge, considering the pressures to adapt ourselves to job market, handle many tough demands of social life, face many doubts (including self-doubt), and try to curb our debilitating idiosyncrasies, too. Thus, usually, we neither realize our potentialities (to feel self-actualization), nor eliminate our bad habits and flaws (to revive our spirits). We do not find the time, willpower, or guts to do these kinds of 'self' explorations and cleansing. Accordingly, we lose the opportunity of grasping our identity and spirituality attributes to live happier on a rather independent path of life.

Many reasons exist for neglecting our potentialities, while we eagerly pamper our flaws, such as egoism and aggression. **First**, societies have not yet explored the inherent boundaries of human potentialities other than measuring people's general aptitude and intelligence for performing some tasks. This outer limit of human potentialities (e.g., creativity, spirituality, or possible connection to the universe) is still a mystery for us. Throughout the human history, only gurus and odd spiritualists have delved into higher limits of consciousness. The rest of us either do not bother with these seeming supernatural stuff or at best adopt a religion to get the matter over with, hoping that we have done an adequate job of satiating our spirituality need. **Second**, our aspirations, greed, and social norms usually encourage us to either exaggerate or misuse our potentialities. Our misperceptions of our potentialities, in fact, often mislead us, thus we lose the chance of tapping this source of energy and wisdom for proper use. **Third**, we ignore humans' deep limitations, especially our needy personalities and crooked perceptions of life. Instead, we believe we can achieve everything we put our minds into, simply because the positive thinking slogans say so. **Fourth**, our need for 'practicality' goads us to pursue only good-paying jobs and wealth accumulation goals and lifestyles, which consume all our physical energy and mental capacity.

Even when we are fortunate enough to notice the streaks of our genius and innate potentialities, we have a hard time utilizing them. Sometimes, they are wasted on trivia or evil thoughts and deeds. Sometimes, they seem useless in the context of our social standards and the criteria of success. Accordingly, many of us feel incomplete and depressed when our potentialities are not appreciated or used properly. Our spirit sinks when not even our seemingly marketable potentialities can help our subsistence or bring us peace of mind. This hurtful epidemic is saddening many of us, though our negligence regarding our 'self' and our divine potentialities dampens our spirits the most, as noted in Chapter Thirteen under the heading of 'knowing (about) ourselves'.

Nonetheless, we should know that our unique potentialities are hidden treasures bestowed upon us, perhaps for some divine purpose, which we have not figured out yet due to personal and social limitations. Therefore, self-cleansing (by overcoming our limitations) and self-realization (by nurturing our potentialities) remain the main objectives of a *lifelong* self-awareness regimen, beyond the common need for an initial, timely self-assessment during youth to choose a viable life path.

The Makeup of Our Potentialities

A person's potentialities (knack for creativity) set the outer limits of his innate capacity (cognition), which is usually not explored and developed fully within regular lifestyles. It entails his higher mental, physical, and spiritual abilities to perceive, feel, think, reason, act, react, and connect with others and his surroundings at a high level of consciousness. Self-awareness builds and reveals the amount of cognition (or potentialities) that we have learned to master at a conscious level rather systematically every day.

We have unique potentialities to do some tasks better than others. We also have an intrinsic capacity to feel life's beauties, moments, and values in our own special, imaginative ways. And we have divine potentialities that can provide the wisdom and mental energy we need to face major doubts and decisions of life effectively. Potentialities include our intelligence, but intelligence per se does not indicate or induce our potentialities adequately. Intelligence is a common criterion and a measure of our mental ability, yet it does not pinpoint those creative areas we can apply for finding our 'self,' and it does not stir the wisdom and energy that magical experiences of spirituality and self-fulfilment induce. Only by exploring our innate potentialities, we stir self-fulfilment, spirituality, tranquility, and capture the essence of life.

We usually think of our potentialities as those abilities in which we seem to excel, mainly for social adaptation and success according to common norms and values. We are drawn to those fields of expertise and activities that offer the highest financial rewards. Thus, we choose a particular education and profession to become an expert in that field. Meanwhile, we find little time or incentive to explore other aspects of our potentialities that stir our creativity and insight, in particular for grasping who we really are. In our materialistic societies, we have no serious motives to seek our essence and potentialities, while we follow a deceptive path of success obsessively.

We cannot sense or measure our potentialities objectively in line with humans' real needs, because we are distracted by either our struggles for survival or our ambitions driven by superficial needs. Applying even those abilities that we muster consciously is a tough task in our dynamic and demanding societies, let alone the huge amount of our potentialities that remain unchallenged at unconscious level. In this kind of hypnotic setting, achieving self-fulfilment and tranquillity becomes a matter of accident for many of us, rather than a conscious pursuit.

We have an inherent potential (or nature) to look for a 'self' controlled and 'self' driven life, but do not receive the family and social support to recognize and accomplish this basic instinct of humans. In this context, our personalities and attitudes towards life and relationships actually reflect how little humans' overall logic and potentialities have so far been developed. Our haughty, phony personalities and crooked social values are obstacles for discovering our potentialities, including our spirituality potentials for guiding us towards a more harmonious humanity. How can we ignore the simple fact that the world's incredible poverty and misery is an irrefutable proof of our miniscule use of intelligence and human potentialities? Sometimes, we feel our innate need for divinity in the latter stages of our lives when our lifelong gloomy experiences shake our belief systems. Ideally, though, we should not limit ourselves to this likely late discovery with a much lower chance of helping us at that point. By grasping all aspects of our potentialities, including spirituality, we can increase the quality of our lives and inhibit our agonies significantly.

The Functions of Our Potentialities

Our life path and success result from the type of potentialities we nurture for, 1) building our careers and pampering our artistic passion, and 2) exploring our divinity and 'self.' Let us refer to these dual purposes (functions) as career and divine potentialities respectively. Besides the purpose of making a living, the main goal of *career* potentialities is to incite our creativity and attain self-actualization, which provides inner satisfaction and fulfils our need for achievement. Conversely, our *divine* potentialities are for connecting us to our spirit and Creation. We find our 'self' and attain 'self'-actualization, as we perceive ourselves a part of humanity, feel global pains, and show everlasting compassion. Thus, the terms self (for career) and 'self' (for divine) are used as two distinct actualizing virtues of our potentialities. Within this context, 'self'-actualization surpasses self-actualization when one ultimately attains selflessness and connects with his soul and the universe. In a sense, merely our creativity can link us to Creation.

Of course, our potentialities fulfil other purposes, too, other than building our careers and satisfying our sense of spirituality.

Actually, exploring our potentialities is the essential process for activating every one of the seven elements of 'self', as discussed in Chapter Thirteen. We like to contribute to society by offering our potentialities (perhaps our simple thoughts). We like to be a little genius in some respect if we could. Even in the absence of this ultimate capacity, we believe we have some creativity and ideas to offer to others or ourselves as a symbol of who we really are and what we have done with our lives. As bare minimum, we like to ascertain our identity for our own sake, and for an honest self-presentation to others. Therefore, our efforts for realizing our potentialities could ideally address the question of, 'What am I here for?' in line with the question of, 'Who am I?' While our socioeconomic motives for using our potentialities are deep and urgent, our instinctual motive to grasp 'who we are' and 'what we are supposed to achieve' always prickle our subconscious, too. This strong urge reflects the unique essence of our being—our spirit.

In our conventional thinking, we ignore the main functions of our potentialities quickly and move on to explore only those skills that we enjoy doing or appear practical for making more money. We attempt to measure our potentialities merely in terms of tangible results and a perception of success, which are usually gauged by monetary rewards. This narrow perspective is rather warranted in most situations as a practical means of living in our tough societies. However, this prevalent view of our potentialities undermines the depth of who we are or can be. It demonstrates our tendency to bypass all the clues about our inherent need to know who we are. It reveals our one-dimensionality. We forget that the ultimate purpose of exploring our potentialities is to stress on our humanistic needs properly, much more than we waste on satiating our artificial needs. In effect, our exaggerated sense of practicality is killing our spirits as we are conditioned by daunting social norms about pragmatism.

The *ideal* option would be to recognize and nurture our innate potentialities regardless of their financial and social appeal. Some rewards might flow in as well, but taken only as fringe benefits, rather than the goal. However, this may not be wise or practical for most people, nowadays. Thus, the implications of career and 'self' potentialities are discussed in some detail in the next two chapters respectively. The objective is to get a better grasp of our approach toward our potentialities. We must know how our being (spirit) might benefit from our higher scrutiny on 'self' versus career potentialities. Maybe it is time at last, in the 21st century, to invent a better social structure and wiser criteria for living and success, by stressing on more important aspect of 'self,' instead of pampering the same old habit of thinking merely in terms of money and success to define ourselves—for God knows how many more centuries. One thing is clear, though: We are not compelled to follow the crowd like a fool!

The Collective Treasures of Human Potentialities

Our personalities, logic, psyches, and spirits stir our feelings, thoughts, and actions, which in turn reveal our potentialities and quirks. Our divine potentialities inspire our views of the universe and outlooks on life. Therefore, while we are always disturbed by external information and atrocities, our inner strengths and divine potentialities could still help us view our world as a beautiful place with all kinds of sensational experiences; or we could just let our quirks lead us in a horrific life journey filled with suffering and controversy.

We can discover our potentialities during our exploration of the infinite offerings of the universe as well as some elite humans' creations. It is true that all the valuable things in life are free! Not gold or diamond, but rather the creations of Mozart, Beethoven, Monet, Van Gogh, and many other masters stir our imaginations and creativity. This vast, collective treasure of potentialities is not private. We can all enjoy them, get inspired, and supplement our personal potentialities to the extent we can observe and absorb the world's and Nature's treasures privately. We would always have more potentialities of our own and others to explore and enjoy in a day. Alas, we would never have enough motivation and time to explore all these treasures and feel all these pleasures. Time constraint is, in fact, a kind of *joyful limitation* in life, as we always look forward with divine anticipation to our next day's discovery and self-fulfilment. And of course, in no way this time shortage is comparable with the kind that workaholics and people in search of wealth struggle with.

The unfortunate reality is that even when we recognize the true purpose of life, we have difficulty to think straight or reduce our mundane activities to use our time more wisely. We still must sustain a family and struggle to pay the bills. Therefore, we keep working in an environment we do not care much about and do a lousy job that seems like a total waste of our potentialities. We still have to deal with sales people who try hard to convince us purchase more useless stuff. We must deal with unending family quarrels and demands. And we must fight the traffic and waste time in line-ups in supermarkets, for social services, etc. It gets hard to find a few minutes for ourselves, to do the things we like, and to explore our potentialities. Even for those few minutes that we need to spend in solitude, we may be accused by our family of being selfish and uncaring. Nonetheless, we keep searching for, and enjoying, the universal treasure of potentialities offered by geniuses, including ourselves, while we bask all along in the vast treasures offered by Nature, too, of course.

We often recognize the bad and sad sides of our personalities causing our conflicts and unrest, besides the social limitations and injustice imposed upon us. However, instead of giving up on life, we can create a life of our own by drawing on our potentialities to connect with Nature and the simpler stuff of existence. Luckily, life is not bound by crude social rules or our naive perceptions of people and the world. Outside those stressful boundaries, life can actually be quite fulfilling and peaceful.

Our struggles continue…!

CHAPTER SIX
Career (Genetic) Potentialities

Career potentialities refer to a person's genetic abilities to think and act for creating a valuable product, while enjoying the work process and output at least somewhat, too. These special abilities comprise merely the first layer of a person's overall physical and cognitive capacity to grow personally in order to enrich both his/her and other's lives. However, how many of us get a chance to explore and enjoy at least this basic level of our potentialities and apply them in our careers? What are the consequences and value of any career that does not use our potentialities?

At home and school, children are asked what they want to do when they grow up. They are trained to envision a particular life structure they must follow rather blindly merely for getting rich and powerful. They sense an urgency to imagine a profession and guess the level of skills needed for it. Moreover, they feel obliged to guess their capabilities, passion, and potentialities for doing those kinds of jobs. But who can do all these assessments and decide realistically, especially as a child or teenager? Therefore, they get confused, instead of learning about the role of human potentialities more logically and naturally. They merely attempt to pinpoint a profession that appeals to them for some reason. If they cannot think of a smart answer, they simply make up an ambitious one, anyway, because they do not wish to appear like fools with no clue about who they want to be. If they are shy with major doubts about this whole shenanigans and the presumed urgency, they might even rely on feedbacks from their teachers, parents, and classmates regarding their intelligence and temper. Children's answers often reflect their brainwashed minds to look ambitious for choosing a fancy career, anyway—unless it ends up to be a silly or funny answer that surprises their teachers and parents. In all, children only imitate what they have learned from TV or adults' conversations. They merely want to become rich and famous like all those celebrities out there. This is the general mentality that everybody builds at childhood and follows for the rest of his/her life.

Both society and parents play a major, and often misleading, role in directing kids' perceptions about the purpose of life and the role of a profession in line with some common social norms. The emphasis is placed on the highest paying profession they can handle, and sometimes regardless of how good they can handle it, if they can learn to fake it. This is the closest everybody comes to learning about the purpose of, and applying, his/her potentialities. That is, most people learn to supposedly assess and develop their potentialities mainly by some rudimentary perceptions about the means of satisfying their career needs and serving their Egos.

Besides the fact that a majority of us never gets a chance to explore our potentialities, we do not even grasp the main role of our potentialities for personal growth. There is not even adequate concern about how our services can benefit others, but how much it can serve our greedy minds and ambitions. Modern societies and most parents cherish this shoddy mentality. We merely focus on our professional success, while ignoring our need for 'self' realization that requires a deep excavation of divine potentialities, in particular.

Another obstacle for exploring our career potentialities relates to college or university education. Financial or social limitations might hinder this development. Our marks may not be sufficient for admission to some particular fields based on our passion or potentialities. We may also be misled by job markets for planning our career and field of study. Or, the job market changes by the time we graduate, thus we feel obliged to adjust our career plans to adapt to the new requirements.

The Reality of Job Markets

The urgency and pressures of 'career planning,' adjusting to market demands, and job insecurities, throw the idea of search for our potentialities out of whack. Facing all these constraints and expectations, we often do not get a chance to *choose* a profession compatible with our primary talents and education, let alone in line with our real potentialities. We simply follow the mainstream in terms of our perceptions about work and the need for career planning, including educational requirements, etc. We strive to prepare ourselves for the available and/or lucrative jobs by any means of training. Of course, some groups try to emphasize on their dreams or ambitions for wealth and power, and some lazy or careless people might simply ignore even the basic rules of career planning, the type of job they might do, or the severity of finding a profession.

Meanwhile, most of us have learned to produce an acceptable level of product or service mainly for survival or possibly profit purposes. Jobs get done, often inefficiently and ineffectively, and our efforts at least support our subsistence. Nowadays, jobs are becoming routine and automated, anyway, and performed by incompetent, egotistical people who occupy those jobs not based on their potentialities (qualifications), but rather due to their power games and socio-political affiliations.

Nowadays, professions and professionalism hardly coincide. We bring enough intelligence and shrewdness to organizations to keep our jobs with limited efforts and expertise just to make as much money as possible. This type of lazy mentality and lousy work ethics give people little motivation to worry regarding their potentialities. We feel lucky to find a job and a source of income. Thus, all other factors, such as social responsibility and exploring our potentialities, feel quite irrelevant, too. In fact, such idealistic ideas or questions do not even occur to most of us in a timely, serious manner, as we all are trained to be allegedly practical. Our brains appear to be trained to think only in one dimension about our careers with minimal or no regard about the opportunity or necessity of using of our potentialities for our own sakes, let alone for the benefit of humanity. Nowadays, in particular, our juvenile dreams and crude ambitions for fame and fortune mislead many of us in so many fronts, including the benefits of exploring and using our potentialities.

Giving 'job security' priority is especially a realistic attitude, nowadays. After all, we should somehow pay our bills. Survival takes precedence over self-fulfilment and our personal aspirations that socioeconomic systems cannot necessarily offer to all. This becomes particularly truer as our societies face newer restrictive socioeconomic challenges in the years ahead.

Some of us might learn to *create* our own professions based on our potentialities and psychological needs. And some of us might have the willpower or resources to *pursue* only professions that match our passions and potentialities. However, these groups would always be in a minority. They should have special talents, intelligence, and patience to sustain themselves throughout their lives and stay sane. Therefore, most of us must learn to cope with the rising mismatch of our potentialities and job markets. Yet, we should at least beware of the effects of the social disorder and deteriorating job markets on our personal welfare and plans.

The Implications of Unfulfilling Professions

On the one hand, even if we can determine the kind of profession that matches our potentialities and temperament, we still face a tough decision to pursue it if it causes inadequate income, social isolation, or financial insecurity.

On the other hand, life feels boring and aimless if our innate potentialities and needs are not explored and used. Especially, our work feels laborious, frustrating, and stressful if not driven by our passion and potentialities. We might feel or pretend to be happy and successful in our jobs and moneymaking schemes. However, most intelligent people feel the vanity of their lives and pleasures if they are not doing some meaningful work every day, especially since marriages are also becoming unsatisfying. When motivated only negatively by financial needs and a sense of job insecurity, the chances are high that we resent the work, the environment, and often even our colleagues. Luckily, some superficial factors make up for the absence of more genuine motivating factors. For example, we get either trapped in the games of promotions, work incentives, affluence, rivalry, recognition, and power, or lured by other management tools to keep our Egos amused and happy. Nonetheless, we feel unfulfilled and hopeless deep down. We feel immense stress, but cannot pinpoint the real cause of it. Thus, we blame our boss's attitude, colleagues' lack of cooperation, or family and personal problems, etc. Most people try to focus on wealth accumulation at least as a remedy or to replicate the sense of true achievements and amuse their brains.

Our lifelong struggles with our jobs remain a deep source of stress, as we seem to have limited choices for both subsistence and success. This modern social reality would always cause a big dilemma for most people, as we have been conditioned to believe in a lifestyle that evolves around money, a career, a family, etc. Many people must accept this harsh reality at the end, no matter how much their spirits object. Yet, initially, when we assess our potentialities and professional choices, and then throughout our lives, we must remember why we made those major decisions as we did. We must always admit that our fulfilment in life depends on the realization of our potentialities and not necessarily finding a high paying job, raising a family, etc. We should remember that as long as our potentialities are ignored, we remain anxious and doubtful about every work and challenge we undertake. We soon lose our work motivation and a chance to grow psychologically. We remain doubtful about our identity, self-worth, family values, means of self-fulfilment, and even the purpose of living. Unless, of course, we conclude that we have no potentialities and are so useless, even despite all the wealth we have gathered.

At the same time, not building a basic career, just because we cannot figure out our potentialities and niche is a bigger risk for our Ego, self-image, identity, and psychological health. Social needs, including need for a companion, are also important factors for our decision. We must somehow resolve this big life dilemma for ourselves. We must gauge the risks of making a wrong career decision when we are young and inexperienced. How we then convince ourselves to live in the atmosphere of our choosing all our lives is our business.

Ultimately, the criterion for solving this major life dilemma and making such a critical decision is our own sense of judgment about the prospect *(ultimate outcome)* of what we would do, now and during many decades in the future. Naturally, making a right decision at young age is tough for many reasons. For one thing, grasping the merits of self-actualizing jobs and imagining the feelings of self-fulfilment are impossible unless a person has had an opportunity for those special experiences. These personal (and often scarce) experiences do not occur to everybody equally and easily. Therefore, the chance of one's drive for self-actualization becoming an incentive is low. Yet, if we are lucky to imagine or experience these deep, authentic feelings, they provide the right clues about our neglected potentialities. No amount of wealth and social recognition can replace those sacred feelings and rewards. Therefore, our decision regarding our path of life becomes easier. Conversely, our egoistical feelings and satisfactions often reflect our negligence about, or deviation from, our unique potentialities.

By he way, 'need for achievement' is an innate human urge that evokes our deeper potentialities, although some people feel it more urgently due to so many factors, including their genetics, upbringings, and social teachings, as noted in this trilogy.

The outcome of most people's career choices is that seldom anybody works effectively and feels fulfilled, nowadays, because life structure and options are limited with little regard for people's true potentialities and spirits. Acknowledging this common social deficiency, however, may at least help us learn to make our long life plans more realistically, and to mitigate the repercussions and stress of our unfulfilling profession. We may admit the need to do something about the effects of this universal deficiency on our psyches. We might at least look for extracurricular activities or thoughts that could activate more of our deeper potentialities and lift our spirits. Some of us might think of a side career or hobby. Some might focus on humanitarian causes, etc. The main point is to stay vigilant of our need for some means of self-fulfilment, since our professions can hardly do that. As a rule, our professions cannot constitute (or be viewed as) a meaningful purpose of life. No matter how hard we work, how much money we make, and how successful our Egos make us feel, we remain unfulfilled and shallow if our real potentialities are not challenged. Of course, most people do not realize their lives' shallowness or the lack of fulfillment, which is probably a way of existence!

At the other extreme, sometimes, a person is drawn to several self-actualizing activities. In this case, s/he is one of those luckier individuals blessed with a chance for a lifetime of enjoyments and fulfilment, sometimes even at the cost of missing some other joys and opportunities of life. Yet, at the same time, s/he is more likely to get into trouble, since s/he is more susceptible to losing his/her senses of practicality and routine life realities, which most of us need for adapting to socioeconomic environment.

Judging the viability of our potentialities is a difficult task by itself, of course, especially when we face the added responsibility of finding one (or maybe a few of them) that appears exceptional and most fulfilling. Usually some seemingly justifiable areas of potentiality or professions mislead us to assume we are good at them. For example, we might think and decide that we can be a good politician. However, in reality, this might have been only a dream or premature judgment behind our sneaky crude ambitions for power and manipulating others.

Aptitude tests such as SAT can help us understand our basic potentialities, at least as preliminary information. However, only our own judgments and decisions based on high self-awareness and true feelings of fulfilment and satisfaction count. We should detect our niche (potentialities) by testing and feeling them. We must do this along with our efforts to learn about our personality, values, life philosophy, stamina, spirituality needs, etc., perhaps with the aid of experts. Realistically, finding a fulfilling career, or even a hobby, entails the tough task of knowing our 'Self' and special potentialities first.

> This chapter's discussions are equally relevant to the topic of **'Work Objectives'** addressed in Chapter Three of Volume III. Therefore, it will be useful to reread this chapter at that point.

CHAPTER SEVEN
Divine (Organic) Potentialities

Organic potentialities signify a person's innate capacity to sense, cultivate, and apply spiritualism through devotion and efforts for realizing his divine 'self.' They induce creativity and contentment that soothe our spirits and smoothen our socializing and working routines. In return, contentment, peace, and creative energy stir a sense of spirituality much beyond the initial, sacred feelings of self-realization. Thus, the following crude conclusions are drawn:

1. Cultivating our divine potentialities is a natural urge (a sacred human attribute) that drives our spirituality efforts.
2. Human spirit is a manifestation of the finer, divine power of our potentialities accordingly.
3. Spirituality is mostly an inner, organic exploration of human potentialities, although it might also lead to a sense of external connections to Nature and humans.

Contrary to 'career potentialities' reviewed in Chapter Six, studying our 'divine potentialities' (our spirits) is for exploring 'self' and spirituality in order to bear inevitable social hardships easier. We can also say that, while all our potentialities help us make a living, no amount of wealth or power reflects humans' essence, organic potentialities, and worth. This mindset offers some radical life options (questions) to ponder when we face the philosophical dilemmas about 'Who we are and what we are here for.' Can we justify our existence without nurturing our divine potentialities? Can we imagine, for once, that wealth or products we create do not measure our success in life? Can we think, for one day at least, only in terms of the authenticity of our characters and the quality of our lives, outside the phony identity that society affords us?

Ideally, our career and divine potentialities should coincide to maximize both our social and spiritual needs. They can become complementary when the sense of self-actualization from our work and thoughts soars beyond normal life experiences towards divinity, like the examples that Maslow has provided about the subjects of his studies. In such cases, no inner conflict grows in our psyches about who we are.

In reality, however, hardly anybody gets a chance to nurture either his/her divine or career potentialities in our modern culture, as even his/her basic means of survival always seems in jeopardy. Despite the rising depression in modern societies, we are forced to ignore the main causes of our stress and instead get absorbed deeper in our depressing jobs and relationships. Realistically, we have no other choice, while hoping upon hopes that things would improve somehow eventually. Sometimes, we run away from one employer or profession to a similar or worse situation. We try to relieve ourselves from the agonies of some career or marital issues and then turn around and get into an equally unfulfilling profession or relationship. Until we feel the necessity of fostering our divine potentialities, we merely keep searching for different professions and lifestyles unsuccessfully. All along, our spirits get vastly suppressed. 'Self' exploration remains an idle ideal when our need for social adaptation occupies all our time and energy. We suffer for ignoring our 'self' that can fuel our mental energy and induce our sense of fulfilment and divinity.

If we care to dig out our divine potentialities, the first step is to pause and ponder the question of, 'Who am I or have become?'

While career potentialities stress on *self-actualizing* virtues of humans' careers and thoughts, divine potentialities emphasize on *'self'-realization* that awakens one's sacred attributes of humility, selflessness, passion, compassion, transcendence, and connection to the universe and humanity—all manifesting now in our feelings, thoughts, and actions. Our *career* potentialities might fulfil our basic needs for achievement and self-actualization, but our *divine* potentialities can potentially hoist our spirits within the thresholds of the universe and spiritualism. During such divine experiences, our cognition, potentialities, and 'self' coincide as related concepts for explaining thinking human's attributes based on the strengths of their consciousness and feelings. If we study and develop the seven main elements of 'self', as discussed in Chapter Thirteen, our divine potentialities emerge automatically clear from socio-economic demands and obligations. Conversely, exploring our potentialities, mainly for self-realization and finding inner peace (not merely for work and social adaptation), manifests our real identity—the 'self.'

We can choose to view our potentialities as a hidden treasure requiring a deep excavation of our minds and souls, leading to a core of personal awareness and a tranquil path of life. Yet, sadly, we usually remain doubtful regarding the role of our potentialities for either divine or career purposes, since we are often forced to think and act pragmatically in this chaotic world. We undermine our subtle urges for piety due to our sense of practicality, quest for social acceptance, or self-doubt,. Instead, we usually depend on people's flashy feedbacks or rewards to gauge the value of our deeds and achievements—the kind of alleged success we then naively attribute to our genius and potentialities.

Surely, our divine potentialities, including spiritualism, cannot be tapped in the course of mundane social life and relationships. Once we get trapped in the mainstream (the imposed social path), we abandon life's natural path and our divine potentialities even if we get the chance to learn about more natural options of living. We get carried away with life's trivialities and our lifestyles' vanities, thus miss the opportunity of exploring the simpler, but more profound, options of living. Most of our natural senses have been desensitized during our efforts for social adaptation. Thus, while our spirit strives to know 'who we are,' our pressing sense of financial and emotional practicality keeps us faithful to our fake identities and social rules, and we merely wander on a shaky social path. We feel so needy for people's opinions and approval, even when our self-deceiving sense of ingenuity and talents make us too arrogant. All along, we get mixed messages from people and our conscience about our needs and potentialities. We fight our doubts about the chance of ever exploring our potentialities and never get a chance to grasp the meaning of living free on a healthier life path a bit outside the addictive social path. We feel trapped, unappreciated, only meandering aimlessly and worrying about our day-to-day emotional and financial survival. We simply get attracted to good paying jobs, instead of pursuing what we are passionate about.

In such dire setting, finding and using our innate potentialities remain an ominous challenge and a major life decision. We must eventually make a major decision and choose a path of life that could at least fulfil a bit of our spirituality need. Some people might build the willpower to overhaul their life philosophy for a chance to explore their divine potentialities. After all, it is up to us to choose the right balance among practicality, social survival, and nurturing our divine potentialities. We should recognize that our divine potentialities could at least make up for our failure to develop our career potentialities properly due to socioeconomic hurdles. Despite our career and family pressures, we can nurture our divine potentialities with some sacrifices in our routines. This is a good, practical compromise (life option) and a likely remedy for the agony of our drowned career potentialities. Our divine potentialities can enrich our lives even when we are stuck in our dead-end professions. In the end, resolving all these stress, inner conflicts, and 'self' dilemmas is our responsibility.

'Self' Dilemmas

'Who we are' depends on the strengths of three complementary attributes. That is, in general, we are a sloppy fusion of what we: i) feel, ii) think, and iii) do. A person with pure thoughts, proper deeds, and authentic feelings has a much better chance for both self-fulfilment and spiritualism. Thus, 'who we are' also becomes a philosophical notion of *primary self* that reinforces the need for our realization and development of our potentialities towards an *enlightened 'self.'* Feeling, doing, and thinking are sources of energy and intuition to follow and fulfil humans' full range of needs. Meanwhile, the more these innate human dimensions are developed in societies, the higher people's knack to fulfil their personal needs becomes. The more authentic and purposeful our feeling, thinking, and doing, the more 'self' grows and resolves the dilemmas of living within our complex and callous societies. And the more selflessly these three attributes pervade personally and socially, the closer we get to a definition of a complete and pure human being. In particular, humans' divine potentialities cannot flourish in current social setting. Instead, our rising misery and looming demise only reveal the crooked nature of humans' thinking, feeling, and doing all around.

The same attributes of 'self' (thinking, doing, feeling) prevail in our professional lives, too, mostly in contaminated forms, since we have failed to invoke ethical values in work environments. At work, we do some ineffective (and often crooked) thinking, we perform our jobs rather inefficiently (often out of spite or due to our incompetence), and we usually ignore the feeling dimension regularly (save for all those tactical or tactful pretences, sucking up demeanours, manipulations, and rivalries). At work settings, the 'feeling' dimension is, in particular, difficult to manage and make less antagonistic due to humans' egotistical, greedy nature. Despite all the science in the fields of management and human behaviour, we are still quite helpless in recognizing the 'feeling' aspect of our potentialities in work places. To remain competitive, organizations have become too practical for managing workers. Feelings and compassion have been sacrificed for productivity and higher profits or merely surviving in economic markets. Thus, both our personal lives and careers are infected deeply, just because organization mentality and the nature of work revolve around many crooked personalities as well. This pervasive, rooted problem is discussed in detail in Volume III of this trilogy.

Collectively, our divine and career potentialities develop our characters and define 'who we are.' Meanwhile, the three aspects of our personality manifest who we have become. Our demented behaviour represents our ideologies, idiosyncrasies, preferences, knowledge, logic, wisdom and many other personal traits. We can study our thoughts and beliefs in terms of their origins, logic, and purposes. We can then try to justify or modify these thoughts and beliefs according to a particular life philosophy that makes sense for us. Next, we can study the incentives and forces behind our thoughts and beliefs. We like to know which of the 'model,' 'ego,' or 'self' aspect of our personality stirs our actions, feelings, and thoughts, how, and why. If they are driven solely by Model and Ego, we are less natural and modest than we could (should) be. If we have a Model personality and needs with pure feelings and humanitarian thoughts as well, we still have a better chance than an egoist to become a reliable and conscientious individual by thinking deeper while evaluating 'who we are.'

Our potentialities and limitations characterize 'who we are' and 'what we are here for.' Yet, we are characterized in terms of how we handle our opportunities and limitations for becoming a better person within the context of our general life philosophy. In all, we all have a potential for being a better, more natural, and happier person if we, i) want to become one and are willing to do some soul-searching to revamp our beliefs and Egos, and ii) can elude the perils and evils of society and people largely.

Understanding the essence of 'who we really are, what we can do in this world, and for what end,' imposes major dilemmas for people seeking fulfilment and freedom. In particular, these dilemmas haunt us on two specific occasions: When we strive to choose the right (fulfilling) career, and when our spirit feels low and we look for spiritual guidance. Yet, most of us dismiss these instinctual urges for self-analysis outright, often due to a lack of foresight or laziness. Another group finds these 'self' dilemmas too philosophical to tackle, thus remains reluctant to spend time on them. They feel overwhelmed already sorting out their daily routines, needs, and potentials. Besides, how could anybody care about his/her identity (or self) when s/he knows so little about his/her true essence? "Who cares anyway?", they decide and move on. Only a few of us eventually find enough time and motivation to explore these basic 'self' questions. Even so, we usually get to this point in older ages when so many opportunities have passed us by and it is impossible to exploit our potentials. By then, it is often too late to rear and rejoice the essence of our being.

Who Cares 'Who We Are?'

Our regular feelings of defeat and emptiness reflect the depletion of our spirits. This happens because we focus only on the world outside us and how best to exploit it. Thus, we become conscious of our existence mainly when we feel sad, anxious, and lonely; otherwise, we follow a routine life structure and certain habits in search of an occasional sense of pleasure. We are conditioned to seek happiness outside ourselves and get sad when we are alone. This raw perception of life is quite contrary to reality, though, as external sources only cause pain and gloom, whereas happiness comes only from inner exploration and self-realization—a lone experience. We can reflect on valuable thoughts in line with our interests and potentialities, determine and do the right things regularly, and most importantly, learn about our authentic needs and feelings. With our feelings, we can create the most delicate and beautiful experiences, and at the same time get acquainted with our potentialities and need for spirituality. With an objective assessment of 'who we are,' we can find our identity, modify our personality, and become a conscious and conscientious person.

Therefore, we are (or must be) the main person who cares 'who we are' or can be. Other people benefit from our efforts to grasp the neglected 'self' within us. However, ultimately, we are the one benefiting from evoking our spirit and the potentialities hidden inside us, so that we can change our outlook on life and means of living.

Following a long self-awareness regimen is a tough decision, however, as it requires self-sacrifice and commitment. Nothing results from a short and shallow self-analysis, since we should focus not only on our own lives, attitudes, and potentialities, but also examine our relationships with the universe and other human beings. Learning 'who we are'—self-awareness—needs a good knowledge of the seven elements of 'self,' which are explained in Chapter 13. We must question the validity of our daily routines over a long period and grasp their sources, purposes, etc. And we should assess and grasp the rationality of our urges behind our feelings. Self-awareness exercises performed in reference to our three personality aspects can reveal the mechanisms, causes, and motives behind our thoughts, actions, and feelings. In all, with major determination and patience, we can learn the art of self-awareness and make it an integral part of our daily routines—a permanent ritual. Then, we learn more about 'who we are' *every day* and notice our gradual divine transformation. In this process, our potentialities surge and blossom as well. Naturally, this is a tough challenge for most people. After all, it is not easy for most of us to create a right balance between 'life' (our worldly desires) and 'self' (our spiritual aspirations). However, the outcome would prove quite worth our efforts.

Self-awareness also makes us a more insightful and intelligent person. It raises our sensitivity as well, in terms of our actions, thoughts, and feelings. Then, we become more compassionate about other people and the world, too, as we learn more tolerance and humility. We acquire added power in seeing and sensing our surroundings, and sometimes even the things beyond our normal senses. As we become receptive and critical of our feelings and deeds, our Self grows, while Ego and Model's influence declines. With awareness, we step beyond the seeming facts we observe on the surface and see the urges, motives, and innate flaws behind our own and other people's behaviour and reactions. Especially, we learn not to judge others or react hastily. First, we try not to taint our own moods and personalities just for retaliation or to handle other people's attitudes and defects in their ways. Second, we gain a tendency to attribute people's shortfalls to some type of psychological and personality flaws beyond their control. Third, we recognize that people's expressions and our impression of them are not necessarily a reflection of their true personalities or intentions. We realize that people's personalities are largely a manifestation of their self-defence mechanism, developed due to their ignorance and uncontrollable idiosyncrasies. Therefore, we accept them more patiently with some compassion. Accordingly, our rising knowledge of 'who we are' also helps us grasp, or at least sympathize with, 'who they are.'

All these exercises lead to a wiser cognition and a deeper comprehension of human potentialities, including the nature of their thoughts, feelings, and actions. Our potentialities are not restricted to those things that we *do* best. Our thoughts and ways of thinking (e.g., logic, outlook, and analytical ability) definitely reflect the strength of our intrinsic potentialities behind everything we do and excel in. This should be obvious. However, the fact that our feelings are in particular a vital part of our potentialities is not quite appreciated.

The 'feeling' dimension of our potentialities ('self') has been suppressed and often misguided purposefully to the point where we have lost our sense of basic compassion and morality, while getting radically oversensitive and demanding. We expect a lot from others, but have no pure feelings ourselves beyond our showy expressions of passion and compassion. We expect lots of love from others, but lack passion and patience ourselves. At the same time, occasionally we get surprised when, in some special moments, our soft feelings suddenly surface and we do not know how to deal with them. We are shocked by these unexpected surges of sentimentality and try to hide them, because they may be seen as signs of weakness and vulnerability.

In all, we do not know or care how our feelings establish our thought processes, as well as our relationships with the public and the universe. We do not care about analysing our feelings, nor consider the feasibility of adjusting them for our own sake and possibly improving our relationships with the outside world, too. Not merely the effects of our feelings on our thoughts, deeds, and relationships, but also our mental connection with those outside elements affect the characteristics of the 'self.' Our criteria in this regard could always improve in order to become more objective, forgiving, and compassionate, without becoming submissive, pretentious, or snobbish. Grasping and nurturing our relationship with 'self' has its own tremendous impact on our psychological growth and life enjoyment. With our refined feelings, we attain a higher standard of being and relating. Our sensitized outlook and relationships also enrich other people's lives.

Without proper feelings and passion, we cannot excavate our potentialities. Our thoughts and actions remain crude if they do not flow through our compassionate feelings and passion and direct our deeds. High levels of creativity also manifest when an emotional connection develops between us and other objects and beings. The 'feeling' dimension of our potentialities connects us to our souls, with the truth of life, and with the secrets of the real world a bit more than our thoughts and actions can do. At the same time, our sincere feelings, passion, and compassion guide us develop and express our selfless thoughts and actions.

An important role of self-awareness is to raise one's ability to keep one's thoughts, actions, and feelings aligned productively and sensibly. Everybody hopes to keep this mental consistency, yet most of us fail to do so due to many realities of social living, nowadays. We fail, because we like to stay practical and adapt to social demands or fulfil our social obligations toward our families or society. Other obstacles are our lack of conviction to give up our fake identities, our lack of a 'self'-driven life philosophy or outlook, our varied addictions and obsessions, our insecurities or emotional tendencies, our general confusion besieging us at many levels for so many reasons, etc.

In return, our low self-awareness diminishes our abilities to manage and align our thoughts, actions, and feelings consistently. This general condition in humans is apparent in the manner we behave erratically a lifetime and reveal so much evil, lunacy, and idiocy as inherent nature of humans.

What Are We Here for, Really?

This book reviews our options, goals, and basic steps for *knowing* 'who we are.' The related question is, 'What are we here for?'

The creation of the universe several billions years ago started a series of intricate evolutionary chain reactions (within absolute chaos and randomness!) leading to the manifestation of man, plus an infinite variety of immensely complex and precise processes, as we know it today. Only God knows what man would look like even a few millenniums from now, if humans survive that long. As we stand in awe about this meticulous creation and strive to detect how every step of the evolution has taken place, we are just incapable of imagining and grasping what all these seeming facts mean. Except that, we might eventually admit our absolute insignificance within the scope of this amazing phenomenon. Our limited knowledge about millions of species gives us some clues about their instincts, defence mechanisms, living habits and urges. All these life dimensions within the expansive universe on the one hand, and the energy and formation of even a single DNA or atom on the other hand, facts and factors related to us humans become pale in scope. Thinking of our existence and gauging the question of 'who we are' within these huge orderly dimensions must just make us feel most humble and also lucky to be part of it.

Despite our vast science, we still do not know *why* and *how* of so many things, including those matters related to the theories of the Big Bang and the creation of the universe. Yet we continue to ask ourselves 'why and how' about all these phenomena, while we admit the infancy of human logic and brain to find suitable answers. Although we are not sure about the gist of creation, the universe, and God, we can notice that all creatures are directed by the question of 'why' intuitively. We ask 'why' constantly as if we intuitively need a 'purpose' for everything. In fact, this trite intuition seems to emanate in all the living things—animals and plants. All these rudimentary actions and reactions also appear to be for specific purposes.

As an alert human, we are ordained to live with an immense intuition that constantly wonders about the purpose of existence or doing many things daily: 'Why?' Even our sense of boredom is related to this inner voice. We often attempt to suppress this intuition temporarily by artificial methods like drugs or alcohol, but we can never elude it permanently. Is our curiosity a good or a bad thing, then, and how does it affect our lives?

Our observations and research confirm that doing things for certain purposes is a natural and valid process that creatures, and even the simplest steps in evolution, behold intuitively for the betterment of their existence. In addition, this intuition has forced us develop a 'logical process' for solving our problems, e.g., rigid scientific methodologies. Not surprisingly, all scientific researches and methodologies start with the question of 'why?' 'Why' is the focus of every scientific research to provide rationales for every intelligent decision or action. Every hypothesis is an attempt to answer 'why' every phenomenon behaves in a particular manner. Therefore, both intuitively and logically we have come to believe that a purpose is required for everything we do.

The matter appears even more amazing (and absurd) since many of us, including this author, believe that the universe and life have no specific purpose beyond their mere existence. They simply are, as a state of being. We cannot ask, 'Why the universe exists, why humans were created, why the Big Bang happened, or why (and how) nothing existed before it?' In this context, the universe or 'life' has no purpose, or at least any purpose that we humans can decipher; they are merely given facts per se (for the time being at least). This sounds terribly bizarre to us, because we believe that every aspect of 'living' must have a purpose. We get anxious when these conflicting thoughts circle in our heads, yet many people cannot evade or ignore them. We have this innate need to justify our existence, in the sense of knowing the purpose of living, every single day and every minute of it. Besides, the evolution has followed many amazingly sophisticated steps for specific purposes, too. On the other hand, it is plausible that even the most fundamental notions applied in our perceived world, as building blocks of human logic, such as 'fact,' 'purpose,' and 'why,' have no meaning or relevance within the boundaries of the real world. No wonder we have turned out so confused and still more curious!

Often we imagine that since we need a reason to do things, the universe must have a purpose, too. We are eager to impose the idea of 'purposefulness' or 'consciousness' on the universe for our benefit. Some people insist that humans' sense of purpose is actually a reflection of the universe's general purposefulness, maybe in line with our unified consciousness. They believe both our purposes and consciousness derive from the universe's. Yet, we have no mechanisms to prove, or even find rational grounds for claiming, these types of raw observations or conclusions.

Of course, it seems logical to suggest that when every simple action or decision should have a purpose, how can the universe or a person's life (his living, not his accidental existence per se) be left undefined in terms of purpose. We can safely assume that the overall purpose of living is not supposed to be the sum of all the simple and single purposes that we set for our varied actions and decisions. Could we, then, say that the whole purpose of living is merely the objective of 'being' per se? And, of course, right away we might question the 'objective of being per se.' In which case we may even demand a purpose for the universe and 'life' per se, too. Why not? But that would be a totally crazy cycle of thoughts much deeper beyond any humanistic logic or prime speculations —rather in line with the old dilemma of who created the God. For the sake of our sanity and making even some basic levels of speculation possible, we must assume that the universe and 'life' are mere facts (for our purpose at least) with no ulterior purposes.

On the one hand, it feels quite rational to believe that even the universe (let alone the mere existence of an individual) has no purpose, at least because we can never prove otherwise.

On the other hand, within this seeming purposeless dimension of existence, humans, and the evolution as a whole, still need a sense of purpose to grow. There is no harm in that and actually impossible to avoid our innate need for purpose and reason. The old cliché, 'Everybody should have a purpose in life,' merely reflects a basic human instinct. Nevertheless, the important point here is that, regardless of the purposefulness of the universe in general, now the whole material existence (including humans) appear to be bound and driven by a basic urge to constantly ask 'why,' as a justification for survival.

While our routine actions and decisions are often for specific purposes, the ongoing process of human life in itself (living) has a much more fundamental objective, in fact, so much so we refer to it as the philosophy of life. The word 'philosophy' has a much broader connotation and meaning than 'purpose' as it includes not only the objectives (whys) we must define for living, but also the processes (hows) we choose for achieving them. It does not really matter which word we use, 'purpose' or 'philosophy.' However, the latter is preferred and used only to emphasize the importance and wholeness of the 'purpose' of living in relation to all other single purposes we set for our actions and decisions. Actually, once we have a wholesome, encompassing life purpose or philosophy, all other purposes that we set for our daily actions and decisions should remain subordinate to the main philosophy. Every simple purpose has to pass the test of validity within the general framework and guidelines of one's life philosophy—our beliefs. This shows the value of a life philosophy to guide us thru life. A life philosophy gives us a yardstick for all our decisions and assessing our doubts. Maybe we all even share one unified life philosophy, someday, to minimize human conflicts. Whether that is possible or desirable is another big philosophical dilemma in itself, of course!

The question of 'what are we here for?' is thus only another attempt to refine our personal life philosophy. By this question, we set out to establish a fundamental (but personal) purpose for staying alive (beyond our purposeless accidental existence), for doing things that would empower our spirits, and for achieving peace and self-fulfilment. Thus, although we are not here on this planet for any specific purpose, we must define one for humans in general (beyond people's personal purposes), and refine it, too, occasionally for our personal use for many purposes, but mainly for keeping our spirits and humanity intact. The complex topic of life philosophy as a tool for synthesizing our thoughts is tackled in Volume I.

'What we are here for' promptly stirs many related questions such as, 'Why do I do certain things, follow a doomed structure of life, or even live, and for what end?' These questions demand some major purposes for living. And, of course, it is implied that life objectives (or purposes) should have perceptible values for self and others. However, the answers to these questions should come from personal research and contemplation rather than only following the norms and imitating others. We must figure out life personally. Religions and cults have made people see things their ways. However, submission to some prophecies or philosophies is not the way to answer the question of, 'What we are here for' even if some answers sound profound and spiritual. One should find the answer personally the hard way, although reading and listening to others might help if one learns to be objective and stay free from influence, false sentiments, and fast conclusions. Ideally, some scholars should eventually offer plausible purposes for both personal and general human existence, which would then make it easier for us to ponder their related theories as well.

'What we are here for' surely implies our valid contributions and accomplishments. However, the question is, 'What are the meaningful and worthwhile things that one can accomplish?' The general criterion is that it should affect and enhance self and other individual(s) in a positive way. Many life purposes might fit this criterion depending on a person's talent, vision, and mood. The public opinion is ordinarily considered the main yardstick for worthwhile achievements, like when 90-95% of people believe in those contributions to society. For example, a doctor practising abortion definitely assumes that s/he is doing a worthy service for the community and many people agree with him/her. Still, a large population considers abortion a crime, instead of a contribution. *Ordinarily,* this service might not quite pass the test, as long as it is burdened by high degree of controversy about its value. Yet, the judgment of a majority must neither justify a purpose, nor affect us in choosing the worthwhile things that we can do. At the end, we need the conviction to make the judgment personally merely based on our life philosophy.

The best test of personal achievement lies in individuals' deep convictions about the value of their contributions today or in the future even though people may or may not appreciate them right away. As long as the purpose is pursued selflessly, and s/he is not insane, fanatic, greedy, or criminal in relation to the thing(s) s/he does, those purposes and contributions can be considered worthy. Making a living along the way would not discredit our choices, either, as long as greed or recognition is not the main purpose.

Many things we do regularly have some value and affect us and perhaps others. However, they most likely do not qualify as personal life achievements. The difference is in the nature of our accomplishments, of course, but more importantly in terms of their 'purpose.' Only those achievements resulting from one's conscious decisions, in line with some divine philosophy and purpose, followed by conscionable actions, qualify as indicators of 'who we are' and 'what we are here for.'

Ironically, the two questions of, 'Who are we?' and 'What are we here for?' are the cause and effect of each other. We can view 'who we are' as the *cause* and 'what we are here for' as the *effect*, and vice versa. It makes sense that our existence should have a cause and an effect. Yet, this clear relationship is not the whole essence of the two questions. Who we are cannot be justified by what we do, nor does the mere purpose of our actions determine who we are. Rather, we must establish many detail characteristics of our 'self' by objective thinking, free from parental and societal influences. During this process, we determine the REASONS for our living, the purposes of our actions and decisions in life, and the integrity of the value system that we choose. Conversely, the causes (motives) and effects (outcomes) of our decisions should validate our life philosophy and existence. All along, only the *legitimate* purposes (causes and effects) of our deeds, thoughts, and feelings polish our spirits and the essence of 'who we are.'

A counter-argument against having a life philosophy and a real purpose for living is that life is much easier, and perhaps happier, without all these disciplines and thinking. Why waste so much of our precious life worrying about these intangible issues even though they feel like instinctual dilemmas always haunting us? Why not try to forget all this mumbo-jumbo even if we must resort to alcohol and drugs to do it? Why set life objectives or justify our actions and decisions, and even existence as a whole? This group might argue that since human life feels random and outside of our control, we must stop fussing so much, and instead leave everything to destiny. Many other arguments may be easily offered for or against this view. However, we should eventually agree that the answer depends merely on people's characters, preferences, and personal outlooks. We could blame our crooked outlooks and priorities (leading to our deep naivety and doomed choices of lifestyles) for our purposeless pursuits all our lives. Alternatively, we could blame our naïve idealism goading the nagging voice in our heads (intuition) eager to know the purpose of living and working so hard tenaciously and painfully. Chapter Two's discussions about Humans' Quest for the Truth elaborate this point and offer some plausible answers.

Either one of the above options define a type of personal life philosophy, although people often adopt a path of life passively, merely based on their personality and habits, without assessing their life options quite carefully. Yet, developing a personal life philosophy is so important it should be considered a major life decision for any intelligent person, instead of just living randomly and imitating the mainstream norms. Having a life philosophy is essential regardless of our lifestyle and the life path we choose to follow. Most importantly, however, our life philosophy should establish 'what we are here for,' even if the ultimate answer is at least a resounding 'nothing' whatsoever! Therefore, maybe soon more people realize the need for, and the benefits of, developing a personal life philosophy and how to go about doing it.

Self-assessment Challenge

Pressured by daily conundrums at work and home and engulfed by so many personal and social limitations, which are discussed at length in Chapter Nine, self-assessment to know 'who we are' sounds absurd. 'Self' sounds like an abstract concept at best, anyway. Our efforts to nurture our potentialities would also feel quite challenging and hopeless in the middle of daily mayhem we cannot avoid. However, some blessed people might succeed to find basic answers regarding their existence gradually through patience and determination during a long, diligent process of self-assessment. They learn to study their thoughts, feelings, and actions as well as the motives behind them. Then, perhaps, they plan to become someone worth being if they realize the necessity for some adjustments, which is usually the case for all objective students of the truth.

Exploring the depth of our 'self' requires refined guidelines, of course, which perhaps some rational experts could put together soon. However, personal reflection in line with the basic concepts suggested in this trilogy can be the first step. After all, exploring spirituality and finding 'who we are' require the same type of inward reflections and judgements. Selective probing of people with objective viewpoints regarding life can also help us stay on a self-awareness path. Sometimes, a simple question or comment even by a child may raise a deep thought that might help answer some of the more complicated matters of life eventually. In all, doing profound thinking is the main step to cultivate our basic wisdom towards self-awareness and enlightenment, usually by choosing simpler lifestyles and learning selflessness.

The sign of being on the right track is a sense of humility that grows as our egotism and neediness decline. We start to see life in an objective and independent manner, instead of just feeding our dogmatism or imitating the norms of prevalent life structure blindly. We start to notice our nothingness, instead of gloating incessantly about our importance. Only by gaining the capacity of doing an honest self-assessment, we become the best judge of our deeds and personalities with fewer doubts about who we are. We may offend others rather carelessly or callously by our words at a moment of weakness, but would realize our error when we sit alone later for a sincere self-analysis. We also find the courage to go back and correct our mistake or rudeness, and perhaps get a chance to reconcile with people we have hurt. Our search for 'self' is incomplete if we still detect in ourselves signs of malice, greed, self-serving conclusions, debilitating parental influence, irrelevant social values, and prejudice. Only through a selfless, divine self-assessment, we might test the value and validity of our conclusions and judgments.

Another purpose and benefit of self-assessment and awareness is to grasp the nature of our doubts and the importance of some major life decisions that we should make in timely manners. This extensive topic is addressed in detail in Part VI.

Naturally, being honest and critical of ourselves is hard if we do not know how or when we naively believe in our sincerity. Yet, fooling ourselves and believing to be honest stubbornly—when our hypocrisy is bugging even our own conscience—is even a sadder case. Without an ability to control our prejudices, both our self-assessment and judgments of others are worthless. One way to test our sincerity is to recollect past experiences and re-evaluate them based on their merits then and now. Do we still consider our response or reaction appropriate today, based on our new objective (rather selfless) values? Would a similar judgment today be valid using our present mindset and principles? Are we humble enough now to at least go back and apologize for our error in judgment and rudeness? If answers to above questions do not show our change of attitude, our efforts to reach selfhood have not been effective yet. We should gauge the strength of our criteria and beliefs used for gauging our reactions and judgments. We should convince our conscience (if we have one) about the rationality and honesty of our current judgments.

Reviewing a true story from my college years in Los Angeles when occupied with self-assessment thoughts might be helpful. I had a friend who seemed quite smart with a B.A. in architecture and doing his graduate studies in urban planning. He had many friends and girlfriends and had travelled extensively, while still depending financially on his parents, who had strong faith in him. One day we were relaxing and chatting by a swimming pool when he whined about his recent conversation with his father. In response to his request for more money to travel to Europe, his father had apparently told him that he could not afford or did not wish to pay for this trip. My friend was furious about his father's sudden reluctance to provide for his life's essentials, including his regular summer travels to Europe for a couple of months. Naively, I tried to explain his father's decision and added that perhaps time had come for him to build a sense of responsibility and financial independence, *like what I had been doing myself, in spite of the immense pains of working so hard just to pay for my education!*

With disbelief about my stupid remark, he yelled, "They must handle my needs since they brought me into this world."

Surprised and offended by the way he saw me as a total idiot, I realized the futility of continuing this conversation.

This example has a few angles for analysis beyond the clear conclusion that this friend had been spoiled. However, the most relevant point here is his life outlook and perception of himself. To me, his view of 'who he was,' as a 24-year-old man, appeared bizarre. It was also interesting for me to note how his knowledge of 'who he was,' his value system, and judgment were directly related and collectively tainted, especially since he always bragged about his sense of modesty and energetic show of philosophical approach towards life.

The big obstacle for self-awareness is obviously our egoism and the effects of crooked social norms cultivated in our heads, which give us wrong impressions about life. How could a reliable value system evolve from a faulty trained mind? How could one hope to assess and analyse the question of 'who am I?' without a proper value system and self-assessment abilities? How can one even grasp the concept of self-awareness and self-assessment without some basic mental preparation? The point here is not to condemn or analyse someone's viewpoint and choices. But rather to demonstrate how my friend and I were both surprised and mad at each other's comments, views of life, and 'who we were' as two young graduate students regardless of our parents affluence.

I always wished to believe that this educational incident with my friend many years back might have a different outcome if we could relive that moment in the following years and decades. Had my friend's mentality had changed over the years, I wondered. I imagined that his father's decision might have in fact pushed him *finally* to adjust himself to the new realities and perhaps build a new outlook and lifestyle eventually. Thus, whenever I thought of him in the following twenty years, I imagined him as a rather changed person. Recently, I heard he was looking for a new rich wife. His first rich wife had apparently kicked him out at last.

Meanwhile, he was also contacting his long-forgotten friends, including me, for some handout!

Well, I laughed a bit, happy regarding his relaxed personality even in his forties and taking life in his reckless strides in such a peculiar manner. Then I was surprised more of how much I had changed myself than how he had not! In particular, I was amazed regarding the nature of our argument when he had insisted on his father's obligation to pay him every year to go to Europe for fun. His mentality and demand, then, as a young man rather coincided shockingly now with my recent philosophy about parents' guilt for bringing so many helpless kids into this chaotic world and raising them so terribly as well. (Maybe children reaching legal age should have a right to sue their parents for their ignorance about the requirements of parenting!)

Gosh, it is hurtful and disheartening to learn so much when it is too late to rectify our errors, if at all!

Life is the best teacher, but we are the worst students. In fact, we all seem to have a nasty gene that makes us self-destructive mostly by our persistence to remain stupid.

The risk I took to write this presumably funny story was rather calculated, as I believe this friend would not find out about my comments even if I gave him a copy of this book personally and begged him to read it. My only risk has been the tiny chance of a mutual friend reading the story and mentioning my derogatory remarks to him. Well, I do not care, anyway! Yet, my openness, courage, and arrogance to include this story here also show the flimsiness of my enlightenment after all these years. I admit, I still have a long way to go. Why could not I resist including this story, even if only for humour?!

On the other hand, it feels even more important—and not at all funny—to mention my rising disappointment, as I have aged, about the accelerating level of naïveté, narcissism, and negligence among us humans in our chaotic, directionless societies towards the doomed destiny of humanity!

Selflessness Attributes

'Humility, resignation, and nothingness,' are main selflessness attributes that have been discussed in this book sporadically, yet explaining them needs a book by itself. They are finely related principles that require deep wisdom and spiritualism to grasp and practise together harmoniously. Still, clarifying their basic natures and purposes briefly here is important.

Humility is a holy *feeling* developed along with an individual's inner strengths to perceive and live independently without any sense of timidity and submission. Humility develops vastly upon our sincere *thoughts,* grasp of our nothingness, and our *act* of resignation, but humility is never meant to reflect vulnerability or humiliation. In fact, humility demands alertness and agility to fight personal and social evils without letting our crude ambitions and needs besiege our judgments. As such, humility is real and reliable only when grown into a natural sentiment deep inside the person. Otherwise, it would be just another personal sham.

Resignation is not an act of abandoning the world or people, but rather embracing the whole universe and society within a divine framework, while cutting our attachments to life's trivialities and materialism. Resignation is also for gaining the inner strengths to avoid so many powerful sources manipulating and dominating our minds and souls. This means that contrary to the implied meaning of the 'resignation,' this fine personal attribute actually requires lots of actions and consciousness regarding our place in society and during our civil relationships with people and social systems.

Nothingness reflects an individual's deep thoughts and inner strengths to recognize humans' absolute, irreparable naiveté and vulnerability despite their colossal, comical egos. It also refers to a person's delicate soul and independence from outer approval or power. This inner strength helps the person think properly and build an authentic identity for him/herself, instead of depending on a fake personality and arrogance to satiate his/her superficial needs and desires. Thus, 'nothingness' requires a lot of thinking to detect and admit our eccentricities and defeat our wild egos. We appreciate our nothingness when we ponder the intricacy of Nature and the universe. In return, our sincere realization of our nothingness makes us dig deeper within ourselves, receive sacred insights, and discover so many beautiful things inside and around us. These are merely some precious benefits of learning about our nothingness, yet most of us only focus on, and pamper, our egos and believe in our perfection. Therefore, we never notice, or just ignore, the depth of humans' idiocy, defects, and helplessness, especially for appreciating the reality of existence or our precious personal potentialities. What a pathetic, sad, non-thinking species we humans are!

Such a colossal waste of our powerful and beautiful brains is simply disgraceful!!!

Humans' Main Functions: The above basic definitions of humility, resignation, and nothingness demonstrate the manner these three selflessness attributes relate directly to the three main human functions, i.e., feeling, thinking, and acting:

The selflessness attributes	Humans' Main Functions
Humility	Feeling
Nothingness	Thinking
Resignation	Acting

We can explore and manage all kinds of *feelings*, including an ultimate sense of nothingness, until we are finally blessed with a full, genuine feeling of **humility**.

We can *think* deeper and purer about ourselves and the whole premise of existence, until we appreciate our **nothingness** with a divine wisdom eventually.

We can *act* at many levels of consciousness to pinpoint and fulfil our potentialities and serve our personal and social duties, until we finally learn the art of stoic, purposeful **resignation** with full consciousness and sense of responsibility.

Selflessness Structure

As shown in Diagram 7.1, selflessness is a special state of being, which is achieved when a person learns humility, resignation, and nothingness after years of self-assessment and likely awakening. Accordingly, through humility (feeling), resignation (acting), and nothingness (thinking) one's selflessness structure is developed.

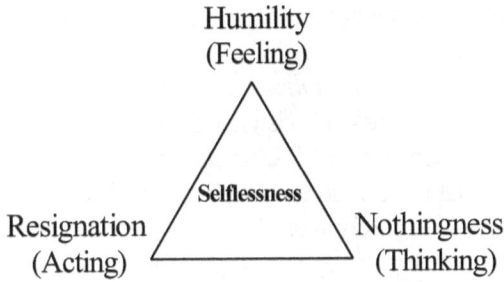

Diagram 7.1: Selflessness Structure and Attributes

The Final Judgment

The goal of raising self-awareness through high consciousness is to build a valid self-image and learn about our potentialities and limitations. We become wiser by thinking more often and deeper, learning about our quirks, refining our value systems, sharing our thoughts and beliefs with others patiently, and contemplating the existential points discussed in this trilogy—all for making better judgments about our being, needs, and relationships with people. Especially, gauging our idiosyncrasies and raw aspirations might help us realize their negative effects on our thoughts, actions, and feelings, which in turn usually cause our stress and misjudgments that hurt others as well.

Ironically, major life decisions should be made at earlier years when we lack the wisdom we might gain only decades later after getting the mindset to do a deep self-assessment. Now, the youths should also try to save humanity and elude the climate crisis we have imposed upon them with our idiocies. Obviously, mastering all these tough tasks objectively outside their youthful dogmatism and thirst for self-gratification is tough for them and so far they have failed. Sadly, their parents and teachers do not have much wisdom about life themselves as alleged role models, either.

Accordingly, self-analysis is a continuous endeavour for those seeking a meaningful existence. Most of all, however, making a viable judgment about our being, ideally when we are young and have more options, is crucial for planning our lives intelligently. We must realize and *internalize* our limitations—including death—to keep the tough task of existence in proper perspective, while also always remember that life limitations compound with time and restrict what we can do and 'who we can be.'

A lifetime, we merely work harder or get lazier depending on our personalities, try to cope or forget our haunting experiences, and doubt the value of our hopes and positive thoughts. We also try to fathom our potentialities and limitations passively in vain usually with scepticism. Often lost within a hazy mindset, our zeal and plans serve neither our natural needs nor a viable goal. Even our struggles to remain content and 'practical' feel merely like another form of 'pure compliance' within a disorderly world, although we take pride in our alleged achievements by pursuing the common aspirations of getting wealthy and famous, etc., like all important people. Worst of all, so much stress and nagging depress us a lifetime, while we also feel shameful of our being on some days.

Accordingly, finding and exploiting our potentialities are also hard these days. Yet, we can at least learn about our limitations in order to get a better sense of our inner 'self,' and benefit from our improved perspective of existence. In particular, appreciating our vulnerabilities and nothingness gives us the chance to view all other life (social) limitations with some degree of wisdom, care, and scepticism in line with a purposeful resignation. Death, as the saddest indisputable truth, is, ironically, a perfect topic as well for gauging the meaning of life and grasping 'who we really are!' It might help us realize our options better and choose a smarter way of living. In particular, the youths must develop solid criteria for guiding them in the early stages of their growth.

Surely, learning about 'self' would be slow and evolutionary if we ever get serious about this matter. Instead, we often wander confusedly in awe and wonder who we are or what we are doing. Our inner conflicts and confusion are rising as humans' clashes and zeal for materialism accelerate every day with no relief in sight. We should face these depressing hassles of living exactly at the time so much efforts and sacrifices are needed just for eluding human demise and repairing all the damages that climate crisis and wars are causing us! Sadly, we all should wrestle with many life dilemmas forever, mostly intuitively, not only as an offshoot of social living per se, but also for appreciating life's inherent values as a 'self'-oriented person seeking salvation.

Of course, self-analysis and self-cleansing for self-awareness at a universal scale to save humanity is a huge expectation. Then again, even a basic level of self-awareness might help us a lot personally at least, although we all should also make an honest judgment *eventually* about the life and society we have built for our children. *How can we feel so proud of ourselves every day?*

CHAPTER EIGHT
Humans' Insights and Foresights

Last three chapters outlined many natural, social, and personal limitations that prevent us from discovering and nurturing our potentialities. Defeating these many obstacles to maximize our life opportunities and possibly find enlightenment, too, is hard. Still, we cannot give up. Rather, we feel obliged to draw on personal insights and foresights that our spirits evoke naturally to recognize and defeat life's limitations. Meanwhile, we hope that fate would also support our efforts to attain the high spirit and dignity that we deserve in line with humans' inherent potentialities. Humans' foresights and insights are, in fact, natural urges that manifest our potentialities for boosting our spirits and existence.

Potentialities and Opportunities

For success in society, one's potentialities and opportunities must coincide to produce some marketable goods. We also need the right type of personality (often a pushy or haughty one) to sell our products and services. Moreover, people are trained to judge their success and self-worth based on the perceived world's norms and approvals. Accordingly, social opportunities bring people more personal deprivations, pains, and stress by abating their attention to their natural needs and discovering their inner self. Ironically, this means that both social barriers and privileges limit people's mentalities and chances to nourish their potentialities.

Nonetheless, social opportunities and setbacks are inevitable facts of modern societies, since we prefer social life to solitude. The more we embrace social rules and values, the more alluring opportunities are made available to us, too. Most of us cannot bypass the temptations and privileges of living in this perceived world merely in hopes of finding peace and divinity in a rather stoic life. Accordingly, 'who we become' (compared to 'who we are' capable of being) reflects our 'adopted' personality (Model). It demonstrates our (dis)ability to recognize and exploit life's (not society's) authentic opportunities and deal with both our personal and social limitations. This personal dilemma was addressed in Chapters Six and Seven somewhat. The main point here is that we have a choice in the way we perceive and deal with social opportunities and setbacks.

Surely, it sounds cynical and bizarre to say that current social opportunities merely reduce self-development chances. However, this is the sad reality of modern societies. Following social norms entails the big risk of losing more of our spirits and freedom, in spite of the seeming big rewards and deemed security offered in the perceived world. Most socioeconomic opportunities limit our chances of finding 'self', since they encourage us to focus on, and worry about, irrelevant life purposes. They mislead us, since they prevent any normal person to build the right values necessary for exploring and living somewhat closer to the real world. We only grapple with life's traps that are disguised as alluring formulas for success and happiness. In particular, our obsessions for wealth and pleasures prevent us from pursuing a more natural life, and exploring our potentialities. We are not taught and cannot see the merits of a simpler lifestyle and nurturing a modest personality. In the end, social living privileges sabotage humans' opportunities and dilute the content and integrity of 'who we are.' They stir immense psychological limitations and dampen our spirits.

An opposite argument prevails about society's limitations, when our failures and disappointments finally force us think and act outside the box. Social setbacks, such as unemployment or failed marriages, sometimes make us find our innate potentialities and peace away from the hectic socioeconomic environment that intends to control our minds more every day. Society's seeming limitations and pressures sometimes compel us dig deeper within our inner self and redeem our divine potentialities and spirits.

Overall, while we are bound by socioeconomic restrictions and rules, life's opportunities might always abound to give us a sense of peace and being at least. Thus, finding a right balance between adaptation pressures and personal growth is the basis for building our life purposes and philosophy. Recognizing life's real opportunities for personal growth is a major life challenge and decision for every intelligent person. We should disallow our misguided perceptions of life opportunities and success affect our chances for exploring our essence through our careers and divine potentialities. Accordingly, developing a peaceful lifestyle, based on our authentic needs and life philosophies in line with a finer perception of life's essentialities, is a huge personal responsibility. Our decision about this matter delineates 'who we are.'

Potentialities and Confidence

Despite our high Egos and exaggeration about our intelligence, we usually have nagging doubts about our potentialities and 'who we are.' Even geniuses often suffer from this condition. Many renowned composers, including Tchaikovsky and Rachmaninov, had doubts about their masterpieces. And some artists, including Van Gogh and Mozart, have suffered psychologically when they did not get the recognition they rightly believed they deserved. Many geniuses have destroyed their artistic and scholarly works, because they had felt inadequate to them. Naturally, a good share of these psychological reactions relates to these artists' drive for perfection. Yet, these sufferings and destructions are often due to our self-doubts or neediness for outer recognition and approval. We let a lack of social validation or criteria for gauging our self-worth make us *doubt* our achievements' ultimate value and dull our potentialities. We sabotage our identities, confidence, and chances for spiritual growth, when we let the perceived world's phony values besiege even our self-actualizing plans and moods.

Normal people can never be quite confident about the value of their feelings, thoughts, or creations. Our feelings, in particular, are often misunderstood even if we expressed them with the most powerful lyrics and sincere intentions. Sometimes, someone may truly appreciate the essence of what we create or say. However, understanding each other's sentiments and intentions is difficult. Nevertheless, the main purpose of developing at least some of our divine potentialities (a basic spirituality) is to curb our endless craving for external validation. Confidence must derive naturally merely from one's spiritual energy and authentic self-fulfilments. While one satisfies one's artistic and spirituality needs, external factors should not distract the process of exploring one's essence. At the same time, often a person's negative sentiments about his/her thoughts and actions is warranted, as it might rightly relate to his/her naïveté and the need for finer plans and insights.

Yet, the opposite is even more prevalent, nowadays, when so many people have become haughty through self-hypnosis or due to commercialized publicity of their substandard creations, such as the messy music that has become popular amongst the youths, in particular. Accordingly, they sabotage their chances to explore their innate potentialities realistically and find who they really are, humbly and confidently, just because society pushes them to be shallow and needy for approval. They prefer to hide behind their phony overconfidence, shoddy creations, and dire self-images.

Both overconfidence and over-doubts hinder the natural flow of our potentialities. Our superficial societies reward even false confidence more than real performance, thus mislead the pursuit of one's real potentials. People mostly judge one another based on their phony appearances and assertions rather than honesty and modesty. Thus, we feel forced to produce a fake personality to adapt and prosper, while hiding our self-doubt and self-pity. We use Model to show a fake confidence just for social purposes.

Of course, even if others could or cared to support us, we still feel insecure in fear of them withdrawing it any time and leaving us helpless and needy again. Actually, people do this quite often intentionally for controlling or manipulating one another. Often, it appears that we have to damage someone else's confidence and pride or belittle him/her in order to feel superior ourselves. This happens especially in work environments, but also in families and friendships. We undermine others, often deliberately, to boost our own Ego and confidence. Sadly, humans would hurt one another deeply as long as their zeal for boosting, pressing, and proving their superiority and potentialities feels vital for social success.

Inner strengths and confidence evolve from needlessness—contrary to social norms where external validation should always feed one's Ego to parade a show of confidence. Ironically, even if enough people were smart, or cared, to offer the right feedback for building our confidence, it would always remain shaky as long as we do not know how to internalize confidence naturally. We would always doubt even people's feedback and judgments if we were not truly convinced of our authentic potentialities—when our confidence lacks divinity and our spirits' backing. At the same time, rational doubtfulness is always a sign of wisdom and humility, which is quite precious as long as it does not lead to chronic self-doubt.

For building our confidence, we need self-reliance to cultivate our insights and mitigate self-doubt. We need inner strength and foresights to dig deep into the hidden treasure of our potentialities with perseverance when some sparks of ingenuity or inspiration strike us. We need strong convictions to build our self-awareness gradually for realizing 'who we are,' while sympathizing with 'who they are.' Accordingly, we build inner confidence about our thoughts, emotions, and deeds. We grow enough confidence to respect other opinions, too, even if offered by people with a lousy perspective of life, whose values we no longer share or care for. Despite other people's wicked views of us, we remain objective about their feedbacks, while stay clear from their manipulations. We internalize our potentialities and who we really are. After all, **only we should care 'who we are,'** as noted in the last chapter.

On the one hand, only through our divine potentialities we can build our genuine confidence, which supports self-awareness and further exploration of our potentialities. On the other hand, authentic, internalized confidence manifests through a real sense of selflessness and needlessness, as our divine potentialities begin to blossom. That genuine self-confidence shows that the process of self-awareness has been productive. This feeling is unlike the ostentatious overconfidence (arrogance) that many people exude, nowadays, to conceal their low potentialities, shallowness, and egoism. True confidence comes from a sacred feeling of humility driven by our high spirit.

Potentialities and Fairness

We all believe we have huge potentialities to offer to society and also deserve substantial rewards for what we do and who we are. We strive to prove our potentialities so that people can discover and respect us for all the substantial thoughts, arts, and sentiments we exude. We change jobs, invent things and ideas, and pursue all sorts of business ventures in order to prove ourselves. In return, we often believe that life owes us the best of everything.

However, many forces prevent our dreams from coming true. Most of us realize gradually that our potentialities would never be recognized or rewarded, and thus we attribute this atrocity to the world's unfairness. It feels as though people deliberately refuse to acknowledge us for what we can do, think, and feel—our unique potentialities. We feel they refuse to provide honest feedback, respect, love, encouragement, or compensation, which we deeply crave and believe we deserve. Therefore, we often get frustrated and convinced about both life's and people's unfairness.

We often feel this way. Actually, our sense of life's unfairness and people's malice are usually warranted. We indeed deserve to be understood and appreciated, but it is irrational to expect others care enough or grasp our feelings and thoughts accurately. People have too many personal problems and agendas to understand or care about other people's depth of pains, feelings, potentialities, and thoughts. Their views and judgments are at best hasty if not malicious. This is the rule of the perceived world. This is human nature, since we have not built our spirits, especially the spirit of fairness. Worst of all, we forget that most people's feedbacks and approvals are totally worthless for building our proper self-image and realizing our self.

Nevertheless, we must accept the reality of unfairness, despite the pervasive prejudices and discriminations at work and family life. As another step for self-awareness and building our divine potentialities, we should adjust our perspective of unfairness and our expectations from people in this regard.

The truth is that while everybody is self-centred and mostly concerned about his/her own needs, desires, and Ego, fairness becomes an illusion automatically. We are not unfair necessarily out of spite, but mainly because we are self-serving individuals and must be fairer and nicer to ourselves first. We need the most and best of everything for ourselves and those whose friendship and loyalty we need. If any charity is still left in us to share, we might be less prejudiced occasionally. These are real facts and we should remember that we cannot do anything about the matter. The truth is that most people lack enough compassion toward others, especially strangers—the primitive law of survival and success! As much as we love to instil justice in our societies, the situation is getting more out of hand every day.

Another point is that we are often personally responsible for our feelings about unfairness by exaggerating our potentialities and setting excessive expectations. This, actually, shows our own unreasonableness (unfairness) when we expect people appreciate 'who we are,' while we keep overstating our capabilities, brag, and remain arrogant. Even if we were somewhat honest with our presentation of who we are, still it is usually impossible for others to appreciate who we are accurately, since everybody is often too busy and shallow themselves, anyway. Therefore, in the end, both epidemic social prejudices and our own misconstrued sense of unfairness for varied reasons are behind these added sources of stress and confusion in societies. Still, we should somehow learn to come to terms with this sad reality, too.

'Causing and suffering unfairness' is a sad human condition. This awareness provides a basic consolation, as we can blame humans' vile nature for feeling and acting this way. Still, some people can handle unfairness and injustice better by disallowing self-pity or aggression overwhelm them when facing systematic unfairness and prejudice. They do not measure their potentialities and self-worth in terms of external rewards and recognition, thus feel unfairness less often. Most of all, when a person grows his/her inner confidence and actualizes his/her divine potentialities, the question of unfairness hardly inflict him/her.

We have a choice on this matter, nevertheless. One option is to accept unfairness as an irreversible reality, like so many other limitations of social living, including the growing mistrust within societies and families. This mentality is hard to adopt, but it can save us a lot of agony and energy. The other commoner option is to let self-pity aggravate our stress and aggression towards others.

Taking fairness less personally and seriously helps us make better life choices. Instead of growing self-pity and/or aggression, we could seek the opportunity of pursuing a rather independent life, while only dream about a miracle to make humans less self-serving and selfish and more trust-worthy eventually.

At the same time, we can bask in a consoling, finite reality: that the only, ultimate fairness in this world is that we all die eventually, no matter who we are or who we think we are! This is a big irony, indeed: That we all know about our inevitable, often painful ending, and yet do not realize our inherent nothingness!

Potentialities and Interests

Discussions in the last two sections reveal the reasons we follow many activities and adventures that feel interesting and fun to us. They satisfy our curiosities and sometimes earn us money, too. Yet, these *activities* are often unrelated to one's real potentialities when they do not entail profound thoughts, productive actions, and soothing feelings simultaneously and consistently in line with a practical life philosophy and plan. Therefore, even our sporadic interests should mostly fit within our some deeper life purposes.

In particular, at younger ages, we are drawn to many fields of education, jobs, or activities that appear 'interesting' or earn us a living. Of course, testing our aspirations is admirable, while we explore our career potentialities and life priorities. This approach feels natural, especially when job markets and demands cannot match the immense supply of potentialities that youths offer. Still, pursuing random interests without a general plan can mislead us in the end and waste many precious years of our lives. While the learning aspects of our youthful experiences are useful, pursuing interests or activities just for testing the waters over a long period might damage both our sense of self and our chance of building a career. These types of pursuits often lead to more confusion, stress, self-doubt, and disappointments, not to mention the big risk of losing the main direction of our lives. It might hinder our chances of exploring our potentialities and opportunities, too.

The point is to, 'Not lose sight of one's real responsibilities and needs in the midst of the rising social chaos and cause further depletion of our spirits.' Unfortunately, it is getting harder every year to cope with socioeconomic, especially career and marital, demands, which then also reduces our chances, interest, and time to explore our divine potentialities. Thus, most of us never realize our life mission to define and boost both our career and divine potentialities regardless of the joy of our fleeting interests and the money attached to our efforts. We might wish (or feel obliged) to gauge certain activities, careers, or interests, but must mainly find and focus on our ultimate plans. Sporadic interests and ambitions (e.g., being a professional singer) must not slow the development of one's long-term plans according to a sound life philosophy.

Potentialities and Perseverance

Talking about the importance of perseverance for nurturing our potentialities seems redundant. Then again, not mentioning such an important factor would be negligence. The simple fact is that real potentialities are like hidden treasures buried in the depth of our unconscious away from our depleted spirits. The only tool for excavating these treasures is perseverance. In order to reach the depth of our being and unconscious, we should believe in our abilities and the strengths of our convictions to pursue our goals without self-doubt or procrastination. We need resilience and a high spirit to conquer the depth of our unconscious and redeem our potentialities. We must break the normal living barriers, build our confidence, and revive our spirits, so that our potentialities erupt and flow fluently. When we whisper the right tunes in our unconscious mind, the self-awareness path becomes automatic and natural, and our divine potentialities resonate musically. In fact, perseverance is merely another manifestation of our spirit. It requires an initial incentive, determination, and a lengthy search for an opening to our treasure of potentialities.

Discussing social limitations and mayhem is not for getting cynical or seeking seclusion. Rather, the goal is to raise our spirits and maybe help humanity, too, by refining our thoughts, actions, and feelings within a divine domain. The goal is to step outside of social boundaries and create a more meaningful life for ourselves through spiritual thoughts and feelings. After all, the only way to redeem our souls is to discard our erratic thoughts and struggles. Only by boosting our 'self' and divine potentialities, we may find peace, build our spirits, and discover the beauty of Nature inside and around us. The most exciting role of our potentialities is to get a chance to establish our connection with Nature.

PART IV
Limitations and Victories

CHAPTER NINE
Living Limitations

Four types of social and personal limitations impede our efforts most deeply to unravel the power of our spirits and potentialities. They hinder our social adaptation efforts and personal growth, and they affect our doubts, decisions, and course of life. They are:

1. Social and Economical Limitations
2. Natural Limitations (Physical and Mental)
3. Personality Limitations
4. Self-imposed Limitations

Social and Economical Limitations

Sadly, we are becoming more susceptible to erratic forces beyond our control every day. We are not talking about fate or natural forces in the universe, but rather the manmade socioeconomic systems that dictate our way of thinking and living. Our social structure has become too rampant to understand and cope with. We no longer know how to live naturally, while our attitude and values shape around many superficial social norms. Meanwhile, we have lost our faiths in social systems, including our political and judicial institutions. Family values have also deteriorated a lot due to socioeconomic pressures. The nature and purpose of family relationships have changed vastly in the last few decades. Couples have major difficulty to relate or respond to each other's expectations. Everybody dreams and demands quite erratically in their relationships, because no logical and moral values exist to guide the public objectively. We have discarded our traditional family principles, but have no new principles to curb our wild imaginations and rising idiosyncrasies. We are living in fantasy with our naïve life outlooks in dire relationship settings. While struggling hard to adapt and prosper by building fake identities, we lose our chances to explore who we really are and what the purposes of our being and socializing are. These routine pressures impose immense limitations for building a simple life and family.

In particular, our children are seriously confused about social values and ways. They lack reliable criteria to develop their life plans and recognize their personal and marital needs, while social living feels hard and frustrating to them. Many of them desire to free themselves from the anxiety of living in this sad setting, but do not know how or often end up choosing a lousier alternative for living and thinking. All we need to do is to look around and witness how senseless crimes in the recent decades have become and how unhealthy our world and living conditions are getting. The other day, on Friday August 16, 2013, three teenagers in Oklahoma City gunned down and killed an Australian student, Christopher Lane, since, as one of them said, "We were bored."

The other night, a documentary on TV highlighted the life of a bunch of university graduates turned prostitutes in order to pay back their student loans. It is hard not to wonder about the deep demise of our social structure and values. It is hard not to wonder about the youths' mentality and our teachings to them or about the value of university education without making the youth grasp the realities and limitations of social living, nowadays. All that high education does not even teach people anything regarding basic human integrity, self-worth, and ethics. What are all these efforts, taxes, and expenditures good for, then?

Random shootings, families kidnapping or murdering own members, teenagers becoming criminals for a few dollars or out of boredom, police shooting innocent people unnecessarily only out of arrogance, unemployment and the absence of an economic infrastructure in line with population growth, disproportionate distribution of wealth and greed, pollution and destruction of natural and economical resources, obsession with sexuality, dire consumerism and capitalistic ideologies, senseless suicides, on and on and on. The list of crazy acts and values we are supposed to grasp and deal with, and the limitations that we are expected to plan our lives within, are growing fast. The outcome of all these pressures is a deep state of confusion and helplessness to grasp the meaning of our lives or anything around us. Many of us have already lost self-control and attempt crazy acts, such as bombing buildings and killing hundreds of innocent people. Who can truly find a meaning for his/her existence in this wild environment when every one of us has become a cause of the problems mostly due to epidemic arrogance, dogmatism, and naiveté? We hurt one another somehow even when we try to be a better person.

Despite our children's potentialities and efforts to achieve certain goals, the impact of external limitations, i.e., social and economic systems, is immense and capable of crippling so many able individuals. The road to success and basic happiness was much clearer in the past. Now, it is full of whats and ifs and insecurities. Not long ago, we believed education and personal initiative led to job security and a somewhat healthy family life, but not anymore. How have we brought this chaos and shame upon ourselves and why do we accept living like this? Do not we have any other option? All we need to agree on at this time is that so many important factors that affect our financial and emotional welfare and mindsets are out of everybody's controls, especially those to whom we have trusted the construction and maintenance of social and economic systems.

In all, the shallowness, unfairness, and irrationality of social structure are making our lives too obscure and unmanageable.

Making sense about this complex system or coming to terms with it would continue to be the most challenging task for people and governments. Still, for recognizing 'who we are,' we must understand and defeat the effects of these erratic forces. **First**, we must somehow accept and cope with the fact that understanding and justifying the existing socioeconomic conditions is beyond our abilities to a large degree. The intricacies and crookedness of socioeconomic environments that we have inherited, and perhaps helped create for ourselves, are unexplainable and unsustainable. Why cannot we, especially our leaders, see this and do something about it? That is amazing! **Second**, we could get smarter and at least resist the temptations of getting absorbed in these systems. **Third**, we should find ways of flourishing as an *individual* within these substandard systems both spiritually and mentally. We can make the best of the bad situation without being pushed to despair completely about existence. Handling this convoluted dilemma is quite difficult for most of us, of course. However, we can at least remember that a person's identity and wisdom manifests only through his selfless and self-reliant character and not the phony social identity s/he strives, so idiotically, to build.

We have been conditioned to blame 'life' and fate for our miseries, instead of our own rampant needs and socioeconomic pressures to live so superficially. We do not explore the roots of social evils and our own inability to find better means of living or stopping our own roles in feeding the monsters ruling the world. We can do so very easily, in fact, simply by stopping our phony social habits, mostly consumerism, and instead encourage others to do the same until perhaps some miracle brings about a better socioeconomic system for this broken species. We can insist on and help build more ethical and practical norms and cultures.

The growing socioeconomic limitations around the globe are, naturally, making the task of evaluating 'who we are,' as a person and human, much harder, too, in line with people's rising malice and naivety. Nevertheless, our only option is to build more self-discipline and spiritual power to defeat the forces of despair and confusion and to focus on grasping 'who we are' and 'what our mission is' in this chaotic world. What other choice do we have?

Natural Limitations (Physical and Mental)

Everybody deserves a peaceful life and a chance to develop him/herself to the highest levels of wisdom and piety in our allegedly civilized societies. This is a noble objective. Yet, our genetic and upbringing limitations always stand in our ways. In addition, both formal and social educations, at home and in society, jeopardize the growth of our natural attributes, self, and spirit. They mislead us about the right values of life and our choices, so we lose our chances to learn about, and promote, our natural urges, while our mental limitations rise rapidly. Society is causing us more doubts, insecurities, and confusion daily, but we also make life harder for ourselves by our decisions and lifestyle choices. Especially, our delusions and unrealistic expectations cause additional limitations that hinder our ability to know 'who we are' and why we choose a particular lifestyle.

Our genetic limitations infect our personalities drastically, too, which then leads to a variety of other self-imposed limitations that contaminate our decisions and judgments as well. Therefore, it can be appreciated how quickly and wildly personal limitations keep piling up and ruining our lives, as discussed in this chapter.

Our mental and physical abilities are mostly hereditary. The bone structure, height, weight, and intelligence are humans' basic limitations, though we can influence their growth somewhat with nutrition, exercising, and learning. Despite genetic limitations' deep roots, which we must recognize and live with, e.g., athletic or mathematical shortfalls, wisdom and awareness might help us mitigate them somewhat after recognizing our mental limitations and pursuing a long period of training to curb our old habits.

On the one hand, we must plan and train our brains for their ultimate potentialities, like body builders who create big muscles regardless of their heights and bone densities. On the other hand, overestimating our mental capacity and logic, and getting more arrogant all along, shows our mere naivety. It hinders our chance to nurture our brains even for our own benefit. Formal education per se or egotism cannot help us prepare for real life challenges. Actually, education seems to be hurting our natural learning and growth as elaborated in Volume III of this trilogy. Accordingly, we need to pinpoint and learn the essential means of living and relating in a more unconventional manner, although learning the right stuff about life and self, including our ultimate limitations, requires lots of patience, modesty, and efforts.

Often parents have motives and a chance to teach these facts to their children, if they were not preoccupied by life's trivialities themselves and could think somewhat objectively outside social norms and teachings. We try to recognize our kids' talent, such as athletic abilities, memory, artistic talents, creativity, vocabulary and language, etc. Sometimes, teachers and mentors might play a positive or negative role, too. Some objective parents succeed in pinpointing their kids' potentialities and limitations and possibly guiding them properly. However, nowadays, most parents spoil their children with their shoddy value systems and their naïve intentions to maximize their kids' confidence and self-image. Therefore, they ruin their kids' chances to recognize their natural limitations and working out their life options realistically. These days, people do not appreciate the repercussions of over or under developed Ego and confidence mostly due to bad parenting; in particular, parents' overindulgence in hopes of raising their kids' self-esteem. Parents only put more psychological pressures on their kids and themselves by ignoring social and humans' natural limitations. They kill their kids' spirits, instead of helping them figure out their potentialities and limitations properly.

Gauging our mental strengths and limitations is a natural and perpetual process that starts at a very early stage of our lives, but our Ego and dogmatism often sabotage our chances for doing a proper assessment. The purpose of gauging our innate limitations is to set more realistic life targets by enhancing our objectivity and self-awareness. Ignoring our limitations, or hoping to curb their symptoms superficially, eliminates the chance of realizing our simpler potentialities that we can nurture naturally and often have divine and lasting purposes. In some cases, self-awareness might help a person overcome even his/her deep idiosyncrasies, e.g., jealousy or spite, after a long process of training and finally revamping his/her debilitating habits. Yet, our main objective of assessing our natural limitations is to set realistic life targets and enhance our self-awareness and objectivity.

Personality Limitations

Personality limitations manifest mainly in the following forms due to a large variety of genetic and upbringing factors:
- false personalities we adopt for social survival or success,
- pomposity and dogmatism,
- lack of identity and knowledge of 'self,'
- inability to grasp life and cope socially, and
- inability to build and maintain a healthy family.

In particular, our phony personalities cause us big headaches, as we lose our chances to find our 'self' and build a self-reliant identity. In addition, we attract people who are incompatible with us in terms of their needs and aspirations. Thus, we go through a long process of trials and errors before accepting that our lifestyle and relationships are only making us too depressed and desperate, instead of enriching our lives. Meanwhile, the lousiness of most relationships, nowadays, is due to our lack of strong personalities, family guidelines, confidence, inner power, and integrity.

As discussed in detail in Volume I of this trilogy, our abilities to communicate, run our relationships, and find happiness depend on the way our three personality aspects, i.e., Ego, Model, and Self, operate. Personality limitations increase expeditiously when Ego and Model become dominant.

Self-imposed Limitations

Our erroneous, hasty judgments and decisions create too many self-imposed limitations. Furthermore, we make our lives tougher and gloomier when we do not build the courage and willpower to reverse a bad decision, or at least acknowledge it. Addiction is a good example. Even smoking and drinking habits start for many reasons. A person with a good judgment would not be dragged into this dire position in the first place, but even if s/he were, s/he would try to rectify his/her mistake. Yet, so many people are not mentally prepared to fight their damaging habits. Not everybody can avoid or defeat the psychological effects of earlier decisions or failures that might linger for the rest of a person's life. This is true even when s/he feels the burdens of induced limitations and realizes how they prevent him/her from building self-esteem and a more bearable life outlook.

Physical limitations due to the lack of exercise and activity, as well as psychological burdens due to shoddy lifestyles, negative thinking, and addictions are ultimately self-imposed if we do not try to do something about them.

We impose major limitations on our lives due to our attitudes, obsessions, and personalities. Sometimes, our false pride stands in the way of establishing or maintaining the kind of relationships we so dearly need. We might even destroy good relationships by our egoism and stubbornness. Thus, we pain ourselves the most due to such self-imposed limitations that lead to substandard life conditions. We often hurt ourselves unknowingly, since our life burdens are the results of our naively conditioned mentality and personality, after all. Of course, our judgments and values are mostly tainted by the effects of our rearing environment and the influence of social norms, which means that our limitations are mainly of no fault of our own. Yet, we are ultimately the ones imposing them on ourselves with our passivity and negativity. We could reflect and acknowledge that only we are responsible for alleviating these limitations the best we can. If we analyse our relationships, expectations, attitudes, and judgments critically, we can pinpoint our self-imposed limitations and weaknesses. Many of these limitations are luckily curable or controllable, if we really care to help ourselves.

Self-imposed limitations often result from the value system and lifestyle we adopt. For example, most people spend beyond their means and then suffer its downsides. They borrow money to buy fancy stuff or pursue a certain lifestyle. Thus, they make life miserable for themselves and people around them by living like mindless robots merely following the crowd. They let their raw ambitions and greed lead their lifestyles, while they get hung up on superficial goals and life trivia. They torture themselves with their juvenile dreams, neediness, misperceptions about happiness and love, or thirst for power and wealth. All these self-imposed tortures and limitations also erode their chances to utilize their potentialities and enjoy self-actualization in a simple lifestyle.

Forces beyond our control, such as social corruption, injustice, and general life dilemmas, usually also impose many limitations upon us. Yet, a wise person considers all these obstacles mostly as self-imposed limitations, because s/he believes that s/he should overcome them somewhat by exploring workable solutions or at least some means of coming to terms with them, mostly the latter. Surely, solutions are often scarce, while conviction, commitment, and self-discipline are needed, too. Yet, most of us compound our limitations by our passivity, ignoring the debilitating symptoms of our self-imposed limitations, or merely whining, instead of working on our willpower to fight them.

The worst kind of self-imposed limitation occurs when we try to resort to lousy solutions to forget, or come to terms, with major setbacks in our lives. For example, we rush to find a new mate to avoid loneliness or mitigate the burdens of losing our spouse or lover. We make major concessions and fight our pride and spirit every day to please a person who is clearly another mismatch for us. Resorting to gambling or other addictions, even for forgetting our sudden, dire loses, is naturally another common self-imposed limitation in modern societies. Then again, some losses are really heartbreaking and nerve-racking for most us, e.g., those related to the loss of our children in rampant school shootings, nowadays!

Timing Limitation

Hasty decisions cause big problems when we ignore our positive doubts (discussed in Chapter 14) or do not build a sensible strategy for the action and decision on hand. At the same time, it is vital to stress here that the 'timing' (for making good decisions in life) is also quite limited, mostly because all social, personal, and life limitations compound with time. Even our extended efforts do not lead to positive outcomes if, 1) We miss our chances to make the right decisions of life in a timely manner, and 2) We do not recognize the right timing for making life's major decisions.

These two related (sounding similar) principles apply to all phases and aspects of our lives with various emphasis and nature. Yet, their importance and effects are clearly higher the younger a person is and the longer his/her future plans must be. For example, we know that children learn languages, music, arts, and sports much better up to certain ages. This 'timing' factor shows that humans' main talents fruit within a tiny window of opportunity.

Living requires many major, timely decisions, as discussed in Vol. III. Although the importance of 'timing' for both our major and mundane decisions is surely clear, our most important plans and decisions should usually be made at the young age perhaps before 30 or so. Thus, analysing life and our purposes of living before making all those critical decisions is extremely helpful. Yet, as young people, we are only misled by social trends and propagandas, instead of finding the right ways of learning about life and our divine potentialities. Therefore, the outcomes of our major life decisions often end up less desirable than we usually anticipate, if not catastrophic. Our bad timing and decisions also affect our families, who then put indirect pressures on us, too, on top of feeling entrapped personally in a meaningless, stressful life alongside our ungrateful, nagging families.

Clearly, our physical and mental abilities deteriorate with age, which means the number of productive years for achieving our (often-essential) objectives is also limited. Not a new discovery, but many of us simply forget this fact or are deluded by positive thinking tricks. We forget that we cannot do most things that should have been done long time ago. We must have made the right decisions when we had had the chance to do so. Most of all, however, without timely decisions, we miss life's opportunities, get trapped within life's trivialities, suppress our potentialities, annihilate our spirits, and limit our chances to succeed in many aspects of life later. Education and learning are best examples, but other simpler life decisions should also be developed timely and wisely for leading a rather peaceful existence. In particular, pursuing unrealistic objectives for looking busy or proactive, or merely due to our naïve positive thinking or dreams, makes us lose great opportunities in life and look pathetic, too.

Education and work constitute the primary structure of life that we automatically plan (and believe is best) for our children. However, societies might soon realize that we are keeping our kids at schools and colleges uselessly for no tangible benefits. Actually, we might be doing them disservice with our present curriculum. This principle of 'timing' must be revisited soon to ensure that individuals and society benefit from human potentials most effectively—or at least better than present. Nowadays, we are wasting vast potentialities that could be applied for personal and social benefits more productively.

By the way, education and work have not always been so structured, rigid, and often useless. Even now, many children in the world do not have the pain and privileges of educational and career planning, since they are forced to labour with much less education, thus feel and face life more readily and naturally. Surely, that is not a proper strategy, but the goals and productivity of current schooling and working routines in modern societies are not analysed and thought through as much as we have now come to believe. This point is stressed in Vol. III in some length.

Another obvious example is the 'timing' for starting a family. Experience shows that the best time to do this is when partners have the financial resources, energy, and patience to handle each other's, as well as their children's, needs. Nowadays, so many auxiliary factors defer people's decision to start a family, or they raise their kids outside a family, e.g., as a single parent option. Overall, a less favourable 'timing,' combined with bad planning, has caused many relationship conundrums in the new era, with much lesser fault of people in this special case.

Therefore, everybody is quite rightly apprehensive about the risks of getting into a serious relationship. For one thing, partners' high expectations of themselves and each other, and the lack of mechanisms to find suitable partners deter people from building families. The damages of customary random dating during the years prior to marriage somewhat diminish couples' abilities to relate, in fact. In many cases, these days we should get into our second or third marriages due to our failures in the earlier one(s) and/or bad timings of various types of decisions.

These assertions are not for condemning people's inability to get married soon enough, but rather to stress that our warranted worries and obligations complicate our decision to start a family on a timely manner. Accordingly, we get entrapped in a graver mental condition, such as lousy marriages. Our relationships (or the lack of good ones) also damage our psyches. In all, timing for marriage is too complex and critical, nowadays, while the effects of our marital decisions often hurt our spirits as well as our children's welfare.

Another example about our decisions' 'timing' is our *natural purposes and interests in life* in conjunction with our careers, so that we can satisfy both our financial and psychological needs. Because of bad 'timing,' many of us live a miserable life due to misfit jobs or careers we get stuck with, or keep switching to no avail. Many people simply choose a career that appeals to them for irrelevant factors, out of necessity, or wrong education. As an obsolete requirement of socioeconomic structure, we spend many years of our precious lives on formal education and training. Then we often decide to ignore all those efforts and pains in order to re-educate or train ourselves in a different field (mostly for staying practical), which usually proves unwise for new reasons. Thus, our decisions about the right fields of education should be made at a proper 'timing,' mostly the first time, after gauging our limitations, temperament, potentials, life plans, and philosophy.

Regardless of our obsession for success and happiness, the bare requirement for health and peace of mind demands timely decisions for building our fundamental thoughts, life philosophy, beliefs, higher spirits, and a suitable lifestyle. We should make timely decisions about a path of life that is manageable with the least amount of stress.

Besides its significance for making life's major decisions, the direst 'timing limitation' relates to the fact that we all miss the opportunity of learning humility and realizing our nothingness before we get old, if at all. This is a major failure and obstacle for humans, to go through life without getting a chance to mature mentally and nurture modesty as a guiding light for choosing their life paths and philosophies. Only if we are intelligent and lucky, we might realize our absolute nothingness before it is too late and apply this wisdom. In fact, this simple timing limitation is the root of human misery and downfall of humanity, because by the time we get old and realize this horrific mystery of life, *if we do,* we have become too rigid and self-centred to change or apply our new wisdom. It is just too depressing and unfortunate that people and societies should suffer so much just because we have not learned to realize this clear, basic reality. It is sad that most people only pamper their childish desires and become more arrogant every day until their last breaths, instead of learning about, and honouring, their nothingness. Ironically, this means that most of us live and die rather senselessly very much like a vegetable, at best, with no clue about the amazing essence of our being—*the awakening mystery we might unravel only when we realize our nothingness.*

The Ultimate Life Limitation

Some astonishing realizations and questions startle us during childhood when we become curious about our origin and wonder what gave us life, and why. What happened that we are here in this weird world? Before finding a satisfactory answer to these elementary but confusing curiosities, we suddenly learn a more shocking fact: Death. It remains a scary and stressful discovery for a few days or weeks. Then, this ultimate reality sinks in our subconscious after we struggle and fail to understand its purpose, even after asking all sorts of questions from our parents. At last, every child somehow surrenders to the harsh reality of death as s/he hides it in his/her subconscious. S/he realizes this ultimate limitation of his/her being briefly, but prefers to deny it. Thus, our understanding of death stays at the perceived reality level, which has a tendency to be rather casual about our convictions and daily lives. Our subconscious does not emanate the force and meaning of death truly—as the ultimate limitation of our being.

Of course, our ability to forget sad realities or submerge them into our subconscious helps our sanity. However, undermining or forgetting 'death' is a major factor in diminishing our ability to grasp 'who we are' and establishing a profound value system. This potential for kick-starting our self-awareness process is lost, as we miss our chance to realize our nothingness. Grasping 'who we are,' our inherent vulnerability, and the reality of death—that our life may end in a second—could have helped us stay modest and mindful. We might have become humbler if we had always remembered we have no control over our most precious asset—our dear lives. Instead, we insist on building pompous characters and brag about our importance so childishly. And we often fight and kill one another foolishly just to prove our importance and amazing intelligence!

The irony is that remembering our 'nothingness' regularly empowers our characters and spirits. We find a deeper meaning for the events happening around us, if we recall forever that our existence is at the mercy of supernatural—or random—forces. At this high consciousness level, other life limitations also become more bearable, and the significance of so many of our struggles for phony success would subside vastly. We graduate to the next level with a big desire to learn something about this outside force that grants us life and death. We try to create a basic personal vision of it at least. We might then decide to re-assess and adjust our life paths somewhat in order to play the limited role we might have in our fates, such as defeating our harmful addictions. Our higher sense of mortality would make us appreciate our existence better, while we enjoy Nature and other creatures, which look so beautiful, but also fragile and vulnerable like us. We feel part of Nature and the universe, and thus become more sensible about environmental damages humans are causing, too. We try to learn from other human beings who have offered their experiences and wisdom. We appreciate how all forms of life have built special mechanisms for both growth and defence against danger and death, yet should yield so helplessly at the end to the powerful forces of Nature when the time comes to surrender their beloved existence. All those fancy defence mechanisms, arrogance, and supposed wisdom would be worth not a grain of sand.

Thus, celebrating death consciously as the main clue about the *meaning* of life, instead of pushing it deep into our subconscious, might raise our wisdom. Repeating the word 'death' must not stir gloom, either. In fact, the more we bring this reality into fore, the more we learn about the *mysteries* and *values* of life. We sense the triviality of all our worries and greed. For example, when a job promotion or recognition is delayed or overlooked, we handle the related pains and disappointment better. Instead, we welcome the opportunity to ponder our life choices more insightfully.

Ironically, nowadays, many people try to keep death in their semiconscious occasionally by repeating the slogans, 'Life is too short, and you live only once.' This subtle awareness is supposed to help us mitigate our fear of taking on challenging adventures. It could also make us stronger and wiser if practised continuously as a ritual, and if people felt the true essence of these slogans. However, most people use those mottos as lame excuses for more laziness or carelessness—instead of alertness—or merely for self-gratifications purposes. Sadly, the slogans 'Life is too short, and you live only once' have become scapegoats for people to get more reckless financially and emotionally. We always insist on missing the boat even when we get a worthy insight occasionally!

In all, while death brings us to the final frontier, it also gives us the best yardstick to gauge our lives and life limitations more realistically. Of course, some exceptions defy this basic criterion. For instance, when an old or terminally ill individual feels pain and self-degradation, the situation could be a bit more devastating limitation than death itself, where it actually becomes a source of relief in this instance, too, as the only escape from another severe life limitation. Or sometimes, we get so bored or fed-up with life, we prefer to resign totally and die, maybe as the only honourable option left.

Anyway, the main limitation of one's life is life itself, which is ultimately significant merely for the opportunity it renders us to trace and enjoy our potentialities, plus the collective potentialities of humans and Nature, for only certain number of years. Even if we are lucky to have a full natural life, we must be quite wise in allotting this most precious resource in a meaningful manner. We have a choice, and hopefully gain the wisdom, too, to spend our lives on activities and thoughts that give us an authentic sense of self-fulfilment and spiritual transcendence. And, for some of us who have passed certain stages of our lives, it is now so clear that life is such a short journey and how ignorantly we, as a child and young adult, had assumed we had so much time to conquer life. We realize how we have wasted so much of our precious lives and mental energies on pursuing shallow dreams and pleasures.

If we truly grasp the gravity of our ultimate limitation—the finality and fragility of life itself—we develop the proper mindset to distinguish life priorities and essentialities more objectively. The journey of life can become extremely joyful and beautiful once we discover that hidden inner power within us—our hearty spirits and potentialities—and engage them consciously to guide us. Death, as life's ultimate limitation, could also make us realize that our inner strengths, which we boost thru self-awareness, may be the echo of an external force. We might attribute this external force to our creator, the God, the supernatural, or anything else that we had not known before learning about ourselves, our inner power, and our ultimate limitation. A perpetual reminder of our finality and fragility thru meditation would become a major tool for raising our awareness and stirring our spiritual feelings, too.

A cute quote from Wolfgang Amadeus Mozart about death is interesting to include here.

"As death, when we come to consider it closely, is the true goal of our existence, I have formed during the last few years such close relationships with this best and truest friend of mankind that death's image is not only no longer terrifying to me, but is indeed very soothing and consoling, and I thank my God for graciously granting me the opportunity of learning that death is the key which unlocks the door to our true happiness. I never lie down at night without reflecting that — young as I am — I may not live to see another day. Yet no one of all my acquaintances could say that in company I am morose or disgruntled." Letter to Leopold Mozart (4 April 1787), from *The Mozart-Da Ponte Operas* by Andrew Steptoe, Oxford University Press, 1988, p. 84.

The phrase, 'I thank my God for graciously granting me the opportunity of learning that death is the key which unlocks the door to our true happiness,' is really precious, although it reflects only half of the picture of this ultimate reality. The other more important half, i.e., death's finality, as a device for putting our existence into proper perspective, is missing in his sentimental wisdom *or possibly implied in it*, depending on his belief about afterlife or the ultimate finality of one's existence!

In fact, imagining any chance for afterlife imposes a major obstacle to understand our existence. The notion of 'afterlife' has been the most ridiculous and debilitating idea in human history that many groups have exploited at the expense of ruining so many gullible people's minds and their chances of gaining their individualism and integrity. That is a sad disservice to humanity, because our emphasis on afterlife undermines the necessity of educating the public about the significance of our existence and the sanctity of our living spirits. Humans' epidemic emphasis on afterlife and religions, instead of appreciating the hollowness of such ridiculous beliefs about human immortality, has been just another clue about the deep-rooted humans' naiveté historically, but especially for this supposedly modern civilization.

To find life, we must forget everything about the possibility of afterlife in order to focus on our 'nothingness.'

CHAPTER TEN
Personal Beliefs and Choices

It is time to agree that humans' intelligence and ingenuity have failed miserably to create social harmony and peace. Instead, they have goaded us fight one another relentlessly or embrace idiotic pleasures in hopes of hiding our pains. They cannot even help us cope with the chaotic symptoms of the socioeconomic structure —which is itself an embarrassing product of our poor mentalities and characters. So far, after many millenniums of contemplation, we have come up with capitalism as our best option to fulfil our socioeconomic needs, yet the majority of the world's population lives in poverty and misery. This is what our logic has told us to do! At personal level, our logic is even less reliable and useful relative to the methodical processes used in social and scientific settings. Our unique emotions, insecurities, and genes make our ingenuity too varied and shaky. Therefore, we feel more helpless every day when our brains cannot aid us communicate amongst ourselves or address even our mundane socioeconomic issues, let alone offer fundamental thoughts and life philosophies. Human logic's frailty is discussed further in Appendices A and B at the end of the book besides the discussions in Chapter Two.

Ironically, with all these immense evidences about our brains' frailty, we still remain so sure and defensive about our demented logic! Our tenacity and vanity are rising astronomically, as we try to build and portray a phony semblance of individualism. Are we just too irrational humans or born stubborn!? Most likely both!

Then again, as soon as we admit that our logic and values are not as useful as we had imagined all along, if not disruptive too often, we get even more confused and agitated about our inability to sort out our doubts and make good life decisions. Under this common, stressful condition, some intelligent and lucky people may eventually succeed in building their beliefs and philosophies to compensate for the shortfalls of human logic. They apply their faiths and wisdom to guide them, instead of relying on logic and social norms per se, or following religions blindly for satisfying their spirituality needs.

Our personal experiences and reflections gradually develop our basic beliefs, which then provide the platform for building the foundation of our thoughts and a life philosophy. In return, a solid foundation of thoughts and a smart life philosophy help us stay focused and objective regarding our beliefs. Together, they offer a good platform towards a specific, and usually divine, lifestyle. Surely, our genetics, intelligence, and even luck play major roles in the manner our beliefs, personality, and outlook develop. Our personal experiences and their impacts on us are always unique, thus our conclusions and convictions cannot be generalized for common purposes. For example, if a person 'sees *the divine truth* when she/he believes in it,' it does not mean that others can also apply this crude faith or rely on this method of self-conditioning to build their convictions.[††] This imaginary condition—blind faith or perhaps hallucination—would never work for everybody and it should at best be considered only another method of mental conditioning (self-hypnosis) with no benefit. As another example, this author's rather sacred experiences shaping his beliefs cannot be replicated or adopted by others as proofs of the supernatural.

[††] Dr. Wayne Dyer's book, *You see it when you believe it* delves into this concept as a method for building our faiths.

They are mentioned in the following pages not for proving any evidence of the real world or a valid basis for his beliefs. They are just examples of things that happen to people and merely help them ponder the possibility of another reality, thus redefine their purposes of living and being perhaps.

These types of real or abstract experiences merely pick our curiosity regarding the existence of a real world beyond our daily perceptions and crude logic. They are only for noting the depth of humans' vulnerabilities when developing the foundation of our thoughts and beliefs—but nothing more. They might also reveal the sanctity of our spirits for leading a saner and easier life, which human logic has failed to avail. In all, the following enigmatic experiences had stirred, at that moment, a deep, confusing sense of curiosity about 'self' and its likely link to a sacred realm, but have also influenced this author many years later when building his beliefs and positive doubts through self-analyses and self-awareness.

Overall, our personal contacts with a mystical force during some blessed moments are scattered throughout our lives, from childhood that is a precious state of curiosity and apprehension until we mature and settle down with or without refined beliefs about existence. All along, two types of divine experiences amuse, if not enlighten, us. First, *abstract experiences* that make us think about the existence of a real world. Second, some life events that feel like magic or blessings ordained by a higher order. They also feel like sacred signs about the real reality, although the messages are often received in indirect manners. We might refer to these events as *real experience* only to distinguish them from abstract ones. Some of us pause and ponder these real experiences long enough to learn some lessons for strengthening our beliefs and spirits, however most people are too engaged to care about the significance of such odd revelations. Overall, building a personal belief system in line with some spirituality notions, philosophical reflections, and magical experiences appears to pay off, despite the impotency of our logic, science, and religions.

Abstract Experiences

'Abstract experiences' noted here signify those fragile events and feelings that do not happen regularly in one's life and are hard to explain by our crude logic. Otherwise, the author still remembers those odd experiences as quite vivid, sensational, and shocking. Other people and scholars have also reported similar experiences, one of which will be quoted later.

In a beautiful spring afternoon, at age 13, I left a relative's house to go home by myself. I walked alone in a shady, long alley that led to the main street. Only the soothing sound of water dashing down a narrow creek echoed, as it ran in the middle of the alley between two rows of huge plane trees at around ten feet apart on the opposite sides of the stream. A bizarre sensation besieged me swiftly and I felt that 'I' was separated from my body. I could no longer feel my steps or any other movement of my body. It kept walking by itself and 'I' just watched it from the other side of the stream. Shocked delightfully, 'I' was looking with awe at the body, as though watching a shadow meander by itself. *Who is that thing, sauntering so determinedly on the other side of the stream?*, 'I' wondered, although 'I' realized it was my body and my query felt bizarre all by itself. It walked unconsciously and effortlessly, as 'I' followed it for about 45 seconds without fuss or even wishing to change anything, although 'I' was quite aware of the lost control. The body was an independent 'entity' outside 'I'. And 'I' was perplexed, more than anything, by this mysterious episode. The whole experience and the fact that 'I' remained in charge of thinking and wondering at that instant felt magical. 'I' did not wish it to end. Then, as 'I' felt content, my consciousness began melting fast, while 'I' noticed the return to normalcy, too, with gloom. The more I had tried to keep myself in that state of separateness, the faster 'I' was pushed back inside the body and soon no trace of a lonely 'body' remained on the other side of the stream. I was in charge of that tricky body again as my steps got heavy like usual. My lumbering began again, as I dragged myself in the last few feet out of the alley, as if my super consciousness had lost its power and freedom as soon as it had merged with the body again. Swiftly, I felt the burden of my body and juvenile worries all over again.

My subsequent efforts to repeat that out-of-body experience, the same day and later, proved futile. I could not recreate that odd experience of separateness of my body and 'I'. It happened once again unexpectedly, though, two years later, but it lasted about only 20-25 seconds. I did not smoke cigarettes, drink liquor, or eat anything out of ordinary that could have caused that sensation (or hallucination) of separateness on those two occasions. Despite my random efforts all along to replicate that state of separateness and likely divinity, it has not reappeared—not even through my meditations. By aging, some obstacle—perhaps the conditioning strength of the perceived world—has prevented it from recurring. The experience could have not been due to any sickness, either, since my awareness had in fact increased during those particular short spans of time, and then the sensation had halted abruptly and my normal, boring level of consciousness restored.

Now, I realize that those questions and feelings during my state of separateness had most likely come from my thoughts and conscious mind that *possibly* resided in 'I', but definitely not in my body. Or perhaps, 'I', a separate entity or soul in charge of my conscious mind and thoughts, had posed the questions, while the body had felt fully isolated and walking on its own power. These logical musings are puzzling, as I recall my conscious and thoughts staying close to 'I'. Either my thoughts and conscious mind had been hanging in midair—as a third entity by itself—when the questions were being asked (by 'I'?), or 'I' had been in control of my conscious mind and raising those odd questions. The main question circling in my head was, 'What or who that body is, then, and how is it operating on its own?!'

I realize that mind can play tricks on people. Yet, the reality of that sacred consciousness and profound questions besieging me in those few seconds, make it hard to believe it was just a trick. Even if it were, its nature and purpose remain mysterious and divine. Dr. Needleman has explained a similar experience in his book, *The Heart of Philosophy*, Alfred A. Knopf, 1992, page 64.

"There was one experience of a certain kind that only much later in my life did I understand. I remember it down to the smallest detail. I had just turned fourteen. It was a bright October afternoon and I was walking home from school. I remember the trees and the colourful leaves underfoot. My thoughts were wandering when suddenly my name, "Jerry," said itself in my mind. I stopped in my tracks. I whispered to myself: "I am." It was astonishing. "I exit." I began to walk again, but very slowly. And my existence was walking with me, inside me. I am fourteen years old and I am.

And that is all. I did not speak about this experience to anyone, and for no other reason than that I gradually forgot about it."

I did not dare or care to mention my out-of-body experience to anybody, either. I simply could not grasp it or even attribute any significance to it, as though it had been a rather normal event at the time, perhaps as part of a ritual for reaching adolescence; yet, too weird to share with others. Besides, I could not explain it easily, not even as much (still sloppily) as I have tried to explain it in these pages. I cherished this experience privately with awe for many years until more recently when I shared it with a person or a group on a few occasions during our conversations about the supernatural. This story probably sounds odd and unbelievable to people who have not had a similar experience. However, it has always remained as a thought-provoking moment of my life (and perhaps a clue about the possible peculiarities of the real world), although it had lasted only around 45 seconds. This type of weird out-of-body condition is reported in million instances during near death experiences—NDE—by the way.

If somebody asks me about the meaning or significance of this experience, I would have difficulty answering. What is the sensation of separateness and what does it prove or show? The basic reaction to, and significance of, an experience of this nature is just in the possibility of body and mind separation becoming a reality for the person who experiences it, even if it is for only a few seconds. I know what happened and I know it was no dream or influence of any outside agent. On both occasions, it happened without prior meditation or any other kind of mind stimulation. It could not be self-hypnosis or effect of mental or physical illness. It happened unexpectedly in full force instantaneously, twice. So, what was it? Perhaps it was the symptom of entering adolescence with its varied imaginations and experiences shattering childhood innocence and bringing him/her to a stance of self-realization. While our minds are reaching the maturity to ponder the realities of the world, the very first inner quest for knowing our self, and the purpose of life that we now have learned something about, erupts naturally, maybe as an instinct. Maybe as a sacred intuition to get to know who we really are (!), which perhaps surges more freely from within us at younger ages. (It probably has difficulty manifesting thoroughly even during adolescence, and thus these odd sensations, since it is so flimsy and tentative when it occurs.) However, as our minds are formed by the rules and values of our perceived world, we lose our capacity totally for experiencing this natural instinct. As our minds get cluttered with perceptions and we get absorbed deeper in the perceived world, we lose our instincts to fathom and feel the connection we may have with our bodies and the real world. Our divine potentialities get buried deeper. Thus, maybe we grow up completely ignorant regarding another dimension of life—, which should have become apparent to us and revealed our essence otherwise—all thanks to the vast influence of the perceived world. Is it then possible to say that the Stone Age humans were more aware of, and connected to, the real world, maybe like dogs or some other animals which seem to have a kind of weird supernatural powers sometimes?

Anyway, consider the above naïve interpretation and a few more in the following paragraphs about those two out-of-body experiences merely as the author's wild guesses mostly for fun with no logical basis—and nothing more.

On the other hand, this experience suggests the possibility of mind and body separation, although we may not know exactly how and why. This is, of course, not in contradiction with the idea of body-mind connection. In fact, they reinforce each other. The unique feeling of body-mind separation and its absurdity, as noted above, in fact, reiterates their connectivity at all other times while we are alive physically. A more relevant question is if this separation can occur only while body is alive, or whether 'I' would survive even after the body is no longer providing the blood, nutrients and oxygen that brain requires to stay alive. Is 'I' in my brain or only *using* it? If the former is true, then our human logic dictates that a separate 'I' would not continue to exist after death. With the brain rotting after the body dies, there would be no more brain cells to think or constitute the 'I' that some of us might believe to constitute our brains, thoughts, and conscious—although 'I' and my brain had felt separated during those abstract experiences. The other possibility is that 'I' is separate from all physical aspects of body, and brain is merely a communication device (an intermediary) to connect the body to 'I'—maybe as our souls, as part of the overall universe consciousness. With this theory, death would destroy the communication mechanism, i.e., brain cells, but 'I' continues to exist in whatever medium and meaning (perhaps not a form) that would apply to it, the way it had existed before I was born and after I die. This latter idea of a separate 'I' outside both mind and body, and that 'I' had existed before birth, sounds even weirder and poses a new dilemma, though. We can ask, "If 'I' existed before my body and mind were created, why I do not remember it, and if I do not remember (know) it, then 'I' is a bizarre entity that has no meaning in the context of my present existence."

Why did 'I' wanted to, or had to, go into this vulnerable body to come to this worldly (physical) form of being briefly, anyway?

One very remote possibility that we may entertain based on this last theory or idea is that, the reason we cannot remember (or know) that elusive 'I', which exits outside our bodies and minds, is because our communication channels, our minds and thoughts, are not tuned in properly. If our thoughts and minds were purified and aimed diligently towards the real world, there would be a good chance that we would recall (and know) the 'I', or the 'self', that we really are. Is the ultimate 'self'-awareness for this end?

The following odd speculations are also good for fun, while training our brains with mystical notions. They are for testing the possibility of body and 'I' separation when supported by some abstract, but *real,* experiences. Still, I am inclined to believe (but never certain) in the existence of 'I', as an entity outside my body and brain that could be contacted through my thoughts if I knew, or learned, how to do so. My big reservation is that why was 'I' initially separate from my body and brain? Or, putting it in a more direct phrase, 'Why was 'I' given a particular body and mind and sent to this world to have a short life with a fragile body and a curious mind? Why connect 'I'—this spirit—to a body and mind in the first place? Why manifest 'I' within a body and mind? Why did not 'I' remain as the 'I'—the spirit—that always existed independently? And why was I born into a physical life we soon learn to love so much in our perceived world, despite so much suffering we must endure, while ignoring and hurting our spirits, too?' One plausible answer is that perhaps everyone, as individual 'I's, is transformed into a mindful body temporarily for a specific purpose and mission. And now we have to know what that mission is! So far, we all seem to have failed to figure this out. Can we ever solve this funny mystery? Is humans' main mission forgotten because of the overwhelming interference of the perceived world?

Nevertheless, this likelihood remains plausible only if 'I', and everybody else's spirit, too, can discover the purpose of being here and living in a chartered body. Otherwise, death is the end of 'I', too.

Another abstract clue regarding the possibility of a spiritual dimension of humans happens to some people through their night dreams. The type and depth of these dreams vary for individuals. Some people, like me, dream every night almost the whole night. These dreams are often quite complex with so many interesting features that I have been studying for years as part of personal curiosity. Some of the main points boggling my mind are noted here. For one thing, we recognize ourselves distinctively in the midst of the stories in our dreams. In fact, the 'I' in the dream has a high degree of consciousness about its existence in those places and events and the manner it behaves, thinks, and feels. The odd settings and landscapes in those dreams are often quite shocking, splendid, and colourful by themselves, which raise the question about the possibility of (and the reason for) brain creating such unworldly images only during our dreams and not when we are awake. Another amazing feature of these dreams is the accuracy and delicacy of emotions, planning, evaluation, negotiations, high awareness, logic, questioning and reasoning, arguments, and the sequence of events that 'I' gets involved in during those dreams. It seems rather imprudent to imagine that only brain's activities can generate such refined accuracy and complexity in so many episodes only randomly without any specific, or divine, objective behind such long sequence of events during so many dreams night after night. These bizarre perplexities make the author spend time to study his dreams occasionally. Yet, the sophistication of these dreams is not only amazing, but also a cause for speculation about the separation of 'I' from daily life during our sleep. Is 'I' in our dreams a clue about our spirit by any chance?

Anyway, please take the above speculations, especially this whole question of who 'I' is, merely as philosophical gibberish that has no value besides giving us a chance to tease or exercise our minds, test our idiotic logic, and possibly build our personal beliefs and spirits. At the same time, we could also ponder the possibility of our dreams and other odd phenomena noted in this section having some kind of magical meanings in a fine realm we might someday enter, at least during our abstract experiences, if not as our eternal resting place.

Real Experiences

Some of us believe that our destiny is set at birth. Our genes play a major role in this matter, anyway, even if we do not believe in God's role or luck, etc. Some people even accept that every event has a purpose as an integral part of their destinies. They put their faiths in their fates as part of their life philosophy. In fact, this mentality often helps people handle unpleasant events, thoughts, and feelings—as pain and torture always push humans' brains into mystical territories. We might not grasp the purpose of an event right away, yet it sometimes manifests as a blessing later. Many little events might turn up to be small miracles for definite purposes. In all, by adopting some faith and adapting to simpler notions of the real world, we may learn to set our expectations and attitude more modestly, make life tolerable or even joyful, and perhaps fulfil some genuine purposes, too.

Real experiences mentioned here are only some examples of small miracles in the author's life. Similar miraculous revelations (divine interventions perhaps) happen to everybody occasionally. However, what goads a person believe suddenly in some realities contrary to the perceived world's norms and values?

I grew up in a family void of religious or spiritual beliefs, which possibly turned me into a pragmatist with little patience for speculation and naive beliefs. Seldom did I believe in miracles, the supernatural, or spirituality. I relied only on facts, reasons, and hard proofs. As I encountered critical decisions and doubts in my life, however, I realized that some matters could not be analysed by facts and hard evidence alone or at all. I became full of doubts as I had difficulty making decisions and, at the same time, felt helpless and exhausted. I felt sad and anxious when decisions were not made or delayed for days and months, and sometimes years, due to the lack of adequate information or my big doubts about all my options. On the side, things happened regardless of my (in)decisions and I started to realize that most of my diligent thoughts and decisions, even after long analysis, had not turned out necessarily useful in the hindsight. On the other hand, many events beyond my control had turned up, rather blissfully, to my advantage in unforeseeable ways.

Many events, which I now consider little miracles, have not only affected my life directly, but also altered my way of thinking and attitude. They have goaded me to embrace certain beliefs, including those related to the inevitability of fate. The point for quoting a few of those *general* experiences is to show how even a pragmatist learns (or is inspired) to break the barriers and elude a lifetime of sticky habits and norms to explore and value mythical principles. These real personal life stories at least provide a short break from so much dull philosophical notions that this trilogy is tackling. (By the way, some other riveting, enigmatic experiences were deemed rather too private or mushy to include in this book.)

The first instance relates to my presumably smart decision to return to Iran in 1976 after nine years of education and work in California. Living in Los Angeles had been quite educational all by itself, with lots of opportunities and disappointments, not to mention the traffic and smog. At the end, I decided to return to Iran and work at positions and salaries unattainable even in the United States. Along with the luxurious furniture and automobile I bought in Rome, my dreamy lifestyle amused me in Tehran for three years. By good fate, however, my routines soon felt vile and addictive with no ultimate purpose. I was just wasting my life away with no thoughts or plans beyond my youthful adventures that could at best be called a dreary mix of pleasure and vanity! I was just living in the NOW every free minute I had outside my highly challenging and prestige profession! Suddenly, however, many odd things changed within a year: The Islamic Revolution happened, I got married, my daughter was born, my father who lived in Los Angeles fell quite ill, and the war with Iraq began. All these events felt quite timely and fated later, in the hindsight, for goading my destiny, despite the gloominess of the last two incidents noted above.

Life's absurdity became more apparent when every night we had to run down fifteen flights to the basement to protect our families and ourselves from the bombs and missiles that Saddam Hussein, with the assistance and guidance of the United States, was dropping on our heads. The pictures of so many young men and boys dying daily in the proclaimed holy war against Iraq, made life feel too vain and depressing. Those so-called martyrs were given a key to heaven and lured into this despicable war of Egos and human folly. In the midst of this mess, my brothers in Los Angeles reported that my father's health was deteriorating fast in the incentive care unit of a hospital where he remained in comma. The borders and airports were closed and leaving Iran had become illegal. I felt helpless and hopeless with no freedom.

I wondered why I had left my rather comfortable life in L.A. in order to face this ordeal with no promising prospect, not to mention the new, cumbersome responsibility for a family I had created so fast quite unthinkingly. Then again, I still remembered how living in the U.S. had felt too mechanical and hopeless in its own way! I was still totally at loss regarding the way Americans focused on materialism, spent so much time at work or in traffic to go back and forth like robots, and bore all that hypocrisy and rivalry at work, never mind the dire smog in L.A. *I had probably been too confused, fussy, or idealistic about the purpose of living already, while living in California!*

My wife and I considered emigration, but the idea of leaving our families and familiar lifestyle to go start all over in a foreign country appeared insurmountable. We had doubts about many issues even if we could get permanent residency and decent jobs. Many risks and uncertainties hindered decision-making. Our tiny savings could not be transferred out of the country legally, and illegally it was not worth much. Most of all, where should we go now that living in both the US and Iran felt equally torturous for different reasons? Then, the new government of Iran suddenly decided to allow people with serious health problems leave for getting medical attention in other countries, along with a relative. I decided to use this loophole to go see my father in his last days. The authorities insisted that my mother, who was in Iran at the time, could go help him, but not me. Luckily, they did not know or discover that my brothers were in Los Angeles already or else the idea had been a non-starter, anyway. After two months of haggling and insisting on the fact that my parents were divorced and my frail mother could not speak English, the officials issued a permit for me to leave Iran, without my family, of course. Thus, I started to plan for my departure.

The bank I worked for was nationalized and I had become a government executive, but under scrutiny and suspicion, due to my lack of religious beliefs and pretences. Thus, overall, hiding my plans to leave the country felt prudent in fears of some bank officials stopping my plan out of spite or whatever.

Just a few months earlier, I had hired an employee educated in the U.S. One day, he came to see me unexpectedly and turned in his resignation for going to Canada as a landed immigrant. In a few minutes, he told me a lot about Vancouver—his planned new residence. I did not know much about Canada or considered living there. Yet, before going home that night, my mind was made (more like a sudden inspiration) to try to move my family to Canada. This was contrary to my initial plan to return to Iran after visiting my father. That night I told my wife that I would not return to Tehran, so she and our daughter must somehow manage to join me as soon as I got our permanent residency from either Canada or the U.S. I realized that my job would be tough and risky in the next few months or years. However, I did not care, as though driven by a divine force with great hopes swiftly.

Another obstacle was getting a visa. The U.S. government had stopped issuing visitors' visas to Iranians regardless of their background due to the hostage situation. (Some 50-60 Americans were labelled spies and kept hostage by the Khomeini's regime.) I called my good friend, a French businessman who knew some people in the economic attaché of the U.S. Consulate in France. He said he might be able to help me with the U.S. visa if I could go to Bordeaux and meet him. Thus, I left my wife and infant daughter for an unknown adventure, with my wife's blessing of course. It was extremely hard for me to leave them behind in the midst of the war and all other chaos, but now it felt like suddenly being on a holy crusade.

Then, the day before my departure, I learned that my boss, a top executive in the bank, was on the same Lufthansa flight going to Germany. There was no time and too much risk to switch my flight. Thus, I disguised myself partially to avoid an encounter at the airport or during the boarding. From my seat in the economy section, I could see him in the first class. I hid in my chair and worried about my family's welfare. I could not elude the shame of abandoning them right in the middle of the mayhem in Iran, despite the soothing sense of freedom satiating me on the plane after so long. At least I no longer had to play a fake personality every day to perform my responsibilities under the Islamic rules, while fearing everything and everyone.

Once the plane was over Turkey, I went to my boss. He was shocked. I told him I was hoping to go to Los Angeles to visit my dying father. "You're not coming back, are you?" he asked with stress and resignation. He complained about my clear disregard for the protocol and not informing him formally. Now I was even more certain that my return to Iran was risky. At the very least, I had lost my lucrative job and a chance for any worthy career in Iran. Bridges were collapsing fast behind me!

I went to Bordeaux, my friend helped me with the U.S. visa—an impossible task in those days—and I flew to Los Angeles. I applied for immigration to the U.S. and Canada at the same time in order to rescue my family with the proper papers from either country. The lawyer for pursuing the U.S. immigration process turned out to be a crook and, after all the money I paid him, the process was taking much longer than he had promised, despite my years of work experience in the U.S. Meanwhile, the rising recession in Canada had created complications. After waiting ten months, I received a letter from the Canada Consulate General in L.A. stating that all regular education-based applications were turned down in line with a recent government policy. First, I took the rejection gracefully and accepted my rising bad luck. Then, a mystical voice whispered in my head that it was not necessary to accept the rejection if I could and should do something. Why not challenge the newly imposed restriction?! What a nerve?

All along, my wife had kept calling me and weeping on the phone for their hardships in Iran. She was also losing hope to be ever allowed to leave the country and join me. At that point, I had spent the worst ten months of my life.

At last, I wrote a letter to the Canadian Consulate in L.A. The words reflected the basic truth in a logical manner, but somehow with a passionate tone I did not know I had in me. The words simply came to me from a divine source I have learned to depend on when I *really* have a legitimate need. My brothers insisted that my efforts were futile considering governments' bureaucracy and the seemingly severe order from the Minister of Immigration or the Prime Minister himself. But I did not lose faith.

In about two weeks, the Canadian Consulate called and asked me to go for an interview in ten days.

After the interview, the Consular General insisted that giving me an immigrant visa was *completely* against the new rules, yet she had been rather inspired to help me. She introduced me to her husband—another official in the Consulate—who had listened to my pleas, too. Finally, they decided to process my application favourably. However, first, the whole family had to undergo a complete medical check-up. I forwarded my family's package to Iran to complete according to the requirements of the Consulate General of Canada in Tehran.

Despite the good news, I was concerned about my wife and daughter, while the war escalated and many obstacles remained for my family's exit. My wife told me on the phone that she had found some smugglers to take them out of Iran at an exuberant fee—our leftover savings after one year of no income and large expenses, including the bribes in Iran, lawyers' fees in L.A., etc. Still, the main risk was my family's illegal border crossing and the chance of harsh punishment if they were captured. However, my wife was adamant to flee, ignoring my pleas to wait at least until I had some documents for her to use for travelling to the U.S. or Canada. She thought that the opportunity to flee was too precious to bypass despite its dangers and risks. Thus, she fled Iran with our daughter after completing their medical checkups and sending them to the Canadian Consulate in Los Angeles.

For my medical check-up, I went to a reputable medical clinic and visited a few physicians for various tests, X-rays, etc. I knew about my old hernia that needed an operation someday. Yet, I had postponed the surgery, since my job had not required heavy lifting and I did not have any pain. One of the doctors noticed it and insisted that I had to undergo an operation or else take the big risk of my immigration application being rejected. He was fast arranging for the operation and calculating the horrendous costs for a person without insurance. I told him that I had to think and let him know the next day. I was worried about my family in the deserts of southern Iran in their attempt to flee and then arriving in Pakistan, which apparently had its own hassle of dealing with the extorting police itself. And now here, a greedy doctor insisted that I would not be allowed to go to Canada with a hernia. I did not want to jeopardize the immigration process or my family's shaky situation, if hernia was indeed a problem. Without a visa to travel to Canada, my family had to live as refugees in a foreign country for months, while undergoing an operation myself would have been time-consuming, expensive, and risky. This was still another major decision to make under duress.

After considering my options, I took the risk and told the ultra concerned, greedy doctor to report the hernia, since I could not undergo an operation in the middle of the commotion around me.

Later on, when my hernia caused no problem, the hypocrisy and exaggeration by a supposedly professional doctor, just to make some money off someone's desperate situation, felt really sad and maddening. Anyway, the hernia story only demonstrates the pressures and the need for another quick, risky decision when I was not in my best state of mind.

The details of the hardships my wife and toddler daughter had to endure to complete their frightening and torturous journey to Pakistan border through the deserts of southern Iran is a long story that I skip here. The journey is unhealthy, especially during the summer time. My wife had told me that she would not be able to contact me for around ten days until they had arrived safely in Pakistan. Arriving in Pakistan would have its own risks, though, I knew. Preying on Iranian refugees' desperation, border officials and Pakistani police could extort as much money from them as they could, and still surrender them to the Iranian police for demonstrating their cooperation with the Iranian government.

When my wife called me from Islamabad in Pakistan, I had just received instructions from the Canadian Consulate to go for the final paperwork and getting the immigration documents. She told me that after giving big bribes and constant intimidation and humiliation by the Pakistani police, they had finally gotten an exit visa. She had also learned that Spain was the only destination in Europe that did not need a visa. Thus, she had purchased a ticket to go to Madrid.

I went to the Canadian Consulate the next day and explained my wife's situation. With the Consular's monumental personal help, all the documents were completed the same day. My wife and daughter's papers were mailed to the Canadian Consulate in Madrid to be delivered to my wife along with my instructions and plane tickets to go to Vancouver in one week. She had visited the Consulate in Madrid every day, but papers had not arrived until the last day when she was booked to fly to Vancouver. She could make the flight and we met after one year in the Vancouver Airport, on September 18, 1982. My wife was extremely thin and tired and my daughter did not recognize me. My bank colleague who had first told me about this great city had come along with me to the airport to partake in this re-union. He surely deserved to be a part of this celebration, as destiny's instrument to give me the insight I needed in one gloomy day in my office in Tehran. It was my fate, but more importantly, my kids' destiny to reside in Canada, where they would surely have much more opportunities —*sadly without my kids ever realizing or appreciating my hard decisions and pains to make their lives' prospect brighter.*

Many coincidences and small miracles had intervened to make our move to Canada over thirty years ago possible. Even my father recovered fully and lived a healthy and active life for another twenty-five years—the same person whom the doctors in one of the best U.S. hospitals had pronounced terminal. To me, it was my destiny making its way through many coincidences and obstacles to bring us to Vancouver; a city full of natural beauty— my ultimate passion—and freedom. Miracles perhaps emerge in the form of mere coincidences, but they sure feel supernatural to me. Accordingly, my divine beliefs seem to have evolved out of these simple personal experiences and tiny miracles.

Life's Miracles

All my life, so many positive or negative events have found a different, often sacred, meaning and interpretation in the hindsight. All the lost job opportunities and promotions, which were given to less qualified people due to discrimination, have turned out to be a blessing for me. I believe so, now, as those disappointments made me find my new ways of thinking and living. Some of the negative events that saddened me at the time have in fact stopped me from getting into a life of continuous struggles for more status and money. I realized this fate many years later, though, when I got a chance to reflect. In fact, those setbacks gave me the chance to do the real things that matter to me now the most. This type of transformation or transcendence can happen to everybody once we see and appreciate the fine clues from the real world. After buying a new house in need of massive landscaping, not having the financial priority to hire landscapers made me do it all myself gradually. Thus, I did lots of laborious and dirty tasks, yet that mission gave me a chance to learn to work with my hands on my knees, something I had never imagined necessary after all that education and building a fat Ego in high positions in the US and Iran. Not only my gardens turned beautiful and refreshing, but also I learned more about the beauty of flowers and plants, how they grow, blossom, and multiply. This experience stirred a deep sense of appreciation for some intrinsic values that only labouring gardeners might enjoy. I feel a special connection to every plant inside and outside my house—a special sentiment I would have not enjoyed if I had not been the person creating my garden, even if it were ten times bigger and more beautiful than it turned out.

Thus, I have come to believe that it is not always the initial perception of, and reaction to, events that determines their final value and impact on our lives, but rather the subsequent surprises that might come later—maybe even decades later—when we see the outcome of our efforts and patience. The amazing beauties and purposefulness of the real world often reveal themselves from beneath our initial perceptions and expectations once we pass the test of imagination and conviction. Then, these realizations and sentiments usually grow along with our deeper beliefs.

Another experience that started badly, but turned positive later, was a car accident that resulted in softening of my back and neck tissues and constant pain. I tried many different treatments, including physiotherapy, chiropractor, and painkillers. Those treatment methods induced some temporary relief, but the pain always returned. One year later, a sports' specialist prescribed an exercise routine to do at home. Adding those timely exercises, along with some light weightlifting later on, improved my health after a couple of months. Now, these exercises have become part of my daily routine. I do not have any more pains and my overall health would most likely not deteriorate too much if I stopped my physical exercises. However, those coincidental exercises made me more conscious regarding my body and I learned more about the sanctity of both my body and spirit. I have learned about the physical and mental connections and the importance of keeping them in harmony and healthy. My spirit has grown drastically after the accident due to the dramatic change I had to make in my lifestyle. Now, I even appreciate my healthy-looking stature after getting rid of the extra fat, fatigue, and short breath. This sudden awakening made me quit my heavy smoking, too, after thirty years of addiction. Therefore, I look back over the car accident as a wakeup call that changed my outlook, *in time*, to realize that a healthy mind demands a healthy body. I learned to take care of the body that must help me for many more years. Prior to this event, I did some minimal exercises only when I had time and incentive. Now, it feels like a delightful duty. Had not I been awakened in time, my physical and psychological health would have gone beyond repair by now, considering the big setbacks in my life, including a bad divorce and estrangement with my kids.

Many other Real Experiences with marvellous outcomes have influenced my life outlook profoundly. They have amazed me in terms of likely miracles that often seem to happen behind the scene. As mentioned before, some of them are rather private, thus unsuitable for this book. Yet, they have all been great examples of destiny and decisions working in a mysterious mix and leading to such wonderful outcomes.

Surely, I have also faced dire failures and disappointments due to both my terrible decisions and what we may call bad luck. Still, those negative experiences have only made the power of positive ones even more crucial for keeping my sanity and beliefs in that divine, mysterious energy that intervenes when necessary. Then, I have also come to believe that, while destiny pushes us in certain directions incessantly, our decisions or indecisions play a big role in the outcomes, thus we should be mentally prepared to face the consequences of our right or wrong choices. It seems a mix of fate, faith, and philosophy have built my way of thinking and feeling in a peculiar manner, probably the same way most people build their beliefs for personal use only! Often, I wonder how long ago I might have lost my resolve to live had not I built a rather strong belief system during the last twenty years after coming to Vancouver as a life-changing event in itself!

Then again, it is sad that we must still face so much setbacks and apathy after all the faith we develop slowly, those sacrifices we make, risks we take, and love we show. Our logic for doing all those things, and the beliefs we still strive to hang on to before and after our failures, feel questionable regularly. Why do our fates sometimes feel like blessings and so meaningful, but then bizarre incidents ruin some seeming blissful features of our lives, such as family affairs and affections we had so naively expected to merely grow forever? I still cannot resolve this one!!

Gosh, I have been all over the map about the validity and value of human logic versus personal beliefs! Is it just a matter of being confused or inconsistent? *I don't know this one, either!!*

It surely feels like we are all so naively inconsistent circling between our logic and faiths in order to justify both, while, in fact, they both remain mostly whimsical forever—unable to support each other or their master. Instead, humans' futile struggle to use their demented logic for justifying their juvenile beliefs, religions, and ambitions has only made them more arrogant and dogmatic. Meanwhile, the outcome of our confusions has been making our lives sadder and tenser, nowadays.

The impotency of our logic, science, and religions to bring us together in a peaceful world has killed our spirits as well. We feel anxious, as we doubt the validity of social values engulfing our minds. We feel lousy and lonely, because we cannot fathom our deeds and marriage purposes. We feel vulnerable and frustrated, while we plough on through life aimlessly and suffer its vanity. We feel perplexed when we cannot satisfy our innate urge and curiosity about spirituality to stir some stability in our lives. We feel lost without a solid identity beyond the fake personality we develop around our seemingly logical perceptions and beliefs.

We feel soulless without a basic touch with the real world, which sounds mythical and confuses our logic further. Yet, we rush to adopt a religion blindly and feel logical about it as well! Are we silly or what?

On the other hand, the option of pampering merely our rowdy logic and living without at least certain divine beliefs built around solid philosophies and spiritualism would make us more fragile, anxious, and pathetic. *I'm convinced about this one at least!*

The Ultimate Victory

My notions of, and contacts with, the real world have surely been limited and remain very much at a philosophical level. Yet, they have made a major impact on my way of thinking, feeling, and doing things, hopefully in a more sensible, compassionate way. My few abstract and real experiences mentioned above merely represent some preliminary clues that have influenced my outlook (positive doubts) regarding the existence of a real world and its significance for building our beliefs and characters. Many other divine experiences have also been influencing my contemplation regimen and strengthening my beliefs during the last thirty years. And that is all that matters. I might never walk on a divine path like a diligent guru, but I rather believe that the little wisdom and beliefs I have accumulated from my life experiences would guide me in facing many setbacks and doubts that keep besieging me on some days.

Now, after going through life stages and making millions of decisions of various natures, along with my indecisions due to my doubts, I feel ready to tally the final score. It seems that a mix of fate and decisions (or indecisions) has accounted for around 70% of my present good fortune and overall success, mainly in terms of finding a simple lifestyle and peace at the end. The other 30% of my life outcome has been negative and mostly related to major decisions of my life, including those related to my doomed marriage and other companionships, career, and potentialities. I made big mistakes in all those vital areas with my hasty or naive decisions, especially during my youth and middle age—*perhaps even for immigrating to Canada if it has affected my family break-up!* Those agonizing experiences have raised my doubts about the validity of my fundamental trust in God, destiny, and human nature. Only the positive outcome of those 70% routine decisions related to less critical life issues and my beliefs in the support of that mysterious fate-maker have boosted my sense of optimism and resilience. Surely, my lifetime efforts and sacrifices to define and practice a practical life philosophy have also played an important role in my present mentality and standing.

My educated belief in the inevitability of destiny has emerged gradually from experiences that have found divine values when their significance had manifested many months or years later. This belief has moderated my sense of mere pragmatism that had directed my actions and decisions in the past. Now, my relative reliance on fate reduces the agony of dependence on information that we receive from so many crooked sources in the perceived world. At the same time, I have been unable to fully eliminate my doubts about the nature and existence of a divine entity behind the scene. I believe humans would never fathom the big mystery behind the seemingly life-changing miracles of life or the validity of our interpretations of them. Nevertheless, I prefer personally to keep my convictions realistic, while cherishing those seemingly miraculous revelations around me regularly as well.

Thus, a balanced belief system between fanatical spiritualism and atheism has been the message advocated in this book as well. Although this conservative middle-ground sounds inconsistent, it offers a sensible path that most of us might feel comfortable to build slowly, while grasping and applying it along with our self-awareness aptitude. All we need to do is to try to 'know who we are' and why. Then, we might explore who we think we are in line with the purposes of things we should do, decisions we must make, doubts we should cherish or overcome, and a large variety of relationships we love to keep with people and society. The ultimate goal is to make our lives as bearable and meaningful as possible and enjoy the wisdom of self-developed spiritualism, too. In the end, we still feel that we have travelled on many paths, but, usually, they had been only exploratory trials and errors that have caused changes of heart, thoughts, and direction, throughout a long journey of wonderment and maturation, all for the best.

Aside from all the above raw conclusions, I have also come to believe that fate is highly correlated to the type of person we are. We should not expect good outcomes and health simply because we believe in destiny. No way! Rather, it seems that good things happen only when we are compassionate, selfless, and realize the need for bettering ourselves every single day. This is probably an important lesson that our beliefs and spiritualism can teach us. It is also a major principle for bringing humanity together within saner societies as intelligent beings. It is just a matter of sensing these truths and building those sacred convictions personally.

Earlier in this book, a question was raised regarding a person's choices when he arrives at the intersection of wisdom paths. Now it is perhaps a good time to address that question somewhat based on this chapter's discussions.

The life path that we choose when we arrive at the awareness intersection would be personal according to our convictions and doubts about a real world beyond our allegedly logical perceived world created mainly for indulging our delusions. At that instant, we are rather aware of the efforts needed to align our inner quest for the truth with the social request for conformity. We feel and accept this challenge, which would keep consuming our energies and thoughts for the foreseeable future, while our conflicts with others and within ourselves ensue. We try to define a practical middle ground that fulfils our needs for 'self'-realization and self-actualization, but also assists us adapt and play our expected roles in society without getting absorbed or ignored.

This rather practical middle-ground path for self-awareness and wisdom can provide a simple yardstick for facing our major life decisions and doubts effectively. At the same time, this basic path may prove to be a trial effort for transcending into higher wisdom paths in a natural manner thru gradual personal growth. We definitely cannot jump or fly to the Summit, but rather we should walk steadily and attentively by testing our sacred wisdom every step of the way. Like a mountain climber, we should keep one eye on the Summit and one eye on the next step, which merely reflects our efforts to know and better our 'self,' while keeping healthy contacts within the world of perceived realities. We ensure we are standing on a firm ground first before taking the next step. This is how we develop a sensible foundation of thoughts and life philosophy to help us grow. This balanced life path, as defined and suggested throughout this trilogy, would be a good guiding light for our actions and decisions without relying on our logic too much or dismissing the chance of God's mercy fully. This basic wisdom can alleviate life sufferings and it might also guide us treat other humans sincerely in hopes of coming closer together and in touch with our spirits and Nature.

The mere sense and significance of arriving at the intersection (of truth) is an important event by itself to remember, however. It means we have succeeded in aligning our doubts, beliefs, needs, and faiths. We have finally passed beyond the foggy layers of the perceived world and noticed that we cannot remain the person that runs around in this world constantly causing all sorts of stress and anxiety for people and our 'self.' Now, we can appreciate the absurdity of many crude ambitions we had nurtured dogmatically as a requirement of social living, such as wealth, status, sexuality, power, and the rest of them. We are now ready to re-evaluate the social requests for conformity against our flourishing inner quests for the truth. And this sacred arrival at *the intersection* with all the revolution in our thoughts and attitude towards life is what we might consider the ultimate VICTORY.

PART V
Commonsense and Self-awareness

CHAPTER ELEVEN
The Conflicting Roles of Our Doubts

While we emphasize on decision-making ability, spiritual beliefs, and assertiveness as appealing personal attributes, we suspect the value of our 'doubts' and the state of 'doubtfulness.' Actually, we often consider our doubts as self-imposed limitations that cause procrastination and hinder the chances of chasing our ambitions. Yet, many of our doubts are blessings, if we grasp their natures and use the right balance of positive doubts and decisions in life. Of course, we also benefit from a good balance in the number of conscious decisions to 'do not make a decision,' compared to occasions when decisions are needed urgently. At the same time, grasping the nature of our doubts is also crucial.

We face an enormous amount of doubts and decisions just for running our daily affairs. Moreover, we ponder many doubtful concepts about life, while feeling obliged to justify our existence every day, too. Our most daunting doubt is about the possibility of afterlife. We try to satisfy our spirituality need (mostly through religion) mainly with great hopes for immortality, which sounds like killing two birds with one stone. The purpose and relevance of these dilemmas and doubts are not too important. Rather, the fact that our minds are so preoccupied with these exhausting doubts and questions needs a review. Why dear God has made us dwell on so many doubts, duel with so many decisions, and still lose most of our life's opportunities, is a big mystery!

Our doubts and dilemmas have increased fast in the recent decades due to the rising social chaos and personal conundrums, which are discussed throughout this trilogy. Meanwhile, we have lost touch with our instincts, as we like to rely more on society to offer the right clues and values for living. Our leftover instincts are not trustworthy now, e.g., when our dire sexual drive either turns us into a pervert or pushes us to marry a jerk out of despair and then submit to his/her whims at the expense of losing our identity and integrity even around our close family members.

Overall, the need for social adaptation has vastly subdued our abilities to think and decide wisely or even gauge the purposes of our positive doubts. On the one hand, we cannot trust even our intuitions, often rightfully, for making our daily and philosophical decisions or for gauging the purposes of our doubts. On the other hand, we rely on our intuitions so readily in emotional situations (like when pride or love overwhelms us), which then leads to another bunch of damaging decisions and disasters. Volume III of this trilogy discusses the enormity of our doubts and dilemmas regarding life, education, work, organizations, marriage, career, parenthood, etc. Sadly, it takes us a long time to possibly resolve some of our doubts. The amount of thoughts and energy we put into them and our anxiety in the process is huge.

Meanwhile, the growing social complexity and uncertainties have mounted our stress and doubtfulness about all facets of life, including our own and other people's integrity and intentions. As we get moulded deeper every day into our shallow identities and routines, our abilities to make natural observations and decisions have declined and we have lost more of our 'self.' The quality and reliability of information, which we are supposed to use for making decisions, have diminished rapidly in society, too. In fact, all kinds of false information and misinformation are deliberately spread in societies to influence and direct the mass in a desired path. Capitalism and consumerism rely on market performance, which is driven by false advertising and propagandas to sustain our fat, incompetent social structure at our expense. Accordingly, we have no reliable life vision or a chance of redemption within a fast declining social environment. We are in a kind of black hole where there is no hope for escape. We just follow this common life path hypnotically and our insecurities keep mounting.

Accordingly, we have become more cynical about the whole purpose of living and struggling for such intangible results. We doubt even our identities, yet we strive to prove our individualism. Then, we doubt our sanity in the midst of this mayhem caused by people's obsession for popularity and pride. Humans' average intelligence has increased somewhat in line with higher education and scientific discoveries, yet the degree of social gullibility has skyrocketed. Thus, the quality of our decisions has declined and we face shoddier destinies and deeper disappointments. To get some relative relief, we have become obsessed with the idea of finding love and happiness *at least*, which has turned out into another painful fantasy. And also the cause of more doubtfulness.

In all, without our instincts, reliable information, or personal convictions, our decisions have become either too mechanical or vastly emotional. As we feel more dependent on social values to set our life objectives and path, the increasing uncertainties and doubtfulness have overwhelmed and contaminated our minds. We feel trapped within an ambiguous mental state and forced to tackle too many dilemmas about all facets of our lives, including social structure, family and friends' expectations, work pressure, spirituality, existence, and human nature. We contemplate these quandaries and other notions publicized merely as philosophical ideas and scientific concepts if we find time, intelligence, and patience. Yet, we usually do not dare to consider, or express our views of, the world differently from the common perceptions of it. Or we simply put our trust in religions, while we often doubt their validity deep down, anyway.

We have extreme doubts about both our inner (self) and outer (social) relationships. Our doubts also grow as our artificial and authentic needs clash, while superficial social trends and structure also cause more inner conflicts. Within this state of doubtfulness, we remain helpless to reconcile the necessities of either our inner or our outer world. We have doubts about our potentials, daily routines, and destination. We have doubts about social purposes in general and our efforts within this obscure structure. We also have big doubts about all the religious and philosophical ideas; especially, we are keen to understand our personal and humans' role within the universe, as if proving our connection to it would resolve so much of our problems and anxiety. We have doubts about the role and reality of our souls. In smaller scales, we have doubts about the purposes of our daily routines, dreary existence, and trusting anybody to help us with our dilemmas and decisions. We have doubts about our thoughts and feelings. We have doubts about our looks, so we check the mirror all the time in hopes of getting some kind of a favourable clue. We do the same absurd thing subconsciously through our conscience—the inner mirror—to handle our doubts about our characters. Yet, only 'gullibles' (gullible persons) and 'egoists' might ever overcome their wide range of lingering doubts.

The Nature and Level of Our Doubts

Several layers of doubts boggle any intelligent person's mind. At the bottom of our fundamental thoughts, we wonder about our identity and destiny—level one doubts. We like to know who we are and what we can logically expect to get from life in general. At the next level, we have questions and doubts about the means of satisfying our primary needs and coping with the demands of social living, economy, family, health, and day-to-day living. Regardless of the ultimate purpose and divinity of life, there is still the reality of hunger, disease, desires, and 'time' as dominant dimensions of physical life. We are forced to make accurate, timely decisions, while we have deep doubts about the conditions that rule our physical and mental growth, social order, and value systems. Then, at the third level, we wonder, with great cynicism, about the means of happiness and spirituality. We want to learn about, and possibly reach, a state of inner peace and happiness, aside from our urge to know our identity and decipher the secrets of creation, and regardless (or in spite) of our unending struggles to satisfy our basic needs. These three levels of doubts are shown in Diagram 11.1. They affect our lives differently and deeply.

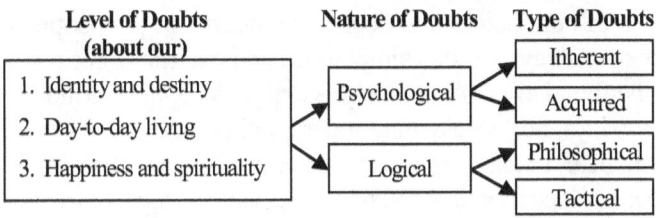

Diagram 11.1: Level, Nature, and Type of Doubts

The Scope and Effects of Our Doubts

A vast number of dilemmas boggle our minds according to the three levels of human doubts noted in Diagram 11.1. These doubts are either psychological or logical in terms of their natures. Examples of *psychological* (and instinctual) doubts include thoughts like, 'Am I handsome?', 'Am I talented?', 'Is my spouse cheating on me?', etc. Parallel to the same questions are *logical* (intellectual) doubts, such as, 'How important being handsome is?', 'How to make a living if not talented enough?', 'How to react to my spouse's infidelity?', etc.

Psychological doubts are either *inherent* due to our genes and human nature or they are *acquired* through personal experiences and building our idiosyncrasies over years. Logical doubts are two types too: Philosophical and tactical. *Philosophical* doubts relate to our options and choices in terms of *what* to do and *why*. *Tactical* doubts relate to *how,* in terms of implementing our choices and options and coping with socioeconomic environment (despite our philosophical disposition and apprehension).

Regardless of the nature or level of our doubts, they affect us psychologically somehow. They might even indicate or induce our deep inner conflicts. Our drive to make good decisions causes stress due to our major doubts and constant conflicts with our convictions, integrity, and conscience. Especially in terms of our logical doubts (e.g., about our sex appeal or wisdom), seldom can we find easy answers to rely on and move on. Even when we choose a life philosophy to relieve ourselves from the constant pressures of our choices and doubts, we doubt our philosophy of life per se. Always various temptations and external forces try to shake the foundation of our thoughts and philosophical notions.

Nowadays, our accelerating inner conflicts create even vaster psychological doubts, since we must face more uncertainties due to fouler socioeconomic conditions and vaguer decision-making criteria. In this chaotic environment, self-doubt also grows fast, while we struggle to build an authentic identity, grasp our roles, and make timely decisions.

Some of our simple doubts eventually turn into fundamental life dilemmas and philosophical paradoxes, which then stir even more doubts of different natures—to a point we doubt even our sanity eventually. For example, a big human dilemma is about our desire to live long, while most of these living years bring us suffering and disappointments! Our doubts about the purpose and value of living long cause us painful dilemmas subconsciously at least. Even the fortunate group who has their basic needs satisfied has vast doubts about many issues, as their lifelong search for that elusive happiness and tranquility feels futile.

Unfortunately, life is becoming too strenuous to allow a stable mindset. It mostly consists of endless struggles for understanding and satisfying our basic needs, confronting people, and trying to survive. The majority of us should rely on economic conditions and job market to make a living. Meanwhile, the level of work related stress has become the main cause of heart attack and other illnesses. So, the purpose of our efforts becomes quite doubtful, at least philosophically. Personal aspirations and artificial needs also keep increasing and putting more pressures on people's psyches. The lack of job security, deficiency of market economy to offer decent and dignified job opportunities to people, the difficulty of finding meaningful things to do, relationship conundrums, family conflicts, and the stressful demands of social living at the early stage of the 21st century manifest the absurdity of our desire for a long life. Sometimes we think that living longer is just an unfair sentence to lengthier torture.

On the one hand, our rising cynicism about life, our incessant misfortunes, and the vanity of our struggles makes us doubt the chance of human life having any purpose, especially in terms of finding happiness. On the other hand, we have an intrinsic urge to satisfy our minds about, and fill our lives with, happiness, which we think we *deserve* and somehow feel intuitively to be a natural expectation for human life. Our naïve innate conviction about happiness, which supposedly shall emanate eventually, goads our naïve explorations, struggles, and doubts. We remain stubbornly hopeful that life has a meaning, although nobody appears to have a definition for it after many centuries of search and speculations. Nevertheless, these rotating waves of pessimism and optimism about happiness and existence create serious doubts regarding the chance of finding peace and justifying the purpose of a long life in such a hectic environment we call civilization.

These kinds of thoughts and doubts about life are not merely the symptoms of an individual's depressed mind. Most of us can relate to these gloomy experiences readily, though the degree and frequency of these negative experiences vary among individuals according to their level of tolerance, naivety, and concerns for humanity. The theme of this book would appear too negative compared with the more appealing ideas suggested in positive thinking books. Sadly, it is depressing to discuss the true reality of life, which consists of our rooted doubts, the enormity of major life decisions in the new era, our obsession to find happiness at all cost, sufferings, endless struggles, and stressful daily routines that we cannot avoid.

The whole topic of 'philosophy' has evolved in response to our humanistic experiences, intuitions, doubts, and expectations, all in line with our struggles to find a reasonable (if not absolute) happiness and tranquillity. The basic premise, which we easily relate to, is that 'peace of mind' is the only tangible definition of happiness and tranquillity. Yet, the characteristics of our lives, causing such extreme level of doubts and struggles, give our minds very little, if any, chance to sustain a steady peaceful state. On top of life's normal conundrums, positive-thinking's naïve prescriptions make the burden of our struggles heavier and less purposeful. Those optimistic ideologies only expand the type and nature of our doubts in all directions.

These depressing facts have necessitated many discussions in this trilogy, including our personal limitations and capacities, the rude and negative aspects of life and humanity, the doubtful value of positive-thinking practices, the role of our doubts and beliefs, etc. These philosophical explorations are not meant to dampen our search for possible relief and peace of mind. Rather, they are for raising our alertness and tolerance, to put all these facts into some perspective and find a plausible path to personal tranquility. Some level of pessimism in this book should not be taken as a full rejection of life and the precious values inherent in it. On the contrary, the point is to find those virtues in life that can bring us a relative peace of mind just by aborting our fantasies, fruitless thoughts, negative doubts, and corny lifestyles.

There is a beautiful world out there behind the illusions and superficialities of the perceived world. It is accessible to all of us while we are 'alive' and can learn to enjoy it with a peaceful mind. This world reveals itself only to those who consciously and forcefully search for it intelligently by denying some of the given rules of our social living, if we can give our brains a break. Sadly, it seems that only through constant thinking and planning we are able to barely sustain ourselves in this super-active, demanding world. Even when we take a couple of weeks of vacation to give our minds a rest, we have a hard time not thinking about work.

We doubt the possibility of a world outside the profit objectives of organizations and we doubt our identity without those fancy objectives, especially for more prosperity and power. It is hard to grasp the idea of a beautiful world beyond the mayhem we live in, and perhaps it is even harder to forego the habits we believe are essential for our survival and social living. It is sad how we humans neglect our abilities to do amazing deeds, create splendid thoughts, and seek tranquility through our divine potentialities, instead of merely nurturing the demons within us.

As another symptom of our growing doubtfulness, we strive (quite rationally) to remain mostly analytical than intuitive. We search for solutions as an endless, routine and keep pretending to be analytical. Yet, even if we had analytical aptitude and could restrain our emotions objectively, we still must rely increasingly on outside information. We are still always at the mercy of others —their actions, moods, and attitudes—to make good decisions, e.g., for getting along with our spouses in agreeable settings. Our sour experiences with people's words, promises, and integrity have made us too doubtful to relax and put our guards down to build even some relative sense of harmony in our lives. Without confidence in our judgments and instincts, the seeds of cynicism have spread vastly in our minds and societies, which then flow subconsciously into our actions and relationships.

Nevertheless, our doubts would keep rising and getting more stressful when we fail to resolve them productively or anticipate gaining a rather steady state of mind and affairs ever in our lives.

To assist in analysing our lives, a few fundamental doubts are discussed briefly in this book mainly in Chapter Fourteen, but one of them felt urgent to discuss in the remainder of this chapter. Understanding human nature is extremely important.

Our Doubts about Human Nature

Our rising doubt about the purity of human nature is particularly troublesome. Our disappointments with people, as we exchange love, friendship, compassion, and services, make us doubt their honesty and integrity, as well as the human nature in general, very seriously. Our anger and harsh reactions reflect our deep frustration about the way others have dealt with us, how damaged we are ourselves, the attitude we adopt to get hurt less often, and why cynicism about human nature is rising. People's low degree of purity and integrity, especially our parents, spouses, teachers, religious leaders, physicians, and colleagues infect our outlooks and raise our doubts at all the three levels listed in Diagram 11.1. Our own impurities, such as jealousy and spite, subconsciously contaminate our views of humans and their nature even more.

Overall, mistrust has become an epidemic and our societies suffer from these personal deteriorations vastly. Corruption has spread fast, and the absence of personal integrity and morality has blemished human nature and humanity beyond repair.

Even more astonishing than humans' big appetite and aptitude for wickedness, however, is some individuals' atypical goodness, compassion, and ability to cooperate for achieving what we may consider a 'humanitarian' cause. It simply feels incredible when humans' divine potentialities erupt from their deep existence and their spirits enrich us all, as well as the person himself. Sadly, of course, these individuals and occasions are so rare we cannot spend too much time to discuss and brag about them when the overall human canvass is painted in such dark colours and people are becoming more corrupt every day. Actually, humans' divine potentialities appear so beautiful and heavenly simply because these experiences are too rare beyond our normal expectations.

Sometimes we wonder about the enormity of human impurity as a sad reality. In fact, we are truly amazed and impressed with the tiniest sign of purity in some humans, as if we were watching some aliens on our planet. Ironically, these rare signs of human goodness cause more confusion and doubts for us, as we wonder for the millionth time about the likelihood of humans' real nature being at least a bit purer than we have so far demonstrated!! Alas, it seems we are only dreaming about this possibility, too. A good metaphor about human nature is the universe itself. While many enlightened and brilliant individuals always shine like stars and give us some level of hope about the chance of a better existence, the deep, dark nature of society and its dire features constantly threaten our being, the same way black holes and asteroids do.

Our doubts about the purity of human nature have affected our relationships extensively, too. We have a hard time choosing a spouse and have a harder time keeping our relationships. We have little trust or faith in our bosses and organizations we work for. We are suspicious of our friends and colleagues' intentions, and we are paranoid about our politicians and officials. Dentists and physicians' embarrassing focus on profit maximization has ruined our basic trust in humans' nature. It is not hard to see how we have reached this level of cynicism about our nature in line with societies and relationships' growing complexities and pains. Yet, the question is whether we can ever overcome our doubts about humans' nature and the chance for a peaceful humanity ever. And if not, how can we live together when our trust towards one another, and social structure overall, is collapsing so fast. How are we going to handle so much personal and social evils?

Naturally, our cynicism about people and social systems will keep growing in line with socioeconomics' rising complexities and uncertainties. This escalating level of suspicions in societies (warranted prudence) about other people's intentions and honesty will further ruin any chance for humanity. We are already badly distrustful of people and social systems' integrity, even judicial system, police, clergies, physicians, officials in top government posts, etc. With all these doubts and suspicions, it is just too hard to imagine the kind of life we may have in a few decades, if at all. All we see in humans already is deepening stress and suspicions, thus can predict only more anxiety, distrust, doubts, and agony.

Especially, witnessing the depth of the wickedness of people we love so much is too disheartening. Even worse, we sometimes resent our own harsh reactions to them, others, situations, events, which show the effects of our latest views of human nature, plus a sense of despair about our own personalities and judgments. Our basic self-evaluation of our purity and integrity—if we ever get brave enough to internalize our thoughts and know ourselves—makes us feel quite miserable and helpless. We resent both our vulnerability and aggressiveness, and for being forced erratically to adjust our attitudes according to situations, individuals, and events, outside our personal standards and ethical convictions.

In all, most of us carry deep doubts about the purity of human nature, especially our own, at least subconsciously. Some days we feel more optimistic and some of us like to keep more faith in human nature's purity as our philosophical choices. Still, we all doubt humanity's future deeply, as people's materialistic interests are always superseding their moralistic values and integrity, and their Egos overwhelm their relationships with others to the point of becoming ruthless, and severely self-centred. Sadly, this author actually believes that human nature is not bad—it is horrible!

More than half a century ago, Carl C. Jung portrayed a picture of the Western man in his book:

"... a complete picture of Western man - assiduous, fearful, devout, self-abasing, enterprising, greedy, and violent in his pursuit of the goods of this world: possessions, health, knowledge, technical mastery, public welfare, political power, conquest, and so on. What are the great popular movements of our time? Attempts to grab the money or property of others and to protect our own." Psychology and the East, First published in 1978 by Art Paperback, page 110.

We have come a long way since Carl Jung made his succinct observation! Not only all those noted traits of Western man have been internalized and intensified many folds, but also we have successfully spread these degrading features of humanity to all corners of the globe under the names of democracy and human rights. Now, the whole world is infected with Western values and personalities in proportions unimaginable to Carl Jung. Ironically, we feel so proud of these values, too!

Our most recent pictures of the Western man and civilization confirm that things will continue to get even worse and our faith in the future of humanity will grow shakier. We might blame population growth and people's higher expectations and greed, while the resources are also declining and our economic systems are getting less efficient and effective. Rich is getting explosively richer, poor is getting pitifully poorer and the middle class has been sinking faster into debts and depression. All these features of our crooked mentality have also affected humans' perspective of life and raised their doubts about humanity and themselves. Their growing hostility, frustration, and insecurities are ruining even the last grains of purity that might have existed in humans.

Human purity has sunk in reverse proportion to the expansion of urbanization, automation and computers, and our submissive devotion to capitalism. Even when some brave experts, who are possibly also in charge of their nations' economic welfare, finally admit that capitalism is doomed, our arrogant authorities deny such facts and just stick to their naïve, self-serving goals to serve the rich. Modern societies, socioeconomic motifs, and capitalism reinforce only more human corruption, ignorance, and evil, while misinformation keep raising our mistrust and naivety and leading to more anxiety and cynicism everywhere.

As hinted above as a rarity, some unique individuals learn to explore their hidden divine potentialities and acquire inner peace, while they also enrich other people's lives. These extraordinary manifestations of goodness are refreshing and usually shocking to us. Yet, even more astonishing and bizarre is humans' dire zeal to neglect their innate potentialities for becoming better beings by nurturing their minds and spirits, instead of only following phony social norms and empowering the demons ruling them.

Managing Our Doubts and Decisions

Our profound doubts and decisions about existence are lifetime rituals. Planning our lives is an intuitive crusade for intelligent people, yet our success depends on how closely we analyse our options, doubts, and decision criteria in a timely routine. Planning is a complex task, as we often suspect information's reliability, social structure, and human nature. On the one hand, proactivity is becoming more important every day, considering our dynamic —and often confusing—socioeconomic settings and the growing contamination of information base. On the other hand, we should understand the nature and importance of our doubts for managing our decisions objectively and patiently, while also ensuring our doubts do not cause more mental stagnation.

Naturally, our doubts' main purpose is to keep our guards in society and avoid getting hurt by hasty decisions. Yet, as a more important and personal purpose, some degree of doubts helps us keep our sanity and humility, as certitude only makes us more dogmatic, arrogant, and stubborn. Without our 'doubts,' we lose our chance for self-awareness. Without our 'doubts' we forget how insignificant we humans are in the large scheme of Creation and the universe. Without our 'doubts,' we would be less natural and instinctual. And without some doubts regarding the existing social structure and values, we would never seek an alternative lifestyle, in which our thoughts and attitudes are not manipulated, our Egos and desire for superiority are not pampered senselessly, and our lives are not shallow and aimless. Carl Jung states:

"Where there is faith, there is doubt; where there is doubt, there is credulity; where there is morality, there is temptation." Ibid., page 123.

At the same time, we can also say that, "Where there is no doubt, there is no genuine faith; where there is no doubt, there is more arrogance and credulity; where there is no doubt, there is no real test of judgment; only where there is no temptation, there is less need for doubt."

Even our most rigid scientific and mathematical knowledge has only relative—thus doubtful—definitions and consequences. Our theories and personal experiences are normally based on a list of assumptions and inductions surrounding the time and space dimensions, stringent conditions, and many presumed properties of some phenomena or event. The relativity theory shows how our perception of time and space has been misleading. Theories of quantum mechanics have indicated that we cannot predict the location and speed of particles with certainty at any particular time. And these *erratic* particles constitute the basic constructs of the universe, the molecules, the energy and matter.

Everything we see and talk about has only a relative meaning and interpretation according to existing situations and conditions at that instant. Surely, we judge many things with a higher degree of certainty and we need not confuse ourselves about them, yet an ultimate interpretation may raise some doubts about their real (and ultimate) certainty. For example, we know about the birth and existence of our children with close to absolute certainty. No practical advantages exist for doubting these facts, at least relative to the prevalent social circumstances. A married person has no reason to doubt the fact that s/he is bound in a relationship with certain characteristics—even though someone might ask, 'what is marriage? What is it supposed to be?' He might challenge the whole concept of marriage and argue that a piece of paper cannot be an inherent determinant of a marriage if the concept and its purposes remain vague or abused.

Our doubts stem from our ability (or inability) to perceive and acknowledge the 'reality' of something based on many personal traits, including intelligence. Gary Zukov states how we see our reality in his book, *The Dancing Wu Li Masters*, Morrow, 1979:

"'Reality' is what we take to be true. What we take to be true is what we believe. What we believe is based upon our perceptions. What we perceive depends upon what we look for. What we look for depends upon what we think. What we think depends upon what we perceive. What we perceive determines what we believe. What we believe determines what we take to be true. What we take to be true is our reality." Ibid., page 312.

The jest of this statement is that perceptions determine our 'reality.' However, how closely this *perceived reality* could ever approach the 'real reality' beyond people's personal urges and perceptions for addressing humanity's needs? Still, we can safely assume that this entity is not dependent upon or subject to our limited vision, logic, knowledge, desires, etc. This 'reality' would always remain beyond humans' capacity to grasp, while a bigger puzzle is how *awfully* far off the chart our perceived reality is?

While we naively accept many of the perceived features of our world as certainties (facts), we ignore that many life concepts can benefit from some level of doubts, starting with doubts about the validity of notions we are conditioned to perceive as facts. Hence, individual differences entail their approaches in defining the real reality within the context of their convoluted perceptions, e.g., in terms of building their beliefs about God:

- Some of us believe in God's existence with absolute certainty— **'Yes'** group.
- Some of us believe in God's inexistence with absolute certainty—**'No'** group.
- Some of us doubt God's existence—**'May be'** group.
- Some of us challenge the meaning of God to begin with — **'What?'** group.

Each group uses its own logic and approach based on its state of mind and personality. The first group consists of those who draw their faith from cultural, parental, or social influences. They have been conditioned to feel certain about God's existence. Although a tiny group might have had odd personal experiences that have convinced them of God's existence, no evidence exists for the rest of us to consent or understand the depth of their experiences. Unless a person is logically convinced of God's existence (what is logic?), s/he would be a fool to believe in such a strong claim just by the influence of others or cultures. S/he is merely provoked to put blind faith in hearsay and accept God with certainty. 'How can such people consider themselves even slightly intelligent?,' is a question that other groups often ask.

The second group consists of rigid atheists most likely due to the lack of concrete evidence or direct personal experiences. Or worse, they may insist on their personal (humanistic) crude logic to prove the impossibility of God's existence. However, one may argue that the absence of proof per se cannot be an evidence for the rejection of an idea. Especially, considering human's very limited knowledge and logic, and considering the vast domain of debatable science and unanswered questions and phenomena, it is unwise to use 'no evidence' argument for the rejection of God. 'How can a bunch of atheists consider themselves even slightly intelligent?,' is a question that other groups often ask.

The third group maintains some doubts with respect to God's existence. For this group, not enough evidence is available about God's existence, while their modesty and logic still let them keep some doubt about the possibility of such existence. They simply abhor rejecting the possibility of God, however obscure social and scientific claims in favour or against it may be.

Finally, the fourth group consists of those who try deviously or objectively to question (or sometimes confuse) the issues. For example, God as a creator may not make sense to them, or they may challenge some aspects of God's definition to such extremes that the whole issue becomes merely philosophical. This group is seeking some kind of evidence that would be less susceptible to humans' tainted logic for building its arguments and beliefs.

Deep down in our psyches, most of us live somewhere within a domain that contains all these four possibilities. This domain depicts the boundaries of our intelligence, doubts, and thoughts. After all, our beliefs are built around our dynamic personalities and Egos, which are themselves a reflection of humans' evolving intelligence, doubts, and thoughts. We all belong to a point on this domain. Clearly, the most desirable points are those along the dotted line drawn between the 'doubtful' and the 'philosopher.' The 'yes' and 'no' groups are the extreme imbalance positions where gullibles and egoists fight one another relentlessly. Thus, if we can envision a balance for the level, nature, and subject of doubts, only the 'Maybe' and 'What' groups might reach that balance, though they are the most doubtful groups. It is crucial to know where we stand on this domain, since our beliefs and Egos affect the quality of our lives as well as others' around us.

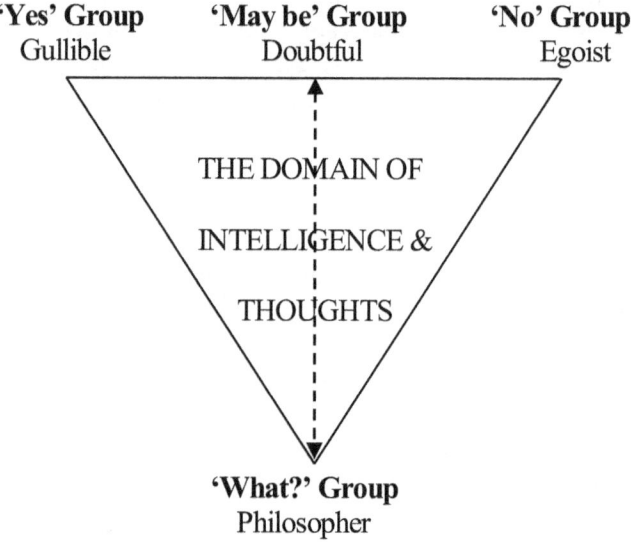

Diagram 11.2: The Domain of Intelligence and Thoughts

The debate over God's existence is a useful example to show that majority of us can be safely classified into these four classes in terms of our naivety, personality, and beliefs. Perhaps a small, indecisive group cannot be easily classified in these terms, but the rest of us have personalities with a tendency to fit within one of these four classes, though perhaps not at such extremes.

At the same time, we are all inclined to convert our doubts into certitude prematurely in hopes of reducing our stress from doubtfulness, showing our decisiveness, and boosting our Ego and self-image. Our goal is to convince at least ourselves about our abilities to manage our doubts and related exhausting anxiety.

However, our rooted doubts about so many issues thrive in our subconscious, despite (and often due to) all our pretences.

'Doubtfuls' seldom overcome their fundamental doubts about life, principles, and social values. On the other hand, 'gullibles' and 'egoists' adopt a position very quickly and stick to their rigid views and personalities. 'Philosophers' are active doubtfuls who keep testing many options and explaining their dynamic views of various phenomena. They never quit their search for the truth and some might sincerely feel that they may (or must) find the secrets of the universe and life with some degree of plausibility.

Philosophers are different from egoists in the sense that when they are less doubtful (or even certain) about something, they can provide some credible description of their thoughts and logic. Egoists cannot do that objectively. Besides, philosophers usually remain flexible to view other evidences, even contradictory ones.

Only 'egoists' and 'gullibles' make their decisions quickly in line with their dogmatism and doubtlessness. Others take their time to develop a plausible value system and a refined personal wisdom for decision-making first. Accordingly, we can detect our own and people's egoism or gullibility easily just by gauging the speed and process for expressing opinions and making decisions. Using this simple criterion objectively and wisely can teach us self-awareness and perhaps even provide some insight about our own and others' minds!

A main step to gain personal wisdom (self-awareness) is to keep a balanced level of doubts about things to avoid dogmatism and fast judgments, and to follow a process of evaluating various options and consequences. The primary goal of self-awareness is to make decisions under a balanced doubtfulness condition, with some philosophical proclivity perhaps. This implies that decision-making and doubtfulness are not opposing conditions, but rather complementary and useful tools. Wisdom contains some degree of doubtfulness. Wisdom develops around one's capacity to align one's scepticism and rationale for maximizing the reliability of one's decisions. Managing our doubtfulness is the art of grasping and acknowledging the purpose of scepticism; it is the process of internalizing and meditating on the question or issue at hand.

Normally, we belong to one group or one point in Diagram 11.2, but pretend to be at a different point for many reasons. Even an egoist often presents himself as a liberal and perhaps even a philosopher just to play along and get social acceptance with his phony communications and pretences. A 'Yes' person agreeing with everybody and everything does not accept for a moment what a sheepish, inferior personality s/he has developed. Instead, s/he may speak of courage and even be rude to others in order to hide his/her gullibility. A devoted philosopher is, by trademark, a bewildered person wandering beyond the perceived world's facts in search of the truth and his real self. However, even he, the big philosopher, has to come back to the world of perceived realities frequently and pretend to cope with the general rules of social living and conditioning. A philosopher or scientist might carry strong religious beliefs, too, *but only as unusual cases*.

The notion of being doubtless is absurd and contrary to the principles of personal wisdom. Returning to our earlier example, doubtlessness about God's existence is a prescription of religions, most spiritualists, and even some positive thinking schools. These authorities promise that firm beliefs would give us the power to see the unseeable, experience the unthinkable, and find mystical wisdom. But in reality hardly anyone can be free from 'doubts' permanently. Our doubts are in fact the remaining inner instincts that we can rely on for reassessing our perceptions and hopefully seeing some clues from the real world. Our doubts, when applied in right measures, protect us from gullibility, and may even incite our creative thoughts. When we attempt to lose our doubts, we take unnecessary risks or make commitments that we might have to carry and regret a lifetime. For example, it is good to have deep doubts when choosing a spouse; this would stop us from relying solely on our emotional state of mind when mistakes and risks could have grave repercussions. Losing our doubts is like losing our natural innocence, although these ideas go totally against the juvenile mottos and mentalities that positive thinking or similar mottos are so keen to spread in our confused societies and make the public phonier and haughtier every day.

While wisdom requires doubtfulness, it also demands timely decision-making in a responsible manner. Thus, self-awareness dictates both alert decision-making and intelligent doubtfulness. The intensity and type of doubts, of course, vary from situation to situation according to the nature and gravity of every decision. Under normal conditions, personal wisdom, which is developed over time through honest reflections, manages our varied doubts the best. Conversely, decisions driven by egoism or emotions only demonstrate our ignorance about the value of wisdom that relies heavily on our measured doubtfulness.

The Benefit of a Doubt

Dilemmas, doubts, and decisions goad our thoughts during most, if not all, of our waking hours. We cannot avoid them because they help the inherent structure of human conscious and because they determine our life direction and destiny. We have introduced these concepts in our procedural and administrative principles and practices as well. For example, when a jury deliberates on a verdict, it is instructed to vote guilty only if it has 'no *reasonable* doubt.' Therefore, we have defined a criterion (reasonableness) for the most important decisions in our judicial system based on the level of doubt, which is supposedly related to the strengths of the evidence offered during the trial. In this sense, the convict is given 'the benefit of a doubt.' His guilt is not established unless proven beyond a reasonable doubt. Moreover, the level of doubt allowed differs depending on the nature of a charge. A higher degree of doubt is allowed for a criminal charge compared with a civil charge even when related to the same case. These seemingly just criteria in some societies are, of course, not followed in many countries, as they are not compatible with their ways of thinking.

Naturally, the notion of 'reasonableness' remains subjective and vague in the mind of every juror, too.

Our decisions are intuitively honed by our doubts, except that the decision criteria vary for different types of decisions as well as the circumstances, person's mood, personality, etc. Often the difficulty of personal decisions is not due to the lingering doubts, but rather the lack of a reliable criterion to measure the doubts against. The rule of thumb usually is that the higher the criticality of the decision, the softer should be the reasonableness of doubt (i.e., need for more scrutiny and doubts). Moreover, for personal decisions, the decision-maker alone has to establish the criteria for giving the 'benefit of a doubt' to someone for a special case. In some cases, we may have to be more, or less, forgiving, and sometimes even feel hostile. These internal emotions of short or long-term nature are the added dimensions influencing our minds about the idea of the benefit of a doubt and our judgments about the reasonableness of a doubt. We often have difficulty to remain objective. We might even rush to ignore the importance of being rational and making objective decisions just for submitting to our emotions fully, despite the likely risks of doing so. We might fool ourselves or hurt somebody else when we forget how significant our decisions are, as well as the importance of the decision (or doubt) criteria, including the two principles of the 'benefit of a doubt' and the 'reasonableness of a doubt.'

As implied in the last paragraph, our doubts and judgments about them are highly influenced by our intuitions (insights and foresights). The other crucial point is that we can benefit from our doubts in a constructive manner once we learn to validate their natures by strengthening our commonsense as explained in the next chapter.

CHAPTER TWELVE
Commonsense's Role

Our reasonable doubts and commonsense are the only tools we have for auditing our judgments. Yet, we cannot stop doubting the value of our commonsense. We cannot trust it even for gauging the reasonableness of our doubts that hinder our decision-making capacity. In return, our commonsense questions the value of our doubtfulness. These circular arguments raise only more doubts about humans' logic and capacity for making good choices.

Sadly, so many clues in society reveal how drastically flawed *the prevailing* commonsense is, while human logic's validity was refuted in Chapter Ten as well. We can witness how ineffectively and senselessly our world is run—like some kind of an endemic 'commonNonsense.' Is not our commonsense driven mainly by our misperceptions and egoistic judgments, after all?

Finding answers for these basic dilemmas are important, since the meaning and validity of commonsense seem too questionable for handling our doubts and decisions, nowadays. We suspect the value of general information and people's advice, too, which are often tainted by malice or emotional factors or do not apply to our unique circumstances or personalities. Especially, for major life decisions, like career or family issues, people's unique needs, personalities, and ambitions cannot be addressed by social norms and advice. Our personal experiences are useful, sometimes.

However, major life decisions are mostly made only once in our lives when we have no experience with those matters.

Commonsense plays two major roles. First, *as an analyst*, we accumulate and measure the information, advice, logic, emotions, and any personal experience available collectively for resolving the question or decision at hand. Second, *as a judge*, we choose an option that feels viable beyond a reasonable doubt. A good judge avoids a hasty decision, while he has some doubts about the validity of facts before him or regarding the risks of choosing a wrong option. At the same time, a good judge recognizes the risks of delaying a decision forever without a justifiable cause. Therefore, the refined responsibilities of *the analyst* and *the judge* constitute a definition of 'commonsense.' Surely, our analytical and judging abilities are driven by our foundation of thoughts, intelligence, philosophy, personality, intuition, etc.

Thus, on the one hand, we should recognize the weaknesses of commonsense, since it is contaminated by our misperceptions, tainted information, biased advice, inexperience, and misleading emotions. On the other hand, our commonsense can be elevated through awareness, as we develop our foundation of thoughts, life philosophy, general intelligence, analytical abilities, beliefs, and objectivity, which we may then call it '*cultured* commonsense.'

Cultured commonsense requires independence in analytical evaluations and objective judgment of our unique dilemmas and decisions. However, the phrase 'commonsense,' as applied here, is also for discussing *common issues* in a *commoner's language* for a *common understanding* of most people. For example, this author believes to have an average intelligence, experience, and knowledge. Thus, the materials selected for discussion in this trilogy are intended to reflect the thoughts and experiences of a common person compared to a pure scientist's or psychologist's way of thinking. Accordingly, the validity of the discussions is expected to be evident in the way the general public may grasp and associate with a good majority of these ideas and discussions easily, and find those conclusions sensible for *practical* purposes.

After all, we like to build better societies based on commonsense shared by most people about social values and principles.

For now, however, even people's general values and views should be challenged on so many occasions when our curiosity is raised. For instance, some readers may agree with the discussions, conclusions, and the approach the author has taken to present them, but some may disagree with certain points. Yet, the overall intentions and suggestions of the author should be at least clear to them. Most of us, including social scientists and psychologists, agree that social and psychological principles hardly submit to solid generalities or conclusions for a global application. Then again, in the absence of scientific proofs and principles for a big variety of our behavioural and relationship dysfunctions, we have no choice but to rely on our commonsense to judge ourselves, others, and the complex relationships that prevail amongst us. We can try to learn *objectively* from one another's experiences and thoughts to boost our knowledge and feelings about others and ourselves, especially for bringing purpose and principles into our socioeconomic systems and relationships, too.

The notion of 'commonsense' suggests that a decision made on this basis must appear proper to a majority of people who are common (average) in terms of intelligence and judgment. This common language is surely necessary for saving humanity, too, by facilitating human connections. However, commonsense, in the context suggested here, is meant to fulfil any average person's analytical and judging abilities, which realistically differ amongst individuals. In fact, commonsense, nowadays, must supersede an average person's analytical and judging abilities, because people are highly influenced by tainted social values, emotions, egotism, and greed the same way their logics are. A constructive *personal* commonsense should exceed the normal sensibility and logic of commoners. Thus, decisions made according to 'commonsense' are not supposed to be necessarily always acceptable to others, nor should they be in line with prevalent social values in order to be valid and valuable. Surely, we are personally responsible for our decisions and doubts based on our *cultured* commonsense' shaped around our altruistic needs, feelings, and values. The main principle is to be highly objective and ensure that our approaches and processes are not biased and rigid out of arrogance or naiveté.

After all, we must rely mostly on commonsense in line with our own and society's sensible wisdom to sort out the roots of our personal and relationship problems and find practical means of raising harmony and peace for humanity. A big objective of 'self-awareness' is to cultivate a sensible social commonsense, which is somewhat more reliable than our logic and raw wisdom per se. Books like this can rely only on commonsense to study humans' needs and attitudes and draw general conclusions—just to build a foundation for making basic communications possible.

Naturally, while the reliability of our commonsense remains questionable, we should judge its strength and quality personally. We must determine if it can be trusted at least partially and learn to boost it through self-awareness. Carrying this big responsibility is hard for us prejudiced, arrogant people!

Developing a 'Cultured' Commonsense

The journey to write this trilogy began about fifteen years ago with my intention to explore the contentious issues and ideas for living in the new era by using 'commonsense,' reflections, and analysis. Soon the project got quite complex and dragged me into much deeper exploration than I had imagined necessary initially. In the process, leaning about myself and the depth of humans' interactions with one another and life became most intriguing. So much of my unconscious beliefs and dogmas surfaced vividly and bridged the mental gaps that usually distort our thoughts and raise our doubts. In a sense, the amount of concentration needed for developing various concepts put me in a much deeper state of self-awareness than I had ever envisioned possible for me. In fact, this experience became a precious practice in self-evaluation and self-therapy, which by itself proved of great value to me. This personal gain happened as I lived through each stage of the book for months and followed my thoughts evolving both in personal and general issues. This long experience had a definite benefit for exploring my unconscious needs, defects, motives, and helped in internalizing some of my general thoughts and beliefs. Although my inability to change myself totally became evident, I learned to adjust my mentality, attitude, and life path to make things easier for myself and others. These general observations and personal convictions also made me realize that grasping and feeling life is a unique challenge that we must take on by creating and pursuing a soul-searching and self-cleansing process privately.

The point is not to suggest that we all write a book, although it is not be a bad idea for learning about ourselves at least. Rather, we could spend time and focus, in some form of meditation, on various issues and ideas raised here or other topics that one may find relevant for living, nowadays. Ideas and conclusions in the book can also be tested within similar or unique aspects of one's life. This exercise could provide deeper insights and a chance to explore each concept and internalize it. This is a good way to turn our raw beliefs and judgments into what we may call a 'cultured, personal commonsense' to support our decisions during relevant events and experiences.

We might relate to some statements and conclusions in a book or study, but our beliefs solidify only through personal feelings and experiences. Still, as we associate with some suggestions and conclusions, they affirm our own thoughts and experiences, and thus mitigate our doubts about the validity of our stoic lifestyles or decisions. Some ideas or issues may be easier to apply directly to one's personal life than others. And, often no final conclusions exist besides some philosophical thoughts—provoking notions. Nevertheless, we take the matter in our hands for analysis based on our situation and our 'cultured commonsense.' For example, the answer to the question at the beginning of the chapter about 'evaluating and judging our doubts and decisions merely through commonsense' remains mostly a personal matter, based on one's self-awareness, rather than a universal guideline or conclusion. Accordingly, the idea of relying on a '*general* commonsense' for everybody's benefit is unwise. Thus, there goes the validity of the general assumption about the commonality of 'commonsense!'

Any valid conclusion comes from an objective review of our questions and doubts, even though no ultimate proof or certainty might be available. Sadly, even if we could provide a scientific proof for any question or phenomenon, no guarantee exists that the principle or law supporting this finding stays valid forever and applies to everybody equally, not even in pure science like medicine. For example, in spite of the immense evidence linking cigarette smoking to lung cancer, non-smokers get lung cancer, too, while many heavy smokers live without getting lung cancer. Worse, no amount of science and commonsense seems enough to convince everybody to quit smoking. This attitude is ironical and a proof of social science's difficulty to draw firm conclusions, especially regarding people's behaviour and commonsense.

Our doubts usually stem from a variety of deeper and stronger unconscious impulses, thus often cannot be affected by straight logic and emotions—though sometimes even our flimsy logic or emotions overwhelm all the facts and our reasonable doubts. The point is that even our seemingly most rational 'commonsense' is not fully capable of helping us with our doubts. Yet, the stronger the foundation of our thoughts and commonsense, a better chance we might get for recognizing the sources and soundness of our doubts. At the same time, not even most intelligent individuals can decide if their 'doubts' are due to their weakness in decision making or their justified scepticism about the risks and pending issues eluding a decision. They have doubts about their 'doubts,' perhaps even more than common people do! That is, we have doubts about not only many life dilemmas and issues, but also the efficacy of our doubting habit. The intention here is not to make complex discussions. Rather, to point out that we suffer more of our doubts about the rationality of being a doubtful person than from our doubts per se. In fact, our chronic cynicism is a quirk that might be resolved only thru personal experience, awareness, and objectivity when we cultivate our commonsense.

A major doubt that most of us share relates to our uncertainty about our mission in life. Many ideas about life and the chance of being a happier and freer person have been raised in this trilogy for nurturing our commonsense. Whether this objective has been achieved, and whether those discussions would really help some readers learn something about themselves and their relationships would remain a personal judgment and ability. A quotation from Krishnamurti shows how these types of discussions and thoughts might be perceived and interpreted.

"When we are young we say, 'well at least I'll be happy'— sex and all the rest of it. As we grow older we say, 'my God, it is such an empty life', and you fill that emptiness with literature, with knowledge, with beliefs, dogmas, rituals, opinions, judgments, and you think that has tremendous significance. You have filled it with words, nothing else but words. Now when you strip yourselves of words you say, 'I am empty, void.'" Truth & Actuality, J. Krishnamurti, Gollancz 1977, page 70.

The Value of Our Thoughts

Krishnamurti's comment makes us wonder and worry about the likelihood of our supposedly deep thoughts and words being just a way of filling our voids. Or if our long contemplations are only for eluding our lingering doubts and sufferings, while we struggle to find a simple means of living or perhaps even our life mission. We cannot help noticing our regular attempts to hide or suppress our fears and insecurities by resorting to philosophy and words. Often, we fool ourselves or others by fantasizing about a serene reality and a chance for immortality, when no evidence exists, except for the messages of some alleged holy books. Still, most people consider afterlife seriously in their philosophies and faiths. Are some of us merely exaggerating knowingly with our fanciful prophecies, certitude, and foolish philosophies, while a rival group remains quite cynical about the possibility of a spiritual reality behind our raw perceptions, contemplations, and imaginations? Are our thoughts and philosophizing *merely* for eluding our voids and fears, then? The answers to these questions are 'yes' and 'no' respectively in this author's opinion, unless our feelings regarding life remain shallow at the level of words and scattered thoughts—despite our sincere efforts to find the truth.

Normally, we do not (cannot) engage in *conscious* learning only for keeping ourselves amused or subduing our feelings of emptiness. At least some of us have deep convictions and keen intentions to transcend beyond the limited wisdom that we have learned to be possible and normal. And for approaching this level of enlightenment, we believe that whatever we learn must be felt internally and practised eternally to realize the real significance of our thoughts or experiences. Yet, those thoughts and experiences are innately significant enough already without any need for us to go overboard and fantasize about afterlife, or even worse, get too dogmatic and certain with our wild visions or philosophies.

Doubting the value of our thoughts, experiences, intuition, and words for signifying our existence—as Krishnamurti implies—would only confuse us even more about our identities. That is, we can doubt the value of our thoughts, feelings, and actions to the point of living like a bum. But, then, we would also doubt the value of living like a bum! Naturally, it would be easier on our minds and souls if we stop questioning life too much, and instead humour it as an obscure phenomenon to be managed practically without going overboard about it with our philosophies or losing sight of it altogether. This is possible indeed. However, how we get to this realization is another significant process and a major life decision by itself. We just cannot wake up one morning and decide that we want to curb all those futile thoughts and doubts that have confused our psyches a lifetime. If we have grown up as a normal person with average intelligence and curiosity, our urges to think are quite strong and demand explanations for many questions that life throws at us continuously.

Curiosity and mental growth are our innate urges, and giving them up is not straightforward or wise. Accordingly, even the idea of 'not caring' about life's meaning and purposes should be an educated, conscious decision in order to make it a reality and find its significance. Choosing any life path or philosophy should be an alert decision in itself. Otherwise, merely more confusions inflict us for lacking a particular vision or plan for life; or due to our activities and decisions' inconsistencies. If we have not made a conscious decision to relieve ourselves from certain, or all, thinking and decision-making, for a superbly valid reason, we must have been forced into that numbness unconsciously, maybe by some external forces or stimuli beyond our control. We are simply a victim of some psychological strains or social coercions killing our senses fully. In this case, we have no ground or criteria for exploring the meanings and purposes of our lives, actions, and thoughts—which means, we must stop assuming and pretending that our minds are clear and functional. Instead, we should admit that our minds are indeed infected by this social epidemic, i.e., the weakness to think and decide independently, *for whatever reasons*. Then perhaps we could do something about the matter.

The point is that our thoughts about life, our missions, and all kinds of doubts that emerge in the process are usually instinctual and have special significance for our minds and beings. They are fundamental and natural requirements of our existence that reflect the vitality of our souls and our allegiance with life dimensions beyond our normal perceptions. The reality of our soul manifests in our doubts regarding the purposes of earthly life. Our search for the truth is indeed an intuitive struggle to access our enigmatic soul. Our positive doubts about the meaning of life and all the rest of it are actually due to our estrangement to our souls. Our doubts render the right clue about humans having souls and a rationale for seeking it. Our dire attraction and addiction to religions is also a big clue about our souls' desperate efforts to emerge!

Accordingly, our doubts also indicate that we have not found the essence of our being—our souls. As such, our doubts render a great incentive to continue our search. Only when we find our souls, our doubts dissolve and the inner peace evolves.

Especially when we are young, we are driven by our untamed Egos that refute our vulnerabilities and naiveties, besides our raw fantasies about an alleged happy life—sex and all the rest of it, as Krishnamurti puts it. We do not have time or patience to think and go beyond the physical aspects of our surroundings. As a young person, we are just attracted to superficial lifestyles and physical enjoyments that maximize our pleasures. This demented mentality is obviously quite harmful, especially nowadays, when major life decisions require a solid foundation of thoughts and care. On the one hand, we need high capabilities in judgment, independent thinking, and decision making to break away from shallow family values and social conditioning. On the other hand, we lack a good platform for independent thinking and decision-making. Our strong doubts about social values are reasonable and rational, but we lack solid values and philosophy to replace all that vanity. The youths, especially, must keep major doubts about their radical (but naïve) values, which they offer as progressive visions of life—supposedly with emphasis on independence and freedom. They must question the validity of their new values and know how they would possibly enrich their thoughts and lives or help them with their real needs, especially the rising contradictory ones, like independence and dependence in relationships. Only resisting obsolete, unfair social systems cannot solve societies' rooted problems, make life easier, or change socioeconomic facts. Resisting, denying, or trying to elude social challenges without finding viable long-term alternatives is merely a reflection of our naivety and egoistic conviction about our personal perfections and invulnerabilities. The challenge for the youths, especially, is to find real solutions for our sick societies without making them even sicker—which is what they are doing now. They just seem vastly naïve and vulnerable these days, which makes the prospect of humans' ever finding a viable social structure too tenuous.

Life's Major Dilemmas and Decisions

Despite our lingering confusions and attempts to avoid too much thinking and worrying about life, we cannot elude our curious nature. Some particular dilemmas boggle our minds intuitively all our lives, mostly as part of genetic programming and biological drives. They direct us in a subtle, but persuasive, manner to make many *philosophical* decisions, too; so naturally, in fact, that most of us do not even realize such subconscious, mental routines. Life dilemmas and our curiosities challenge our psyches as a feature of living—mostly subtly and intuitively. Their main purpose is to *direct* our thoughts, convictions, and life paths. The fundamental thoughts discussed in Chapter One of Volume I are of this nature —and for helping us make some *philosophical* decisions about:

- understanding our *authentic* needs,
- finding peace of mind by grasping the purposes of our lives and choices,
- building a general life philosophy in line with our beliefs,
- staying objective in our judgements and decisions, instead of allowing over-optimism (positive thinking) or cynicism (negative doubts) mislead or cripple us,
- gauging social norms and developing our personal values and ethics,
- discovering our divine potentialities, and
- realizing the scope and importance of life's inevitable major decisions.

In our busy and complex society, most of us never find the chance to grasp the impacts, importance, or even the existence of these *philosophical* dilemmas and decisions throughout our lives. At the same time, our consciousness about these dilemmas and decisions rises as people's intelligence and self-awareness grow. Therefore, it is plausible that the above fundamental thoughts and dilemmas would feel more explicit, discomforting, and urgent *if* human wisdom grows in the next millennium or so.

Nevertheless, we all ponder these *philosophical* decisions in some manner, at least subconsciously, but seldom deal with them effectively and directly. We hardly scrutinize on them, or merely come up with some perfunctory answers and ideas to move on.

Another group of *routine* decisions help us directly to perform our inherent life functions in compliance with a superficial social structure we have inherited and run. These decisions are about:
- our long-term life objectives and a plan to satisfy them, such as education, careers, financial needs, wealth, social growth and adaptation, means of finding happiness, etc.,
- the type of personality we wish to build or present to others in order to cope with social demands, pursue our aspirations, and maintain our identity and integrity, too,
- our risk-oriented opportunities and their timing, including investments, savings, budgeting, etc.,
- understanding and applying our genetic potentialities most effectively for building our careers and living comfortably,
- aligning our careers, passions, and social responsibilities,
- the means and criteria to choose a spouse, and
- our duty towards our children, how to nurture them, and our roles for guiding them in such contaminated societies.

Social demands and personal needs force us to make these *routine* decisions regularly and consciously. Still, our educations and mental preparation is quite inadequate even for these basic, expected decisions. Thus, we usually end up making hasty or forced decisions mostly when we are emotionally vulnerable, maybe in love, or running out of time, patience, or options.

Sadly, even for those of us who somehow contemplate both philosophical and routine decisions, and question our motives in some depth as well, still the answers are never absolute, and the results of our seemingly rational decisions are rarely predictable or satisfactory. Furthermore, we constantly find new priorities and preferences that make us view things differently in various stages of our lives. Therefore, even the value of our fundamental thoughts and philosophical decisions might appear questionable and in need of regular scrutiny and occasional refinements.

All these facts reiterate the difficulty (and importance) of making decisions due to the dynamic nature of our perceptions and environments. Accordingly, developing a decision platform during every life stage helps us function somewhat consistently and rationally. Fundamental thoughts and philosophical decisions are the only means of supporting our routine decisions somewhat based on sensible criteria.

Besides acknowledging the inherent role and force of major life dilemmas, doubts, and decisions in our lives, we also face a big challenge to control, balance, and master them in an efficient way. Instead of getting absorbed in life's mundane duties and decisions, we must doubt our present mentalities and lifestyles and spend time to gauge the essence of life. By eluding the mass of superfluous thoughts we waste on self-preservation decisions, dilemmas, and doubts, we can strive to contact our true self for self-recognition.

The ways we are conditioned to see and ponder life—mainly in terms of dilemmas, doubts, and decisions—are astounding. And the amount of mental energy wasted to align them, just to keep our sanity, is enormous. We are not here on this planet only to solve problems and find solutions, or are we? We are not here to fight and destroy one another just for satisfying our false prides, fat Egos, and endless greed; or are we? Should not we cultivate *serious doubts* about everything we have been doing to humanity so far? Is it not the right time, yet?

Ideally, our thoughts and spirits could help us redefine the meaning of life and humanity. We could relax our minds and free our thoughts and spirits to see the beauty of Nature, the intricacy and grandeur of our inner selves, and establish our real identities. We could tame our desires to boost our spiritual dimension.

"Those fettered by desires cannot perceive the Clear Light. Desires crave for external fulfilment. They forge the chain that fetters man to the world of consciousness. In that condition he

naturally cannot become aware of his unconscious contents. And indeed there is healing power in withdrawing from the conscious world - up to a point. Beyond that point, which varies with individuals, withdrawal amounts to neglect and repression." Carl Jung, *Psychology and the East,* First published in 1978 by Art Paperback, p 125.

All these great ideas about revamping our mentalities are, of course, easier said than done. How can one break away from the conventional and self-sustaining ideas and forms of life that have passed through many generations and become an intrinsic reality of our being? Even more implausible, 'How can we egotistical, modern humans elude our obsessions for self-gratification and idealism?' No easy answer exists. Yet, we may start personally with discipline and perseverance for gradual self-awareness. We can assess the rationale for our decisions and doubts, and then try to validate them with our beliefs, instead of accepting them as facts or acting upon them casually. We can question our naivety, dogmatism, value systems and their purposes. Self-awareness is a process, not a sudden awakening. The latter seldom happens, yet gradual self-awareness can lead to enlightenment thru meditation, reflection, and simple mental practices, which we are capable of mastering slowly. Our *positive doubts* and *objective thinking* help this process a lot, as explained in Chapter Fourteen.

As intelligent beings, we pursue our life plans by constant processing of information and acting upon our brain cells' orders (decisions). Our brain activity and quality to process information for making many critical life decisions is a personal issue. This book, however, will discuss the mechanisms of *decision process*, including decision-making elements, conditions, and criteria in more detail in Chapter Sixteen.

Self-awareness for gauging our doubts and decisions has been stressed in this part of the book, so the next chapter will explain the means of raising it by adopting the seven elements of 'Self.'

CHAPTER THIRTEEN
Knowing (about) Ourselves

Knowing (about) ourselves, or self-awareness, starts with a study of our personal idiosyncrasies, needs, and concealed potentialities. Then we try to detect and analyse humans' chronic illusions about themselves, society, and the universe. Especially, grasping the innate relationship between humans' spirituality and potentialities, as two interrelated, divine dimensions of 'self,' is important for knowing who we are and for redeeming our spirits. We feel empty if we cannot nurture our potentialities that usually stir our personal sense of spirituality as forlorn, curious beings.

Accordingly, knowing (about) ourselves turns into a sacred crusade for understanding our existence and its potential value. The goal is to access our essence as a bewildered human and to explore the urges behind our thoughts and deeds consciously within the finer realms of the universe (and not society per se), *as if driven by a mysterious force!!* Thus, a definition of 'self' has evolved, mostly as a symbol of our ideal for the perfection we seek in ourselves. We hope to discover a semblance of humility and contentment in our souls beyond the contaminated, complex values crippling our minds and societies. However, our search for 'self' also shows our despair and doubts about 'who we are.' Witnessing so much evil in humans makes us wonder if God had really meant us to be this bad or we have just become like this all on our own through utter foolishness—*perhaps even in absolute contradiction to His elaborate design!*

Unfortunately, seeing the depth of widespread malice around us, we have a hard time not concluding that this is in fact the best we humans can ever be! Then again, sometimes, some blessed people portray signs of divine abilities and sensitivities (including compassion), which appear to be instinctual and in many cases sincere. Those qualities and sensitivities raise some doubts about the essence of 'self.' In this sense, 'self' is not just a moral side, or a divine raw characteristic, of human that loathes and defies the selfish humanity surrounding us. Rather, 'self' reflects mostly those innate, but active, aspects of a person who seeks a proper means of relating to the outside world and other humans, but also craves a natural connection to the supernatural dimensions of life.

Our genetics determines some aspects of the self. Parents, teachers, and society also affect our 'self,' how we observe the world containing us, and what we imagine is right for our being. Another vital aspect of 'self' manifests in our dynamic mentality and determination to change things and grow to higher states in order to capture and keep a sense of contentment and tranquility. Each one of these aspects of 'self' must be studied seriously with an open mind in order to reach a tangible level of self-awareness.

The ambiguous usage of 'self' in different connotations and contexts could be annoying for many of us. Even attempting to *explain* what 'self' constitutes or contains is quite cumbersome and subjective. Yet, most people have some personal notion of 'self.' Chapter One of Volume I reviews 'self,' along with 'model' and 'ego,' as individuals' three aspects of personality. In this Volume, however, we discuss the role and characteristics of this elusive 'self' for connecting us to the universe through our consciousness and spirit, but also guiding our daily endeavours according to our level of self-awareness and integrity. For this dual role of the self (i.e., our needs for spirituality and practical living), several aspects of 'self' collectively establish who we are and what we need from life. Using this general knowledge as a platform, examining and understanding 'self' is, nevertheless, a personal, lasting endeavour. It demands commitment, sacrifice and sincere efforts to raise our consciousness about our being and leading a stoic life in an objective manner. The main goal is to become more 'self' conscious and less self-conscious.

For the limited study here, the following seven dimensions (or functions) of 'self' are explored in this chapter:

1. Spirituality
2. Potentiality
3. Individualism (integrity, compassion)
4. Relationships
5. Contributions
6. Growth
7. Social responsibility

Spirituality

Spirituality is the essence of 'self.' It evolves out of our psyches along our psychological needs to offer a much deeper sense and purpose for our existence. As an innate human urge, it empowers our spirits and connects us to the universe, while it also soothes our melancholies naturally. Appendix C at the end of the book shows humans' intricate physical and spiritual dimensions.

'Spirituality need' is, in fact, more instinctual than most other psychological needs that we have built artificially, including the needs for love, power, recognition, or status. Yet, for many of us, our need for spiritualism remains subconscious, or unconscious, simply because we are unaware of its nature or role, although most people try to satisfy it through religions and superstitions.

Actually, the upbringing influence in societies deprives most people from exploring their spirituality need independently. They get brainwashed quickly by debilitating religious teachings and stories, which appear to fulfil (but actually only kill) their innate spiritual need. After all, it is easier and faster to accept a religion based on some naïve illusions and move on, instead of bothering their brains with an elusive idea of spirituality without any of the luring religious promises. Trusting religious stories, promises, and prophesies (nonsense) about the heaven and God's mercy or punishments also relieves, so conveniently, their natural urge for a self-assessed spirituality. In all, most people are simply too lazy or unprepared to think independently and figure out the inherent purposes of spirituality outside the tempting, crooked teachings of the perceived world.

On the other hand, some people's ambitions, pragmatism, or apathy toward religious ideologies dampen their spirituality need altogether. Especially when we are young, we usually have many aspirations and worries, so the last thing we have time to explore is our spirituality need. We normally have a tendency, due to our upbringing and education, to think of physical and material things rather than intangible and inconsequential ideas. Sometimes, we stay away from spiritual concepts during our contemplations or communications with others just in fear of being associated with superstition and naïveté. We think spirituality makes us look soft, outmoded, and vulnerable, which is contrary to what our culture and value system is propagating.

Anyway, for many reasons, including family beliefs, culture, and our erroneous impression of spirituality and its purpose, we suppress our spirituality need. Thus, we often reach a point where only a big shock, crisis, insight, or awakening can trigger our spirituality senses. Of course, in desperate situations, we resort to our spirituality urges subconsciously to seek the extra energy we need to face a major challenge or pull through a crisis. Somehow, we seem to feel this source of energy that lies within our spiritual and non-physical realms. Then again, we forget about it or ignore it when we do not have an immediate use for it. We forget that this spiritual energy manifests merely thru an ongoing conscious acknowledgment of its existence. Carl Jung states:

"There is an undeniable psychological fact that the more one concentrates on one's unconscious contents, the more they be-

come charged with energy; they become vitalized, as if illuminated from within. In fact they turn into something like a substitute reality." Psychology and the East, Carl Jung, Published 1978 by Ark Paperback, page 124.

Whatever the source of spiritual energy, it is hard to prove it scientifically, although some scholars claim the evidence of some kind of psychological and medical nature.

"The possibility that each person is an infinite being is becoming more real now. Gifted with real flexibility in our nervous systems, we all have the choice to build boundaries or tear them down. Every person is continually manufacturing an infinite array of thoughts, memories, desires, objects, and so on. These impulses, rippling through the ocean of consciousness, become your reality. If you knew how to control the creation of impulses of intelligence, you would be able not only to grow new dendrites but anything else." Quantum Healing, Deepak Chopra, M.D., Bantam Books, 1989, page 225.

Other scientists and scholars have offered similar thoughts and personal experiences to confirm the existence of a mysterious source of energy hidden within humans. Yet, it is tough for many of us to associate or even grasp the true implications of claims similar to the above quotes by Deepak Chopra and Carl Jung. Only our random encounters with divine feelings can convince and motivate us to explore spirituality deeply. In such moments, we feel relaxed, high spirited, and mindful, all of which provide a clearer vision of reality for making better decisions effortlessly. We sense the power of insight, like a magical experience, and often along with a divine source of wisdom helping us when it is called upon selflessly and purposefully. Surely, the conditions for seeking and receiving this sacred energy and insight should be proper, including our sincerity and genuineness of our intentions.

For many of us, the 'need for spirituality' should be awakened and brought into our conscious thoughts. Some suggestions have been offered mainly in this book, but also other volumes of the trilogy, about achieving this objective. The most difficult part of it is, of course, to change our attitude and mentality beyond our conventional views of religions versus spirituality. We must stop perceiving and denying spirituality as synonymous with abstract non-physical concepts or superstitions. As Carl Jung says:

"... spiritual understanding ... is a capacity which no man is born with, but which he can only acquire through special training and special experience." Psychology and the East, Ark Paperback, 1978, page 76.

Jung's point about 'the capacity for *understanding* spirituality requires training and special personal experience' is important. Yet, more crucial is to know that the seed of spirituality, as an inherent psychological human need, is already cultivated in 'self' when we are born, and we feel incomplete and lost forever until we learn to nourish it. Through our sporadic divine experiences, we find the naturalness of our spirituality need as an inherent link to Nature. Spirituality arises from our natural belief in a sacred dimension of being ('self'), which we readily feel within us.

Potentiality

The second dimension of 'self' contains our potentialities (knack for creativity). Humans have two types (levels) of potentialities: genetic and divine, as discussed in detail in Part III. The former consists of our unique capabilities, such as artistic, intellectual, or special talents according to our genetic properties and superiority. We are rather familiar with these potentialities and apply them routinely, though not fully, for our careers and creations. On the contrary, divine potentialities are universal capacities of humans as soulful creatures. This inherent human quality, which links us to the universe, is less understood and often abused, although everybody feels it subconsciously, depending upon his/her level of self-awareness, of course.

Our genetic and divine potentialities are rooted in our general characteristics within 'self,' although distinguished here for their opposing roles, i.e., mainly for career goals (mostly thru genetics) vs. exploring our souls (mostly through divine intuitions).

The miraculous insights that surface in *special circumstances* and lead to self-actualization and spirituality, manifest our 'divine' potentiality. This abstract idea about humans' divine potentialities indeed fits Mazlow's findings in his 'self-actualization' research, where peak experiences (and spiritual feelings) occur subsequent to some divine insight or discovery. The question is, 'What those *special circumstances* are that make such moments of ecstasy achievable?' And, 'How is one moved to pursue a wisdom path that makes such special circumstances and moments of spirituality possible?' Clearly, our innate spirituality urges *could* provide the best trigger for stirring our divine potentialities. Yet, as noted in the last section, our spirituality urges are largely subdued these days due to cultural and family influences on the formation and growth of our mentalities.

Divine potentialities reflect humans' inherent capacity to feel and seek a connection to the universe. This capacity manifests thru supreme intuitions and spirituality sentiments, which might be unique to humans (as privileged creatures of God). We also think that a special purpose prevails for this capacity in humans. For one thing, we appear lost and lack a real identity until we activate our divine potentialities and answer many questions about our existence. Definitely, some innate urges initiate the process of inquiry and curiosity in a person, perhaps a need for awareness about self or some matters related to human routines or suffering. We may also say that our previous peak experiences (however small on most occasions) mixed with new intuitions create a state of mind to focus on an idea exclusively and fully. This primary attention generates the energy needed to initiate and pursue the process of exploration. This energy, which goads us to realize and delve into worthy endeavours, is by itself a spiritual energy (our spirit), because it expands our regular span of attention and intelligence. It represents the divine potentiality that exists in all humans, although we have to know how to honour and activate it through diligent self-analysis to a higher level of self-awareness. That is totally contrary to blind faith and religious rituals.

This energy (spirit or potentiality) would not only generate the insights that enrich us immediately, but also leads to still higher levels of sacred curiosity and discovery subsequent to the new feelings of actualization and spirituality. Every time we go thru this fine cycle, we reaffirm, revitalize, and reinforce the level of spiritual feelings and the energy that stems from them.

Spirituality also reflects humans' ultimate level of aspirations (and needs) at the highest spectrum of human potentiality. Thus, it induces a particularly high level of attention and awareness, and it increases our stamina and motivation to understand and pursue worthwhile goals in life. Ideally, if we realize this potentiality at young age, we can better focus on the essential facets of life and grasp life's real opportunities and purposes easier. We would not waste our lives on trivia and materialistic values, while constantly doubting the purpose of our struggles, too. Spiritual energy helps us see beyond the obvious and rudimentary facts, thus brings out the best in us.

The energy from our divine potentiality is not only a spiritual sentiment. Rather, it helps us penetrate our unconscious mind and explore the hidden wisdom beyond the primary boundaries of our intelligence. It helps us discover those dimensions of ourselves that we have ignored and suppressed. In a sense, enlightenment and insight are parallel phenomena that emerge from a person's unconscious mind, as his/her divine potentialities are excavated.

Both levels of our potentialities (i.e., genetic and divine) have several effects, each of which exerts a source of new energy and wisdom by itself. One aspect of these potentialities relates to higher awareness, insight, and creativity that emerge during our endeavours, such as the music that Mozart composed. As said about his music, it appears that it came to him directly from God. Apparently, he had made a comment about waking in the middle of the night and sensing music pouring in magically. He just wrote them down without a single correction. His words and creations are not directly attributed to a state of spirituality, since no clear evidence exists about his level of spiritualism (despite his religious music, remarks, and rearing influence). Nevertheless, his sense of actualization and deep potentialities most likely gave him a unique power and intuition to penetrate his unconscious mind and obtain the energy, the insight, and the genius that one finds in his music. In a way, we can say that his ingenuity was already his personal means of spirituality and enough in itself, since the main goal of spirituality is to give us the power, feeling, and energy for sacred personal imagination and creations. This is exactly the kind of property and value that all religions lack. They actually kill people's divine capacity and power of intuition and instead make people dogmatic and naive.

It is possible that the two types of potentialities converge at some stage of one's life (perhaps even in childhood) to create a genius. People like Mozart and Einstein have definitely benefited from both genetic and divine potentialities knowingly or by some miracle. The majority of us, however, at best use a limited supply of our genetic potentialities for survival and personal growth. For accessing our divine potentiality, however, we can incite our spirituality sense and energies (our beliefs) consciously. Through self-awareness and by building our solid inner beliefs, we can trigger our divine potentiality for insight and wisdom without too much effort. Spiritual insight grows parallel with self-awareness as we attain selflessness and enlightenment eventually.

One aspect of knowing 'who we are' and finding the 'self' subdued within us is to explore and exploit our potentialities, both genetic and divine, most realistically through personal initiatives and intuition or perhaps by the aid of an expert. Detecting our true potentialities has a lifelong implication, as it affects not only our routine activities and major life decisions, but also the level of energy we ignite for choosing the right path of life. Focusing on trivial life issues, pursuing a dull career, stagnation, and acting contrary to our real potentialities cause personal suffering, since we are constantly trying to be the person we are not built to be. Our struggles to pretend being someone else—emitting a phony personality and temperament—hurt us more than anybody else can harm us. Besides negative psychological effects, ignoring our real potentialities would be a total waste of life, not to mention the foolishness of losing our chance to actualize our 'self.'

Ironically, our only relief from life's hardships comes through realizing our potentialities by working very hard every day—an odd mystery of creation all by itself. Yet, we should work even harder and sacrifice even more if we seek real happiness, which comes merely by exploring our divine potentialities. Thus, even for people denying the power of spirituality, excavating their real potentialities requires a grasp of 'self,' which is ultimately the only practical means of handling life's hardships, while exploring its beauties as innate sources for personal serenity. Even if we do not believe in spirituality per se, inner urges for self-actualization eventually awaken the divine potentialities in many of us readily, as a venue for personal achievements and relative tranquility. On the other hand, for reaching our unconscious mind and activating our divine potentialities, knowing our 'self' becomes a necessary task, and a major step, for all intelligent people.

Individualism (Integrity, Compassion)

Individualism is the hands-on manifestation of 'self' mainly for boosting our identity and resilience in society along with a better sense of our being, especially regarding the sanctity of our spirits. Individualism is the nucleus of 'self,' since it should ensure our survival and progress in society, while we fight both personal and societal evils. Its mandate is to boost our integrity, compassion, and spirit. It portrays the innate characteristics of a simple, pure, evolved man with a delicate soul capable of facing others fairly and sincerely. Most of all, individualism reflects the traits of a man in peace with himself and the world, despite the pervasive evils within him and society.

Defining 'individualism' as an improved state of being rightly shows our mistrust in the inherent purity of human nature. This interpretation reflects our realistic view of human character and its influence on our cultures and lifestyles, while we dream about a purer version of what we have become! It reveals our desperate struggle with humans' natural tendency towards immorality as their basic attribute. It shows the evil and absurdity of the phony individualism people are boasting about and propagating these days. In fact, our societies hinder the advance of individualism as a plausible common human quality. Therefore, in the end, true individualism and integrity often sound like some rare virtues found only in saints and highly evolved individuals—like some divine manifestations beyond most humans' capacity.

Humans' low integrity affects them in their relationships the most, but also personally. One becomes what he practices as part of coping with all the hypocrisies and deceit in society. He is forced to become cruel like everybody else, despite his potentials to be a better human being. We notice people who have become so absorbed in their evilness that malice has become their real nature. They cannot do anything without some form of treachery even when it does not have a benefit for them, or even at their own perils. Their bare sense of being has simply collapsed, and thus turned into a mere deceit-brain—a soulless entity. Ironically, they actually fall for their own lies with such deep commitment they sacrifice even their valuable assets in the process, including their families and friends. The world of deceit and hypocrisy that they choose to live in contradicts even the bare social ethics, let alone a sense of compassion and integrity that are fundamental requirements for true individuality. They just float within a vastly crooked illusion of life and behave like the devil. Sadly, now our societies are shaped, and ruled, by this majority.

The Webster's definition of individualism is, 'The conception that all values, rights, and duties originate in individuals.' If not already implied in this definition, it is crucial that all these virtues of individualism must have a purpose as well. It must have some worthy personal and social implications. Therefore, individualism seems like an attempt to gain our independence and establish our identity, not merely in society, but mostly in our own heads. We like to 'know (about) ourselves' and the chance of being a better person with a capacity to choose and propagate the right values and practices for a civilized humanity. Thus, we strive to assess ourselves in terms of values, rights, and duties we have adopted (created) in the process of earning and proving our identity.

We try to understand the origin of our values, their validity, and their capacity to help humanity and us. In terms of our rights, we ensure they coincide with *some practical rights for all*, so that society and people can move forward together towards a peaceful harmony and relative relief from life's hardships. The problem, nowadays, is that a person's rights often turn into self-serving demands on others for personal gains and interests. People have difficulty making this distinction when looking for their rights. They try to impose their misperceived notions of personal rights on others deliberately or inadvertently by their egotistical attitude and unrelenting struggle for power and authority with little regard for other humans' basic rights. Ironically, often they do all these evils under the guise of protecting their individualism!

With respect to our duties, individualism reiterates our social attachments and ensuing personal obligations. Some of them are instinctual, such as our duties towards our children and parents. Other duties, e.g., towards our spouses and friends, are expected to come natural to us, too, if genuine feelings exist. Yet, people are too self-absorbed, nowadays, to keep their integrity and fulfil these types of duties naturally. Thus, they must now extend extra efforts more consciously to discharge their duties to some degree at least. Finally, some duties are mostly moral obligations, such as our duties at work and society. Our passivity in accepting and discharging our duties may be intentional or due to ignorance. Intentional passivity is too hard to repair, as it mostly reflects our pomposity, deep psychological flaws, and the impact of social adaptation. On the other hand, ignorance can be remedied a bit easier through active involvement and self-awareness.

Individualism reflects the quality of our choices, decisions, and actions, as we determine and practice our rights, values, and duties for accomplishing notable purposes. While the objective of 'individualism' is to strengthen the inherent value of 'self' as a wise and humble person, it also stresses on personal integrity to adjust our values, rights, and duties in line with the needs of all humanity. Individualism is not an inner growth and satisfaction per se, but also an outer reflection of integrity and morality for sustaining humanity. The Webster's definition of 'individualism' does not quite reflect the need for the rightness of one's values, rights, duties. Yet, without integrity and compassion, we cannot set the right 'values,' as we cannot see their rightness. And we cannot comprehend the value of people's 'rights,' because our criteria of rightness are personal and selfish. Contrary to common view to interpret individualism as a means of self-absorption, its value lies mostly in a person's regard for other individuals' rights. Individualism is actually a venue for inner exploration, instead of an external ostentatious presentation of one's Ego, as it is mostly implied in our common pretensions of individualism, nowadays.

Individualism evolves only through compassion and modesty, while a person gauges the truthfulness of his connection to other individuals, things, and concepts with a genuine interest and care. Only then, s/he can see other individuals' rights and the values of things and concepts in their purest sense in line with his/her own authentic life purposes. Without compassion and integrity, one lacks the sensitivity and sensibility required for perceiving things or people outside one's rigid and biased prejudgments. The lack of compassion and modesty reflects Ego domination, which is the main hindrance for knowing our 'self.'

Each one of the seven dimensions of 'self' is a big source of energy with the same effects noted for the first two dimensions, i.e., spirituality and potentiality. The energy from 'individualism' stems from the integrity of our choices, decisions, and actions. A sense of 'self' realization lifts our spirit when we finally choose a modest option by resisting many self-serving alternatives, make a compassionate decision, or take a worthy action. We try to make the right choices with integrity and compassion for the betterment of humanity, while strengthening our own spirit, despite our sour experiences of social living and its painful distractions. Perfecting every dimension of 'self' brings more energy and wisdom for living peacefully with divine contentment. Building this lively, proactive mentality boosts our identities and spirits to go through life with minimal confusion and distress.

Relationships

Besides our strong urge for socializing, we have an innate sense of connection with the universe and Nature. Thus, relationships manifests as the fourth dimension of 'self' in terms of connecting to others and outside world by compassion, patience, sincerity, and integrity. Volume III of this trilogy explores organizational and marital relationships in detail as major life mandates affecting our tortured 'self.'

Relationships enrich human existence when people, especially couples, share life experiences together. Moreover, relationships like marriage motivate us to entertain more risks and sacrifices than we might consider necessary otherwise. We work harder and think deeper because of our urge to keep our relationships strong and healthy. As much as individualism stresses on our ability to develop and maintain our independence, relationships reflect our strengths to satisfy our dependence needs with compassion and build our tolerance level for facing people. In fact, 'relationships' is an inherent mandate of 'self' to align our conflicting urges for both independence and dependence, as well as our enthusiasm to develop and express our individualism.

Ironically, relationships often bring us anxiety and frustration, and they keep raising our doubts about humans' true nature. In our relationships, we give and receive passion and compassion; we despise each other and feel deep animosity towards others; we help each other develop things and ideas, but then turn around, kill one another, and destroy so much family and social structures we had built with agony, money, and hard labour. Sometimes we seem to get close and understand a person, but the next day we feel so estranged and hostile. We all seem to be saying the same things, but are unable to communicate. And, while our needs for trust and sharing our thoughts with somebody keep growing, the whole world and society have become robotic and passionless—unwilling to listen and cooperate. In all, our relationships raise our spirits on some occasions and ruin them quite frequently, too. That is why managing our molested spirits is a big challenge and responsibility for 'self.'

Our relationships has the potential of boosting our awareness about ourselves as well when, in some situations, people's hints can be a more objective view of our character than our dogmatic, pompous sense of ourselves. Their points or even harsh reactions provide a good source of reflection for learning about ourselves. Without some feedback or a motive to think, we can hardly be objective about who we are. Our Egos and idiosyncrasies prevent us from judging ourselves honestly. Of course, some basic trust in those people who give us feedback directly or subtly is crucial. Their method of advising us must be effective, too, in order for us to at least ponder their direct inputs or subtle hints. We normally have deep doubts about other individuals' intelligence, intentions, objectivity, and judgment. Actually, we usually believe others are ignorant and biased, and that their judgments are malicious or at least not based on a realistic view of life and us. Our doubts about people's objectivity and characters are often correct. However, relationships and people's inputs usually make us contemplate on 'who we are'—the 'self'—more than any other tool that is out there. At least those inputs are valuable for stirring our curiosity and a chance for reflection, though we should also resist thinking and behaving like others just for the sake of getting their approval or complying with crooked social norms.

In spite of our supreme need for healthy relationships, it is getting harder to build constructive ones, nowadays, mostly due to, (a) people's misperceptions about the nature of relationships and love, and (b) their inability (or reluctance) to communicate and relate a bit less selfishly. They cannot portray a real image of themselves, so their partners remain confused and misled. In this contaminated environment, relationships have become robotic, calculating, and pretentious for the sake of coping and keeping the general appearances as long as possible. We portray a false image of ourselves for the sake of being accepted and popular in society. And we have become more confused about the nature of human beings due to the complexity and vanity of relationships. We are also becoming more sceptical regarding the purposes and sincerity of our relationships. All these obstacles for connecting with people, nature, and the universe have dampened our sense of 'self,' which is the essence of our being. As our 'self' and spirit are becoming weaker every year, we wonder who we really are and why we live.

The massive level of relationship failures and family quarrels reveals the depth of social dysfunction in the new era. It is, in fact, quite bizarre how the situation has worsened the more people's obsessions for socializing and individualism have increased!

The form, depth, and wholeness of our relationships are major factors for studying our 'self.' Spouses' varied personal needs and expectations form their relationship and the extent and scope of their genuine feelings and patience depict its strengths. And the accuracy of people's perceptions of their relationships and one another affects the completeness of their relationships, including the ones we have with Nature and our 'self.'

Therefore, the goal of 'knowing (about) oneself,' demands a study of our relationships with other human beings, Nature, and ourselves. Grasping the relationship with ourselves is extremely important, as it could reveal the level of our objectivity, integrity, wisdom, and a large host of other important information. First, we need a capacity to assess such relationship honestly, however. If we notice a major discrepancy between our perception of the form, depth and completeness of this relationship (with our 'self') compared with the feedback we receive from other people and our conscience, we might try to find the reasons less selfishly or ask an expert to help us with this process. It is also possible that what others think of us is due to their biases and perceptions of us in line with mainstream values that we may no longer advocate. Thus, in some instances, a rejection may in fact be an indication of us being on the right track for our finer purposes, even though it may be making others uncomfortable. Ten again, we should be careful when making judgments about others and ourselves thru personal perceptions per se, or only from our impressions of other people's feedbacks. Both are tricky, since it is often difficult to comprehend the real intentions of others or rely on our raw perceptions of others and ourselves.

We should know what we might reasonably expect to get out of our relationships, and usually keep our expectations modest or even low for building lasting relationships with minimal frictions. Naturally, spouses' expectations often clash in relationships due to their unique needs and perceptions. In fact, their exaggerated, artificial needs often ruin the intentions of any kind of relationship. Therefore, it is crucial to know the real purposes of a successful relationship and its particular requirements, instead of relying on our misleading personal whims and perceptions, which we apply to build a long list of ludicrous expectations. We can then decide what we are willing to give up for making a specific relationship more stable and how comfortable we are in doing so. What do we need or expect to receive in return? Can our partner give us what we need? Can we keep this relationship without imposing our needs on our partner? And if not, how and how long do we think we can tolerate not having our needs satisfied? We should resist our ulterior motives or interests beyond what we express explicitly or can expect sensibly from any relationship.

Overall, grasping and honouring relationships' authentic needs is a vital attribute of 'self' for enriching our routine lives, while respecting other people's rights, too. This reflects the importance of healthy relationships for empowering 'self.' The minute we lose sense of our integrity, individualism, and intentions within a relationship, it is reasonable to expect failure and disappointment, as well as the depletion of 'self.' For example, any relationship for financial exploitation is clearly doomed from the beginning. This sheer love for self is contrary to the love inherent in 'self.' The former kind of love is selfish and merely reflects one's need for attention and dependence on others.

The simplest, most gratifying type of relationship is when a person gives his/her love or attention to someone or something without any expectations in return. The relationship is personal and its reward (the inner satisfaction) is the fine experience itself. When we learn to enjoy Nature, nothing else can substitute the purity and reverence of this relationship. One simply enjoys the beauty, power, and delicacy of this private experience without expecting outer rewards or a lasting commitment. The love of our children is an experience in pure selflessness. Of course, this may change when our kids grow up and the parent-child relationship creates a new atmosphere and form. The relationship between grownup kids and their parents would have a new requirement, although it usually continues to stay less selfish on parents' side. The nature of parent-child relationship changes, anyway, because its form, depth, and completeness change.

'Who we are' vastly dictates the type of relationships we can create and be comfortable in, including the option of choosing solitude. Our personal preference for the type of relationships we like to maintain changes based on our personal growth and the life philosophy we choose at any point in our lives. Overall, our perceptions and expectations from a relationship develop based on our personal needs, maturity, and the strength of the 'self.' The more superficial our needs, the more primitive and clashing our relationships would be. If we are still obsessed with our needs for power, egoistic (self) love, social acceptance, popularity, or money, we get stuck in relationships that might support those needs, but destroy our integrity and 'self,' while causing family frictions as well. If self-actualization need drives a person, s/he would enjoy only profound relationships that can help him/her relax and achieve divine goals that sustain his/her individuality.

Certainly, our real potentialities can enrich our being much beyond the superficial goals that we try to satiate in our mundane contacts with people. We merely endure those relationships and perhaps even consider them our happiest life experiences at the cost of ignoring our potentialities and self-actualization needs. These higher personal needs often remain unfulfilled, because our time and energies are consumed on raw demands imposed on us by so many soulless relationships. Sadly, most marriages these days stress on partners' selfish needs that infect their relationship and hinder their chances of grasping humans' innate potentialities that can enrich a person's life uniquely.

The properties of relationships can be studied from different perspectives to highlight the perplexing dimensions of 'self.' Overall, our relationships directly affect 'who we are' or want to be, especially considering the long-term effects of being in some relationships, like marriage. The level of partners' individualism, compassion, independence, and integrity determines the format and strength of their relationship. Accordingly, the growing social conundrums and chaos are very much due to our relationships' lack of integrity—since our friendships and marriages, as well as family and organization relationships have become so calculating and soulless. Besides relationships' headaches and heartaches, we waste almost all our lives quarrelling about the selfish needs and demands of others and our own in many long-term relationships. Therefore, we hardly get a chance to explore our 'self.'

Overall, 'relationships' is an important dimension of 'self,' because it can either boost or threaten a person's attitude towards 'self,' as well as the other elements of 'self' such as spirituality, individualism, etc. The integrity of 'self' is often threatened when partners feel obliged to serve their pompous self or compromise their standards in order to maintain a substandard relationship.

Volume III of this trilogy addresses organizational and marital relationships due to their major effects on our tortured 'self.'

Contributions

The fifth dimension of 'self' evolves when we selflessly devote our thoughts and deeds outwardly only for humanitarian goals.

'Contributions' reflect one's ultimate life purposes. 'Who we are' is also measured by our modest accomplishments—the tiny marks we leave behind as a trace of our existence. In essence, a person's life purposes direct him/her towards certain objectives and possible accomplishments that comprise his/her contributions to other human beings' welfare, although 'self' obtains a sense of actualization and magnificence, too.

Maslow's findings appear to suggest that self-actualization coincides with the philosophy of 'self' and 'being' very closely. He explains 'peak experiences' characteristics when one senses the most significant and pleasant aspect of humanness. Those findings show that any important contribution not only causes self-actualization, but also validates 'self' as an inherent element of humanness and being.

Self-actualization is certainly a valuable personal experience in the way it induces sacred feelings and moments beyond the common experiences of the perceived world. However, its higher significance lies in the mere *contributions* that result through a person's endeavours. Most often, the feelings of a self-actualizer result directly from the anticipation of the value of one's work for humanity, rather than a selfish gratification of personal success. This is true because actualization and peak experiences happen only in pursuit of worthwhile purposes and projects. The main objective is to make a significant contribution. Even a personal capacity to think in these terms is precious all in itself. Maslow has referred to the self-validating aspect of peak experiences as an end in itself without explicitly raising the sense of contribution that a self-actualizer feels automatically as part of his endeavours.

"The peak experience is felt as a self-validating, self-justifying moment which carries its own intrinsic value with it. That is to say it is an end in itself, what we may call an end-experience rather than a means-experience. It is felt to be so valuable an experience, so great a revelation, that even to attempt to justify it takes away its dignity and worth." Toward the Psychology of Being, Abraham Maslow, Van Nostrand Reinhold, 2nd Edition, 1968, page 79.

The self-validating aspect of peak experiences can indeed be justified as an end in itself (*which carries its own intrinsic value*). However, an even more intrinsic value is evident in the initial purpose of a researcher or explorer who begins his/her journey with the idea of making a contribution. That inherent intention is always present as the main intrinsic value behind all the feelings of self-actualization that may or may not follow. We can say that, on the one hand, peak experiences depend on the significance of the purpose and its impact on humanity. On the other hand, we know that such peak experiences happen when a self-actualizer attains a high level of selflessness, and perhaps lives in a state of spirituality. Together, the state of selflessness and the significance of the experience (plus the results of his/her work) demonstrate a person's egoless attempt to make a worthwhile contribution to society. Thus, if we consider a self-actualizer's product a true reflection of his compassion and selflessness, we can easily agree that his contributions surge from pure devotion and conviction rather than a mechanical motion or ambitions induced by shallow personal needs and greed. Only these kinds of selfless, targeted contributions reveal the essence of 'who we are.'

A person receives substantial inner rewards instantaneously when s/he contributes to society, although receiving a reward has never been his/her intention or motivation as a scientist, inventor, writer, or explorer. S/he is merely pursuing his/her instincts and talents for unselfish purposes without any expectations. But this very natural urge that drives him/her to devote his/her life and energy to achieve something activates the inherent 'self' surging within him/her, which then brings him/her unparallel senses of joy and divinity automatically. That is the 'spirit' of the 'self.'

It is hard to imagine the feelings of a self-actualizer and the way his/her spirit ascends the realms of mortal existence. Yet, the lack of spiritual imaginations is what prevents us from actualizing our 'self.' Our limited perceptions of life and our raw definition of success hinder our psychological growth, self-actualization, and the sense of aesthetic values found only on a meaningful path of life. We cannot imagine a life outside the perceived world, so we remain ignorant about this vital dimension of 'who we are,' and how our contributions might grow and signify it.

Growth

The sixth dimension of 'self' is its inner urge to grow and attain the highest level of awareness and wisdom.

We are bound by nature to grow physically, psychologically, and spiritually forever. The physical growth has been accepted as a given fact that extends from birth to death in a steady manner with little personal control. We refer to the physical aspect of growth as aging, although the increase in the size and strength of body are implied as well. The body reaches an optimal growth regardless of its size and strength, perhaps around the age of 30, then starts to decline. Overall, bodily growth might be viewed mainly in terms of aging. After certain age, we resent the growth as one feels the loss of allure and vitality that have high social appeals. With aging, lethargy and body shrinkage or fat replace our vigour and youth, thus the growth after certain age becomes undesirable. We are aware of this aging process, we anticipate it, and become more concerned and conscious about it when we reach probably 30 or 40 and see the signs of old age, grey hair, wrinkles, lower energy, etc. We try in many ways to stop this undesirable aspect of biological growth at all costs, to no avail. In all, while we take the desirable portion of this growth gracefully, we find the second stage depressing. This unflattering growth affects our spirit, behaviour, and outlook. Mid-age crisis that we usually tease one another with has in fact a major influence on people's level of doubts and decisions about themselves, their lives, and their options.

We try to develop methods of mitigating the negative aspects of growth in the second stage, or at least make ourselves look younger. We do more physical exercises, take vitamins, remain careful about our diet, dye our hair, and avoid strenuous bodily activities, cigarettes, and liquor, etc. We try to feel good about our body and looks. Our boosted self-image and self-satisfaction—when sincere—might mitigate the negative psychological effects during the second stage of our physical growth. Besides these weak methods of curbing our psychological depression due to aging, another *growth* factor helps us defeat, forget, or ignore the effects of aging. This factor is called mental maturity—one's psychological growth through self-exploration.

The process of 'knowing about ourselves' definitely involves a thorough knowledge of our bodily needs. We must learn about caring for our body, not only to reduce the negative effects of aging on body, but also to support our psyche to face the negative thoughts of aging and death.

'Knowing about ourselves' depends on how smoothly we can grow psychologically, mature by actualizing our self, use our potentialities to make social contributions, learn humility, and grow compassion, individualism, and integrity to build sincere relationships with others and ourselves. The required strengths to follow this path depends on our good knowledge and control of our bodies and minds—our mental growth. This is even a greater risk during the second stage of humans' aging process, i.e., when the negative physical growth begins.

Contrary to physical growth that goes through two stages of positive and negative bodily experiences, psychological growth is a natural, constant progression, subject to individuals' awareness, participation, and resolve to achieve it. Actually, psychological growth can lead to an endless spiritual growth and enlightenment. Everybody with relative physical and mental health has enough capacity to nurture his psychological growth throughout his/her life by grasping the meaning and methods of heightening mental growth. Actually, a huge objective of 'knowing about self' and doing the right things is for supporting our psychological growth to keep our spirits high. We should develop our 'self' beyond the boundaries of a normal person to a spiritual being, thus.

Growth has a risk, though: It demands the risk of abandoning our existing dependencies in order to enter new boundaries and to experience new concepts and thoughts. We are now addicted to our stagnant ways of living and thinking. In order to grow, we should let go of the past, but this involves losing the security we feel in the existing value systems, or losing the support or respect of others. As we do not have the insight of living in the present, we cling to our pasts and societies' conditioning forces. We may wish to experience and search new meanings for our lives, but they all sound rather threatening to us. We do not want to give up our attachments to so many established forms of whatever (!)—family, status, lifestyle, dreams, attitude, love, sex, etc. The sense of security prevailing within our existing habits, values, families, and defence mechanisms inhibits the possibility of a new outlook and a fresh thought process.

Accordingly, trying new (meaningful) things is sometimes too daunting or painful for some of us, thus our psychological growth might be hindered by our reaction and aversion to this immense risk. We might be willing or even striving to reinforce our psychological growth, but many of our psychological defects prevent it.

Unless we overcome most of our psychological defects, we have no chance for growth; and without psychological growth, we intensify the level of suffering and stress all our lives, as we are not maturing or satisfying our higher needs. We do not build an antidote for aging. It is not easy to get rid of psychological flaws that hinder our growth, of course. This is because we often have difficulty recognizing and acknowledging the sources and depth of our defects, which is the first phase in overcoming them. Psychological growth ultimately leads to, and requires, a personal awakening and spirituality, too. Yet, most of us have difficulty finding an authentic sense of spirituality for all the reasons noted throughout this book.

While we cannot control physical growth—the aging process —, we can have a much better control over our psychological health and growth as well as spiritual maturity. This control of psychological growth, along with a conscious care of the body, to the extent possible, would assist us in minimizing the agony of old age and the inevitable sufferings of life. In order to know 'who we are,' we ought to measure the extent of psychological growth that we have allowed ourselves, what we know about this growth, and how it can be achieved and perhaps maximized to the verge of enlightenment.

Social Responsibility

The seventh dimension of 'self' is its ability to acknowledge and fulfil certain responsibilities.

Whether we realize it or not, like it or not, or practice it enough or not, we all have a responsibility towards one another individually and collectively. We all share a planet, a country, a society, a family, and are members of some organizations. Social living creates social responsibility. We cannot only take from a society and not give back enough to maintain it. The equilibrium has already been lost when a large majority only takes with little enthusiasm to give back something worthwhile in return. A very tiny minority now owns the world, whereas the big majority lives in poverty and agony like some kind of modern slaves. Social responsibility is not restricted to monetary issues, yet most of our social problems are caused somewhat and somehow by our greed and capitalism. We can look around and observe how we engage in many unethical activities to get wealthier, mostly by pushing people to buy things they do not need through sales gimmicks and advertising, which are proudly called marketing. Instead of feeling responsible for the growing social hardships and chaos, this selfish majority just keeps exploiting the helpless public more every day. Their only objective is to find better ways of keeping the public in ignorance and sell them more stuff at high prices. Hardly anybody thinks twice when an opportunity arises to fool or rob others. Our so-called democratic governments let all these atrocities happen to poor citizens, too—actually support all those foolish capitalistic ideals.

A wide range of social responsibilities covers all facets of human life, nowadays, especially when the morality of people's and businesses' activities and decisions have an impact on the overall welfare of the society and Nature. Political and business corruptions, polluting the environment, and destroying the forests and wild life are only a few examples of unethical, irresponsible ways of thinking and behaving by modern humans. We are all responsible for the drastic repercussions of our mentalities and lifestyles on humanity and the future of this planet.

'Knowing about ourselves' needs a sense of social and family responsibilities, which is a natural extension of one's knowledge of *individualism* and *relationships* noted above. This basic sense of social responsibility is also distinguished here from the fifth element dimension of 'self,' *contribution,* as noted above, which demands a deeper devotion beyond bare social responsibilities. Yet, feeling our social responsibilities is the basis for building our character and motivation to enrich humanity as well beyond our daily responsibilities.

In the end, we all have a chance to grasp and build the seven dimensions of 'self' in ourselves for our own and humanity's benefits. But do we ever grow up enough individually or socially to perceive the reality of existence and behave a bit intelligently?

The Integral 'Self'

To understand the integral 'self' and 'know about ourselves,' the seven main dimensions can be defined in a universal phrase. That is, we can say that:

Man is intrinsically built of spirituality and potentiality, which he can explore within himself for developing his individualism, compassion, integrity, and meaningful relationships for making contributions to himself, Nature, and humanity as a whole, and for performing his social responsibilities selflessly. Only through this holistic process, a person maintains a constant growth of 'self' towards enlightenment.

The basic objective of 'knowing about ourselves' is to find a practical compromise between devoting our lives to spirituality in search of 'self' and getting completely absorbed in the perceived world in hopes of maximizing our pleasures and wealth. Most of us are unable, and have no desire or courage, to withdraw from the luring social life completely. However, while attending to the demands of social living, we might wish to find a life path that could help us refocus our thoughts and build our psychological strengths for actualizing our 'self,' while satisfying our profound inner needs, too, at least partially. This approach might give us an opportunity to make life tolerable and meaningful, but also get a better control over our psychological and spiritual growth.

An integral 'self' emerges when its seven main elements are nurtured and work harmoniously. Especially, the 'individualism' dimension can play a central role to ensure all other elements are in balance and functional. Nevertheless, exploring these elements of 'self' provides a general framework for self-evaluation, too.

'Self' and Fate

The fact that 'self' emphasizes highly on personal choices and actions may again appear contradictory to the idea of giving fate at least a modest weight in the foundation of our thoughts. This is a major dilemma, especially since nurturing 'self' demands so much personal efforts and initiatives. In fact, one might ask, 'If one's destiny is preordained for a final (perhaps divine) purpose, then why care about building 'self' in hopes of enriching one's life?' Maybe doing nothing and waiting for fate to do its things is the best approach and least tiresome. The answer is that, while we cannot change or fight our fates, we have a basic role and choice in directing our lives. In fact, 'self' is the best means of maintaining our composure and sanity when fate imposes life's hardships on us and we should depend on our inner strengths to survive the ongoing turmoil. We always face options and choices, and we must learn how to make those decisions properly based on the principles of individualism for a 'self'-driven person. If we were to do nothing or not use our instincts, we would just perish. A simple 'doing nothing' is to not pick up a loaf of bread or a glass of water to survive, or perhaps even not swallow what is in our mouth. Nature stirs our instincts to eat, but we should get the bread and swallow it as well. We could expand on this simple example and notice that showing initiative to do so many 'right things' with integrity and compassion in a timely manner is vital. Chapter Sixteen explains the role of fate vs. personal decisions, but a few highlights about the role of 'self' in line with our beliefs about destiny is offered in the remainder of this chapter.

Without 'self'-determination, we would lose life opportunities and perish quickly. This could be a simple task of walking to the refrigerator to get food, to eat, to have strength, to work, to make money, to buy food, to store it in the refrigerator, and up the scale we go. Perhaps one of these times when we swallow a piece of bread, it goes the wrong way and we choke and die, which would be our destiny, but still our job was to swallow it, because it was the right thing to do with the right purpose when we initiated that step. We should pursue the guidelines and steps we have defined in our life philosophy in line with our instinctual urge to fulfill our authentic needs. In particular, we should show initiatives to satisfy our instinctive needs—starting with the needs for food and shelter all the way up to self-actualization. Establishing this kind of wholesome mentality is a prominent demand on humans, to prevent our physical and psychological deterioration.

Our belief in the inevitability of fate, in fact, demands our high vigilance about many likely surprises in our lives and the need to react to life's varied hardships. The need for this high degree of consciousness also stresses the importance of being proactive in making 'proper and purposeful' choices and decisions regularly. Now, a cynical person might still question even the need to fuss over all these issues if destiny is in charge. The answer is that we do not really have to be proactive or vigilant, but why do things wrongly intentionally if our intelligence could guide us? Why would one prefer to shove his food up his nose if he is no longer a baby or a retard? Doing things wrong intentionally or ignorantly, such as crimes and drugs, is going against individualism and our instincts that we desperately wish to support. By acting against humans' instincts and moral values, we have inflicted so much suffering and stress upon ourselves. To reverse this doomed process, and as part of knowing what 'I' or 'self' is all about, it is crucial to recognize our nature and instincts and abide by some moral rules. For example, while sex is a basic and essential need, becoming slave to it, as has become so common, is beyond the dignity of a 'self' driven person. For humanity to survive, we must learn to do the right things individually and collectively.

The numerous properties of 'self,' as explained within its seven dimensions, direct us in choosing the right options by using a proper value system for us and recognizing everybody's rights, all for the purpose of performing our sacred duties. While one's 'self' stresses on morality, it is not bound by it. In fact, it contains many higher principles for 'self'-imposed thinking and doing the right things independently, regardless of the narrow morality that society publicizes naively. We can and should aim for our highest sense of self-worth and ethics way beyond what society can ever support, e.g., by shallow slogans about human rights.

Since we are not saints and do not work hard on establishing our 'self' and understanding its implications, we all engage in doing both the right and wrong things knowingly. Therefore, as a major step in knowing who we are, we should *consciously* assess the intensity and frequency of those things that we do right or wrong. We should build and maintain a conscious knowledge of our deeds and ask ourselves why we prefer to do them in that manner. Some very small urges, as well as deep habits, make us do the right or wrong things. We must distinguish and keep them in our high conscious. Of course, we first need valid standards to assess our deeds and determine their aptness. We can apply our instincts, conscience, and objective judgments as a preliminary yardstick. The wrong deeds we have been justifying all along should now be reassessed with a fresh mentality outside of our prejudices, neediness, and Ego. Surely, measuring the rightness of an action is not easy, because we need practical criteria and techniques to stay objective and open-minded. Mainly, we must believe that assessing our integrity is the proper thing to do for healing our own sick psyches. To save our spirits.

What makes us do the right or wrong things? How have we come to make a habit of it? These questions should be reviewed for each of the three groups who do wrong things, a) knowingly, b) out of ignorance, and c) due to rearing and social conditioning, and believing in the appropriateness of their actions.

Our motives for doing wrong intentionally or innocently are quite different. When no direct or obvious motive exists, some hidden causal force (or conditioning), including ignorance and naivety, is driving us. Studying our psychological idiosyncrasies, their roots, who or what triggers our bad deeds, and 'how and if' they might be corrected, require a lengthy discussion—although many aspect of these issues are hinted throughout this trilogy. Yet, a more urgent question is, 'How should a person assess his/her individualism, integrity, and compassion, and how can s/he improve him/herself once s/he agrees that self-awareness can help him/her?' Luckily, if we ever get serious about knowing our 'self,' we notice our weaknesses fast in terms of individualism, integrity, and compassion. Whether a person quits justifying his/her errors in his/her mind at this point—when s/he stands on the wisdom path—and whether s/he stops his/her old habits, would become a personal challenge. If this challenge is accepted, s/he would get the opportunity to review the seven elements of 'self' and then decide to help him/herself through self-awareness. S/he would learn to make objective judgments and decisions. Still, choosing this rather divine path of life to reach a higher stance of 'self' requires personal initiative and commitment.

We inherit lots of defects and acquire a lot more through our relationships and encounters in society. Together, our genetic and acquired defects besiege our perceptions of the world, others, and ourselves. Naturally, we do not conceive our defects, or quickly justify them. Yet, we have little patience and compassion towards other people's defects that we detect fast. We believe to be great experts in criticizing social structure, political systems, people, and even God sometimes, yet unable to see our own flaws. Thus, we lose our chance of becoming better human beings with some notion of 'self' driving us. Furthermore, the effects of our biases and misjudgments scatter the seeds of suspicion and distrust in other individuals and society. In general, it appears that neither our basic personal traits, nor the outcomes of our relationships in particular, can help us achieve a level of nobility and purity that we hope to find in human beings.

Our wrongdoings are often the result of social (dis)order and pressures. And it is obvious that unless we redefine and correct the foundation of social values, the remedies for reconditioning the elements of this social system, i.e., individuals, would remain impotent. On the other hand, how do we go about changing the superstructure when the operators, i.e., individuals, do not believe in a need to modify their mentalities and refuse to participate in changing social values? Thus, we should do both simultaneously. We need to appreciate our roles in both making a global change in social order and developing a fresh personal mentality. While revamping our perspective regarding life and our deeds, we must participate in the development of support systems to reverse the process of manipulating and conditioning people in society. Our educational systems, in particular, need a major overhaul. We need to propagate social conscience and a more compassionate foundation of human thoughts. We should learn to respect the sanctity of our spirit, instead of destroying it with our misguided shows of individualism.

Doing the right or wrong things *knowingly* occurs when our conscience at least realizes its rightness or evilness. Correcting those deeds and thoughts is still tough even though for this case at least our conscience plays a direct role in alarming us privately and tentatively. However, our two other types of deeds are much more difficult to handle: The ones we engage in *unknowingly* or out of ignorance, and the ones we do habitually, because we are conditioned to believe in their rightness or enjoy acting in certain ways. Clearly, activating one's conscience and 'self'-awakening requires even more work and most likely professional techniques and therapy if a person is fully incognizant of his behaviour.

We have a very long way to go to attain even a relative sense of human integrity as well as building social systems that would support and allow such qualities prevail. Meanwhile, we should still deal with imperfect characters and personalities, especially our own. We must help ourselves a little at least, while we wait and hope for a bit of universal morality mixed with viable rules of coexistence, too.

If we are seeking, or believing in, an inherent purity of human nature, we are setting ourselves up for major disappointments. We would suffer due to our unreasonableness and stubbornness in placing the emphasis on the wrong faith. Instead of expecting integrity and morality in others, we must seek and develop them within ourselves, and then stay content with the harsh reality of social living. If purity is achievable at all, it can evolve in certain ways and by special individuals only. Expecting it universally as an inherent human property is unrealistic.

PART VI
Doubts and Decisions

Prelude to Part VI

The number and difficulties of decisions a person should make regularly to survive is rising fast every generation, while people face more risks with too much doubts about people and situations at the centre of their decisions—all thanks to the dire inefficacy and corruption of socioeconomic systems around the globe.

So far, in human history, both social structures and personal lifestyles have missed the chance of bringing people some solace, let alone a valid definition for success and happiness. Instead, our cultures and religions have mired our chances for mental growth and exploring our inner strengths. Merely some positive thinking jargons and modern personal obsessions for love and happiness have caused us more confusion. They have just made us increase our expectations from life, instead of learning the reality of living in our complex and callous societies with all sorts of sufferings we endure so helplessly and hopelessly. In general we have either positive or negative thoughts in the following five categories:

1. Social (doubts about our lifestyles).
2. Personal (doubts about who we are).
3. Interpersonal (doubts about who they are).
4. Supernatural (doubts about the essence of life).
5. Spiritual (doubts about our connection to non-physical spheres).

A Cautionary Point about Part VI

Part VI's rather analytical discussions are useful for gaining some insight about the workings of our brains and psyches when facing life's tough situations and striving to analyse our options and their risks. At least, this background might help us remember both the difficulties and essentialities of major life **decisions** when we are facing big **doubts** about the best path for living.

CHAPTER FOURTEEN
Positive Doubts (Vibes)

Previous discussions hinted that our doubts affect us positively or negatively depending upon their nature and the way we perceive and analyse them. Positive doubts increase our caution level for making decisions due to information deficiency or ambiguities. Negative doubts are also alarming, but often reflect a mental state where facts, questions, and options are reasonably known, yet we cannot bring ourselves to decide. We usually present all kinds of lousy evidences and excuses to defend our logic and justifications for delaying a decision. We might think our doubts and hesitation are justified by the lack of information. However, it often relates to our fears of risk, failure, and humiliation, if not mere laziness to act. Anyway, we can study our doubts to fathom their sources and assess their effects on our wellbeing. For one thing, we can ascertain whether our doubts are a symptom of our weakness in decision-making or a sign of unresolved issues and problems begging for attention.

Perhaps it is easier to think of these doubts as 'vibes' that we are more familiar with and use regularly, i.e., as 'positive and negative vibes' that raise some sort of alarm. For example, the phrase, 'He gives me a negative vibe,' reflects our suspicion and doubts about his intentions or feelings towards us.'

The importance of distinguishing positive and negative doubts also lies in their opposing effects on our perceptions of life and personal image. Positive doubts reflect wisdom and patience and it helps self-awareness and growth, whereas negative doubts stir tension and a poor outlook. Of course, even positive doubts may inflict anxiety and suffering, as we continue to struggle with the dilemmas that all doubts create. However, with a proper view of positive doubts (and distinguishing them from negative ones), we can reduce the overall inner tensions, as we redirect our efforts more effectively—from eliminating our doubts to understanding them. Thus, now, a new dilemma to haggle with is to ensure we have built the objectivity and right mindset to distinguish and apply our positive and negative doubts (vibes) productively!

Positive doubts justify our indecision due to information or evidence frailties. More importantly, positive doubts stop us from becoming dogmatic and arrogant. It also gives us an opportunity to ponder ludicrous beliefs or claims beyond the plausible facts of the perceived world, such as afterlife or similar religious claims! Furthermore, positive doubts keep our minds open regarding the possibility of human soul and mythical concepts like happiness, God, love, truth, trust, etc.

Grasping the *nature* of our doubts is an important objective of self-awareness, as it pinpoints our outlook, explains the sources of our tensions, and might eventually help us put many facts and facets of life in their proper perspectives. To use a metaphor here, positive doubts are like 'good cholesterols' that we had not heard about or knew their value for our health. Rather, we had always focused on bad cholesterol (negative doubts) that we knew are harmful to our health and wished to elude to be a positive thinker.

A doubt is positive (significant) for its two essential functions: First, it reflects our alertness and instincts to question (and remain doubtful about) the validity of any conclusion not supported by enough information and evidence. Second, it stops gullibility and risky outcomes of hasty or emotional decisions. Other benefits of positive doubts are:

- They indicate how thoughtfully we perceive life and live.
- They prevent undue risks, which are not measurable due to the incompleteness of information and evidence.
- They prevent emotional decisions and reactions.
- They make us look inside ourselves for clues and answers.
- They provoke philosophical reflections and insight.
- They raise our self-awareness.
- They are usually a sign of humility and control of Ego.
- They are often a sign of patience, experience, and wisdom.
- They let us ponder, assess, cherish, and apply our intuitions.
- They often hint about myths and obscure realities, compared with the inevitable facts of life (e.g., social chaos or humans' impure nature) that we keep fighting with or blame others or ourselves for.
- Positive doubts help us think, learn, mature, and turn into a better human being.

The level, nature, and types of doubts were shown in Diagram 11.1 (page 207) and discussed in Chapter Eleven. Positive doubts (both psychological and logical) can be studied further according to their categories (subjects) in this chapter:

1. Social (doubts about our lifestyles).
2. Personal (doubts about who we are).
3. Interpersonal (doubts about who they are).
4. Supernatural (doubts about the essence of life).
5. Spiritual (doubts about our connection to non-physical spheres).

Social Doubts

Social doubts reflect our apprehensions about the way we accept, and boost, our socioeconomic settings, while we strive to make a living and support our families. We question the value of a society or family that is often incapable of fulfilling our basic needs in a consistent and fair manner. We feel like slaves, reliant upon such imposing, faltering socioeconomic systems that have tainted our minds and all facets of the modern world. We keep doubting our sanity for cherishing our lifestyles built around fanciful ideologies that everybody seems to believe in, such as democracy, freedom, and happiness.

Accordingly, we cannot elude our sense of helplessness and doubts about being exploited in some form, simply because we want to live in society and not be rejected altogether. Then again, these are our lives that are being wasted in pursuit of futile social and economical values. If we cannot save ourselves, nobody else would care or question our sanity for living the way we do. At the same time, we feel helpless to challenge or change the values and systems that have rooted themselves in the hearts and minds of people so solidly. Actually, most of us are now addicted to the superficial rewards of compliance to the social rules and values. We also doubt, quite rightly so, the effectiveness of our resistance and the point of opposing status quo. We have already discussed how limited the expected level of our influence for changing the existing systems are, although doing whatever we can is still valuable at least for personal growth and satisfaction.

For building our perspective of socioeconomic structure, we should view and accept its shortfalls as an extension of human defects caused by all of us. We have collectively built, and are maintaining, a superstructure that best reflects and fits our nature, abilities, and flaws. We may believe that these systems have been developed democratically or by sheer autocratic forces that some groups have imposed on majority. In the final analysis, however, our submissiveness to these defective ideologies and authoritative figures is a real human deficiency that we cannot deny or change. We admit that people accept the prevailing socioeconomic rules because of their naivety or greed for social rewards. Despite our vast imagination to think of ourselves as a capable and superior species, we can refer to socioeconomic chaos around the world to reconsider and refine our conclusions about our abilities—human nature and intelligence. When we see socioeconomic systems as a symbol of our ignorance and incongruity in vision and goals, we can then better cope with the realities of human imperfection.

We cannot elude the perils of socioeconomic problems, but recognizing their roots can help us minimize our negative doubts. We should stop thinking of these systems as some independent phenomenon that can (or should) provide fairer and freer life for all and bring order and control to all values and ways of thinking. We have continuously tried to make our legal systems stronger and fairer. Yet, we are witnessing more violence, corruptions, and frustration about the way justice seems so fanciful. Does not this suggest that we humans are so eager and capable to circumvent our rules of coexistence and laws when it is not to our advantage to abide by them? And does not it suggest that we prefer chaos and we are responsible for the world's demise as well, in spite of our seemingly good intentions to bring order to our lives? Is not our greed and arrogance killing us? Has not the effects of present social structure made us quite sick and cruel to kill one another just for releasing our frustration with society and life altogether? Understanding the reality and nature of socioeconomic systems makes our doubts positive, because we stop envisioning them as some independent structure that has its own will and capabilities. We know this faltering social structure is merely our thoughtless creation. It is just a perfect representation of humans' demented nature and naiveté tainted by their egos and failures!—a horrific product of humans' tormented existence to date. The only puzzle is how much longer humans will survive if we stay so selfish and silly. How much longer can we allow this monster—our social insanity—grow before it swallows us whole?

Nonetheless, socioeconomic doubts make us feel trapped, as explained in detail in Volume III of this trilogy. Accordingly, we also often doubt the usefulness of our thoughts and the value of our struggles, especially if we have not studied our other positive doubts to grasp our spirituality and real needs. We might suffer consciously or subconsciously for our helplessness to improve the situation, while also playing an active part personally in this chaos. These doubts regarding our roles in the maintenance and promotion of socioeconomic systems and our substandard way of life can be quite devastating for a conscientious person. On the other hand, if we acknowledge these seemingly irreversible facts of life somewhat, we can do certain things to alleviate the effects of such feelings and our demented deeds at least partially. This can be achieved mostly by turning those negative feelings into positive doubts, thoughts, and deeds. *How?,* you may ask.

For one thing, we can gauge the depth of our attachments and involvement with socioeconomic systems. We would feel more positive by striving to find solutions that minimize our reliance on these systems. Exploring new ways of living results in joyful experiences and higher stamina to cope with social living flaws. Finding practical solutions to live more independently can bring us gratification as well, while we handle our personal limitations, learn the complexities of alternative lifestyles, and prepare for the sacrifices we must make to find our 'self' and a solid identity. We would definitely benefit from our new way of living and thinking about socioeconomic systems. While we accept our inabilities to make drastic changes, we learn to cope better with the pressures of these social systems somehow just for survival.

Our self-image and doubts about our existence in this chaotic environment become more positive when we monitor the degree of our involvements and reassess our responsibilities. We would think more positively once we relieve ourselves from the feeling of guilt as a culprit in supporting such greed-based, inhumane systems. For example, we might consider adopting the 'coping mechanism' option when working for an organization or facing marital issues, as discussed in Volume III of this trilogy. We can rather justify our position and optimism, while accepting the risks of further estrangement, and possibly even more family or social havoc due to our passivity and lower involvement. If we avoid promoting abusive values, materialism, and hypocrisy, we can make mostly positive effects in our families or organizations with our positive doubts regarding our associations and involvements.

Our positive doubts would focus on few positive changes that we can bring about, in spite of the huge obstacles, controversies, and disappointments. We might still have doubts about the effect of our efforts, but they are positive doubts that do not stir despair. Most importantly, our positive doubts at this level are valuable for enhancing our outlook, despite our stoic attitude. Sadly, we might still doubt the value of life within prevalent social structure, but strive to stay positive by finding ways of adapting, focusing on our values and beliefs, and tuning our rather simple lifestyle. We might still doubt the value of our big sacrifices and efforts for a peaceful life, but it would be a positive doubt if we follow a sensible life path for self-fulfillment in line with ethical criteria. We might deviate occasionally from our hard principles, yet soon return to our fundamental beliefs and bring ourselves right back on track by analysing the roots of our personal doubts.

Personal Doubts

Personal doubts consist of our curiosity about our personalities and abilities. These are the hardest kinds of doubts for us to grasp, accept, and turn into positive attributes, since we simply cannot see our idiosyncrasies and mistakes. Actually, for most of us, the problem arises from 'not having personal doubts,' which shows how our Egos stop us from having a better appreciation of 'who we are.' The difficulty of knowing 'who we really are' was stressed in Chapters Seven and Thirteen. Having 'no personal doubts' is only another reflection of our Egos being in command. It demonstrates our naive presumptions about our perfection and knowing 'who we are.' Individuals with lesser Ego are sincerer and humbler, thus carry some degree of personal doubts. This does not mean they are less confident or doubtful regarding all aspects of their personalities and abilities. Rather, out of their sheer confidence and modesty, they have also gained enough wisdom to doubt the validity and truthfulness of many aspects of their perceptions, actions, traits, and thoughts.

Personal doubts prepare us mentally for accepting criticism from ourselves and even from others without becoming overly agitated or threatened psychologically. It reveals our grasp of, or willingness to explore, the possible personal defects that hinder our relationships, communication, and growth. Of course, in some extreme cases, personal doubts may portray low self-image and confidence. At this extreme, self-doubts are 'negative doubts' that taint our outlooks and attitudes, as discussed later. Indeed, self-doubts may require professional treatment if negative effects of social withdrawal, paranoia, and insecurity are prominent in one's life. Unlike self-doubts, however, balanced personal doubts are quite constructive in the way they help us explore the sources of our problems and find means of improving ourselves.

Almost everybody has personal doubts in some degree and form. The difference is in the person's level of consciousness and willingness to allow these doubts cultivate his/her mind and how s/he uses them to guide his/her thoughts about 'self.' Some of us might stubbornly insist on the appropriateness of our actions and behaviour, and believe totally in our raw, rigid interpretations of events and situations we create or participate in easily. However, by hindering the opportunity of self-evaluation through personal doubts, we deprive ourselves of the benefits of knowing who we are and why our lives contain many sufferings and imbalances. We just continue to perceive the world and our mission in life based on some predisposed vile values that we have inherited or learned from our parents or society. Without personal doubts, we hinder our personal growth and hurt others with our defects, too.

'Not having personal doubts *ever*' is a rare case and merely a sign of a person's dire psychological disorder or even insanity. In most cases, though, we are only hesitant in acknowledging our personal doubts (positive vibes), while trying hard to repress our natural instincts pushing us to face our doubts and defects. We fear listening to the inner voices that send subtle messages about who we are, our defects, and mistakes. We elude our conscience that often tries to interfere in our affairs. Usually our Ego plays an active role in defusing these voices and suppressing our urges to doubt what we do and who we believe to be. Yet, despite all these efforts and struggles to elude our personal doubts (positive vibes) fully, we still hear the nagging voices inside us and feel the anxiety that results from our actions or behaviours, or from other people's reactions. Our options are to either continue to resist our personal doubts and the feedbacks we receive from our inner voices, or open up our minds to the possibility of reaping the benefits of studying our personal doubts that are mainly alarming us about our idiosyncrasies. We can explore these doubts in some depth, and recall them proactively for more direct intuitions. We can look for sources and causes of our doubts and many personal defects they usually pinpoint.

Often, we subtly question the value or validity of something we do, or we condemn the manner we handle a person or issue. Nurturing these questions raises our self-awareness and leads to positive doubts for exploring our lives realistically. We try to use this information to detect our flaws, ignorance, and their sources, and to remember them for future decisions and actions. However, how successfully we can apply our wisdom to future situations depends highly on the extent of our quirks at any particular point now or in the future. A bad experience would not necessarily prevent us from repeating our heinous acts or behaviour when the source of that experience, e.g., our greed or jealousy, dominates our personality and beliefs. Most of us make the same mistakes repeatedly even when we have personal doubts and feel guilty about our judgment, and even when we realize the repercussions of our actions. We cannot stop our compulsive behaviour and problem-causing mentalities until we learn to control the roots of our defects effectively mainly by raising our self-awareness. We can then use this wisdom and energy to control our defects and their effects on our lives and relationships. Of course, recognizing and doing something serious about our genetical defects on top of humans' vile nature is, especially, tough. However, some special people learn to do it.

Besides helping us pinpoint and defeat our defects, positive doubts help us internalize our thoughts and experiences. In a state of doubtfulness, we are more receptive to input and information that erupt around us and in our heads. We find our contemplation a positive experience to study our lives and become more aware of the values and issues that spur our foundation of thoughts and drive the structure of our lives. This is a self-awareness process stirred by doubts. However, personal doubts' positivity, including its learning and tranquillity effects, depends upon our mentality and attitude. With only little personal doubts, we do not challenge ourselves enough, and thus miss the benefits of divine feelings and tranquillity that self-awareness exerts. With too much doubts, however, we suffer the anxieties of self-doubt and our inability to make decisions or face life effectively. Understanding our doubts' natures is surely a challenging endeavour in itself, after all.

Unfortunately, our value systems and cultures have caused us a misperception regarding the nature of personal doubts. We are conditioned to attribute personal doubts to high self-doubt, a lack of determination, and low self-image. In fact, we strive to hide our personal doubts by portraying (or pretending) an image of self-confidence, toughness, and assertiveness. We strive to appear decisive and confident. We lean towards the extreme of showing, or believing in, a personality of a 'doubtless' person by becoming intimidating and rude in our work and family relationships. We ignore that our doubts are not only normal, but also useful and healthy if personal doubts are distinguished from self-doubts. The latter is an extreme instance of a suppressed personality with low self-respect and self-image due to negative past experiences or genetics. Having personal doubts, on the other hand, is a positive virtue that stems from our vital instinct to grasp 'self.' Self-doubt causes anxiety, paralyses a person, and leads to indecisiveness, whereas balanced personal doubts stir patience and calm, which help us alleviate our defects, empower our relationships, and raise the quality of our decisions. Studying self-doubt's peculiarities in the next pages is helpful for distinguishing it from personal doubt.

The Special Case of Self-doubt

Well, now doubting the nature of our doubts is a major dilemma all by itself. 'How can we differentiate our negative self-doubts from positive personal doubts?' 'How do we know if our doubts are emotionally and psychologically balanced and positive, rather than self-doubts?' In particular, making any of these judgments seem impossible during a doubtful moment or situation.

For one thing, our mood is an indicator of the kind of doubts we are facing. Self-doubt (like any major personal defect) feels like a shell holding us within its tight grips. As much as we try to free ourselves by thinking about salvation—what we like to be or could be—still we cannot escape the cage, thus get anxious. We might even look at the world outside the cage, which reflects the open horizons of potentialities (purity and ethics—in contrast to our general defects or evil), but we cannot get out there despite our desires and efforts. We are imprisoned within our self-doubts (a sense of pity and failure). Conversely, having positive doubts is a state in which we feel free to walk outside the cage already. Gaping through the open door, we are merely trying to establish what path to follow towards which horizon. Balanced personal doubts merely instigate our urges for reflection, relaxation, and learning in order to make a final decision and hope for the best. On the other hand, self-doubt is just an extreme case of personal doubts when our questions and doubts are unfocused and erratic, thus result in confusion, indecision, and pain.

Both self-doubt and positive doubts are rather fixed conditions, although for different reasons. The latter becomes a potent means of strengthening one's life philosophy, whereas self-doubt comes from the absence of life philosophy and personal convictions. If we spend enough time and effort on personal positive doubts on a regular basis, we would gradually learn who we are and what we want to do. This life philosophy eliminates, or at least minimizes, self-doubt, because we have profound value systems and criteria to rely on when we face a decision or action; we do not have to endure a frustrating process of evaluating our values and choices hastily at the time our mind is occupied already by the nature of a particular dilemma. At the same time, balanced personal doubts are usually not related to any specific or urgent need for decision or action. We simply assess our values, purposes for living, or our previous negative reactions to certain situations and relationships regularly. Conversely, defeating our deepened self-doubt is hard. It erupts during every crisis or challenge, but we are just paralysed without a belief system.

Most people can usually detect the nature and type of their doubts, thus manage them accordingly. If self-doubt becomes too deep and painful, the remedy is to review the nature and roots of our doubts deeper and develop a simple foundation of thoughts gradually to stir our deeds and decisions for particular, purposeful objectives. We should delay our immediate decisions and actions, or else choose the most conservative options, while gauging our personal doubts and philosophy for following a simple life path.

Self-doubts are especially annoying and destructive when fast decisions are required. A true example about a soccer player is relevant to mention here. Being put in a breakaway situation, he was carrying the ball forward elegantly. The only obstacle was the goalkeeper, who started to run towards him with a loud roar. The forward's brief loss of confidence and momentum was so clear. His tiny self-doubt (atypical for a 'forward,' especially) made him lose his agility. His minute hesitation (partly stirred by the goalkeeper's rush and roar) just deprived him of a beautiful goal. Instead, he just shot the ball into the goalkeeper's hands impotently, instead of all the open space in the net. In life, we face these situations all the time when others intimidate us fast and easily due to our momentary surges of self-doubts.

In most cases, our self-doubts result from our interactions and communication with others and the authority they impose upon us. We feel more vulnerable in their presence and cannot think as clearly and objectively as when we are alone. We may also have a weakness to resist someone, because we love or need him/her. Yet, this love and need is most likely a sign of our self-doubt and dependence on others. A plausible remedy is to pre-establish our position before confronting the individual we love or fear his/her authority—without becoming aggressive or arrogant, of course. In order to minimize the influence and effects of others on our wishes and decisions, we should first come to terms with our doubts. Otherwise, we would always be swayed away from our positions when we face people who like to exploit or manipulate us or those whom we love. We then regret, and feel frustrated with, our weakness later.

The irony is that while our self-respect and self-image suffer from our perceptions of other individuals' authority over us, we doubt the power of individuals who lack an aura of authority. We see their self-doubt as a debilitating feature of one's personality. Our tendency is to do not respect people as much when they do not reflect some authority or assertiveness. However, honouring people's authority does not necessarily mean we like them. On the contrary, we mostly like people who are vulnerable, since we have a better chance of manipulating them or at least associating with their self-doubt and suffering. These are all symptoms of our defects and social conditioning, which affect our perceptions of others and ourselves in relation to them—the following topic: Interpersonal Doubts.

Interpersonal Doubts

Interpersonal doubts arise from our bad (or baffling) experiences in varied relationships, plus our general mistrust in human nature. Viewing our relationships in such negative light is unproductive, of course, though largely warranted, nowadays.

On the positive side of the coin, however, our 'interpersonal doubts' erupts like a personal wisdom if we rather sympathize with humans' defects as their natural weaknesses for grasping and complying with the rules of ethics and integrity. This wisdom can induce a more compassionate perspective of our relationships, as we try to accept people's idiosyncrasies as an undeniable, fixed reality. We might even strive to become somewhat more tolerant of people's deep idiocies along with general pity for humanity.

Naturally, we always try to avoid defective relationships and people, but it is often impractical or impossible to stop socializing, especially with people we love or care about their welfares. At the same time, our misperceptions and ideals can cause havoc.

For example, our persistent idealism for people's perfection and understanding, especially at a large scale amongst the public, is just another personal flaw by itself. That is, instead of keeping our expectations so high about any likely purity in human nature, we could draw on our basic wisdom, driven by our interpersonal doubts, to admit that humans' innate evil and egoism hinder their ability to communicate and cohabit civilly. In fact, we all should somehow accept and find a way around this irresolvable obstacle for finding a realistic solution for humanity.

A basic fact is that we get hurt more ourselves when we try to change people or expect them to be different, i.e., perfect for our liking! It is hard for us to admit our inability to force or influence others to think like us. Even when we accept this fact, most of us still believe that, by logic and discussion, at least the people close to us might eventually learn to think more properly and change themselves. We hope that people convert eventually according to their own convictions even when we cannot play a direct role in convincing them. Maybe they think deeper about what we tell them and see the merits of our advice at last. However, for our sanity's sake, we should stop hoping. We should just lower our expectations, instead of waiting for others to change. Building this mindset at least curbs our anxiety and interpersonal doubts (deep conviction about people's natural evil), while we strive to get less irritated by people's idiocies; or even laugh about it kindly.

We have a natural ability to make this mental adjustment if we can overcome our senses of hostility, false pride, and rivalry. People would still be annoying, but at least we perceive it as a deep social sickness. It is like watching an old black and white movie that can feel annoying, considering all its technical flaws.

Yet, while the defects keep rushing before our eyes throughout the movie, we can still enjoy it if we lower our expectations fast according to an objective new criterion. Accepting new criteria for judging others and situations, living becomes easier or even funnier. We humans have severe personal defects that are often irreparable. Still, many of us also have the talent of adjusting to new thoughts and situations if only we stop being stubborn and resist being too dogmatic and vengeful. The trick is to recognize, through self-awareness, that our efforts to revamp our egoistical mentalities would make our lives much easier for us, too.

Of course, creating new criteria and lowering our expectations just for the sake of tolerating some annoying people or situations is not easy, if not insulting altogether! For example, how can we explain or develop criteria for our doubts about a marriage that suffers from mistrust? Maybe one or both spouses have doubts about the validity of their relationship, but they doubt the viability of other personal options after separation as well. In some cases, partners might even enjoy their physical contacts, but lack mental connection. Therefore, they cannot erase their doubts about their spouses' intentions, while trying to bear each other's guts, too. Many difficult situations like this develop in our lives at home, work, and society and we keep suffering from our doubts about our options as well as our duty to cope. Often, indeed, we suspect people's intentions and their games. Then, we also have doubts about our own level of patience and tolerance needed to keep such relationships without losing our sanity and self-respect.

Nevertheless, finding proper criteria to subdue our egoism and reduce our expectations remains the best remedy for dealing with interpersonal doubts in most difficult relationships, unless a more specific and viable solution presents itself. We often rush to divorce our spouses or quit our jobs as our best options, but these solutions might hurt us even more in the long-run. We often think of these seemingly rational options, but they are most likely only rash conclusions induced by our hurt sentiments and vengeful Egos, which would prove to be so destructive for us in the future.

Once we have satisfied our urges of spite and revenge, we would feel void and empty, now with even less options to build our lives around.

Supernatural Doubts

On top of our struggles with social, personal, and interpersonal doubts noted above, we are burdened with many questions about humans' seemingly special position within the universe. These supernatural doubts comprise of our curiosity about the origin of life, its possible divine nature, and the possibility and kind of our connection to it—all in hopes of some relief from all the hassles of mortal life. We feel obliged to explore the significance and roots of our doubts and curiosities scientifically for finding some meaning for existence beyond our mechanical social perspective. The extensive philosophical thoughts addressed in Volume I of this trilogy (mainly Chapter One) reflect the nature and scope of our supernatural doubts, too. The big success of religions to keep almost all humans in dark is due to our innate supernatural doubts raising our curiosities and boggling our psyches all our lives.

At the same time, we often try to discard mythical phenomena and supernatural thoughts, as we get tired of wasting our energy on mysticism. We abhor our failures to get anywhere with our most natural doubt, i.e., creation, or the possibility of any purpose for existence. We try to elude the shoddy clues or evidences of a real world beyond our perceptions of prevalent social structure. Sometimes, we wonder why our raw curiosities agitate our minds so often. After all, we wish to remain practical about our views of daily life and appear logical in our encounters and thoughts. Yet, our dreary doubts about our vision of reality linger forever, while ignoring them seems rather difficult and unnatural, too.

Nonetheless, wondering about existence is an innate urge that directs many of our thoughts and choices. Trying to suppress this urge would not only cause stress and sufferings, but also deprive us from a minimal touch with our spirits and a bigger reality that stands beyond our flimsy social structure. Obviously, at the end, we still cannot answer most of the questions or elude our doubts about the essence of life, but we achieve two fine goals. **First,** humouring our curiosity regarding the universe gives us a better, simpler, and brighter life outlook despite our irresolvable doubts. We might even realize our nothingness, curb our Egos, and thus live more peacefully. We also get a chance to explore the wisdom that resides deep in our unconscious and the ones that experts and philosophers, excluding religions and spiritual cults, can offer. **Second,** viewing life in a finer perspective helps us transform our confusing, negative doubts (that we misjudge or try to elude) into positive doubts and energy. Thus, we build our spirits to manage our daily challenges and struggles. We develop a wiser lifestyle and grasp the nature of our social, personal, and interpersonal doubts a bit more deeply. We learn to draw energy from Nature.

The five categories of positive doubts (i.e., social, personal, interpersonal, supernatural, and spiritual.) are complementary and interrelated for building and explaining the foundation of our thoughts. Collectively, they indicate how we perceive life and live it. As we are often absorbed and distracted by our artificial habits and pleasures, we do not find the incentive and time to look beyond our limited vision of life. Most people just adopt a religion to fulfil their inner voices and curiosities, since they are too lazy or naive to grasp the meaning of their positive doubts and explore their urges for spirituality on their own. The situation is worse for the mass on this supposedly prolific, compassionate planet. They are facing so much misery and daily challenges of work, war, famine, and family problems that their minds cannot wander and wonder beyond their urgent struggles for survival. Of course, in their busy heads, still the same questions regarding the essence and purpose of living circle, perhaps even stronger, as their sufferings are quite deep and permanent. Yet, despite the ongoing encounter with life's fundamental questions, they have time only for dealing with their urgent needs and challenges of survival. They are too lost and engaged in their daily routines to entertain even the idea of turning their essential and existential questions into positive doubts in order to nurture their outlooks. Yet, for the rest of us luckier people enjoying a higher level of personal freedom and economic welfare, letting society dominate our minds is a definite failure. Merely feeding the prevalent life structure with our greed and neediness is even more pathetic and a crueller crime.

Of course, modern societies impose their own obstacles for nurturing our supernatural curiosities. In fact, modern people get too deeply absorbed in a mechanical and physical life to feel or care about the nagging voices regarding the metaphysical world or the benefits of finding at least some tentative answers about it. They somehow convince their brains that these questions and thoughts are fruitless, irrelevant, and a waste of time. At the other extreme, many of us keep struggling with our doubts, because we cannot get the basic questions about the essence of life out of our heads. All our lives, we feel lost and agitated for our inabilities to relax, while so many absurd questions regarding life burden our exhausted subconscious minds too frequently. Especially, these days, many of us like to know the meaning of life.

The evidence of our efforts to cope with our deep, unrelenting curiosities about our connection to supernatural is all around us in the forms of religions, superstitions, spirituality notions, myths, etc. During humans' rather short history, we have invented and adopted so many shoddy ideologies in search of a better meaning for life to soothe our sufferings. However, we have so far only caused ourselves more confusion and inner conflicts by making odd interpretations about the essence of life or by adopting crude ideologies, such as 'living in the now,' according to our erratic moods and insecurities. Most of us believe, nowadays, that the purpose of human life is to find happiness! So, out of desperation, we seek refuge in extravagance, sexuality, and other exaggerated means of living in search of happiness, simply because no other answer satisfies our curiosities about existence. Our conditioning habits and attachments stop us from finding any other meaning for life. We speculate, theorise, or philosophise many ideologies, sometimes according to scientific evidences and human logic, yet they all remain mythical and contradictory at the end. A big body of scientific knowledge is also accumulated, especially in the last century, about the workings of the universe. However, we are still unable to answer many fundamental questions about life, while our curiosities keep growing and humanity's chance for survival keep declining due to uncontrollable climate and social crises. Thus, we try to suppress these nagging questions somehow and dismiss our supernatural doubts, or even turn them into negative thoughts and cynicism, e.g., atheism. Some use drugs, alcohol, and other artificial stimuli to escape their basic instincts seeking answers about life. In the worst-case scenario, of course, we just adopt a religion to curb our curiosity and sense of helplessness.

The consequence of people's varied approaches to define life and deal with their supernatural doubts is that they have difficulty these days to understand one another and relate effectively. Our inability to resolve all these dilemmas is causing the social chaos we face and suffer from daily. In fact, the extremely wide range of people's interpretations and doubts regarding the nature of the universe and our connection to it—the big picture of existence—is amazing. Naturally, people perceive life differently based on their intelligence, lifestyle, and realism. Yet, it is so depressing to witness these deep mental incongruities causing so much conflict, quarrels, and confusion among humans—mostly due to human ignorance and man-made religions.

As part of our supernatural doubts, we also talk a lot about destiny, which we believe is some form of fate, luck, or karma. It seems that we are in a kind of joint venture with God, in the sense that we make many decisions and pursue many challenges, while we ponder and depend on the mercy of some supernatural power to support our decisions and challenges. Our religious teachings definitely have a lot to do with this type of (tenuous) mentality and approach. No religion dares to say which attitude is more realistic, i.e., a rigid planning for our lives or depending merely on God's mercy. So we are told to do both! *God will help you if you help yourself* is the common suggestion (hidden scapegoat) by religions. Yet, even this notion about the 'joint venture' with God sounds perplexing and intimidating, to some of us at least! Then, our faith in fate also reflects our personal experiences of certain events and coincidences happening to us so miraculously, which we cannot attribute to any other source other than fate and the interference of a supernatural power watching over us.

We can never fathom destiny, but might get a sense of it from those subtle clues that emerge from our experiences and the way our spirits occasionally make us *feel* connected to some obscure power. Naturally, the closer we come to our souls through self-awareness, the more we witness and accept the role of destiny in our lives. We can never overcome our doubts about the nature and role of destiny, but we can feel and use the positive energy that results from putting some faith in it. We might even stop doubting (and accept) our triviality within the universe and the fact that all parts and particles of life are somehow interrelated. Although humans are such an infinitesimal piece of this grand phenomenon, we are still affected and driven by the same forces of Nature and rules of existence. Although we cannot observe these inherent connections, many people can fathom profound meanings and explanations infinite folds superior to our immense boundaries of science, imagination, logic, and thoughts—way beyond what our Egos can ever envision. Therefore, destiny may simply be the offshoot of all these innate correlations between human conscious and the universe.

Overall, our relentless thoughts and doubts about supernatural phenomena can affect us in two opposite manners. If we judge their peculiarities lightly and naïvely, instead of taking them as clues about other possible dimensions of existence, we simply subdue our spirits and psyches. Alternatively, our doubts start to become positive and productive if we nurture our curiosities and let life's odd clues arouse our imagination and doubts, to explore and envision other dimensions of being. We can try to achieve this enlightenment through philosophy and spirituality, on our own, without recourse to religions. And we can do all this search mainly for bringing a relative sense of purpose and tranquility into our lives.

Spiritual Doubts

While supernatural doubts are general regardless of our spiritual beliefs, spiritual doubts are for defining the nature and purpose of our *connection* to the universe or God. We question (doubt) our divinity and even humans' basic capacity for divinity in general.

In our minds, we have a mishmash of concepts about afterlife, God, religions, and spirituality. We have grown up with religious models that proclaim God as the creator of life, who gives us both a physical form and a non-physical identity we call our soul. We are exposed to these ideas even if not born into a religious family. Some people claim contacts with their spirits and some offer evidences of spiritual existence. However, at best, all these claims remain doubtful for most of us with good commonsense. They are speculations and models we have built with our limited intelligence and gawky perceptions. Still, we cannot deny that some possible truths or significance might exist for some of these thoughts and imaginations. We cannot refute the chance of some type of reality, including afterlife and human immortality, beyond our perceptions.

As an *instinctual* urge, our sense of divinity raises our *logical* 'spiritual doubts' to explore our essence as a human in general. Meanwhile, our feelings and doubts about spirituality instigate our curiosity about the chance of afterlife and a fuller dimension of being, too. We wonder about our connection to another form of life or the world of realities that engulf our minds, bodies, souls, and perceptions. Has a super being created us and watches over us? Are we only what we are in this world, just a biological form per se? Or our physical existence in this world is only a shadow of what we really are? We are both optimistic about our immortality and fearful of death. Only fools might guarantee or trust eternity, thus we remain doubtful regarding our destiny after death. Even dogmatic individuals face regular surges of doubts despite their hypocritical persistence about certain convictions. Religious fanatics also reveal their fundamental, hidden doubts by committing all kinds of outrageous sins, while insisting on God's punishment of sinners. Everybody loses his/her blind faith in God (and begins to doubt all the nonsense about eternity), at least on some peculiar moments of truthful contemplation. This happens after we suffer enough or when our sinful urges override our beliefs at last. In fact, doubtlessness is usually only a *show* for justifying a radical life philosophy that supports our demented desires and innate weaknesses. In all, our doubts about spirituality have been driven by our subtle scepticism about both the idea of immortality and the purpose of our daily deeds.

In our pressing lives, most of us deal with our spiritual doubts in two ways: 1) We perceive or practise spirituality *merely* as a (defence) mechanism created by humans only for soothing their souls. We might value it somewhat according to our upbringing and intelligence without appreciating the purpose of our nagging doubts about spirituality. We ignore our curiosity about this high personal need in all humans and never satisfy it properly. So we feel unfulfilled. 2) We stick to our religions (or dogmatic beliefs) blindly in the fear of mortality. In both cases, we lose the chance of exploring spirituality personally. We do not experience it truly as a tool for freeing our spirit, validating our daily routines, and knowing our 'self.'

Alternatively, we can be creators of our thoughts, actions, and feelings, if we learn spirituality personally, instead of rejecting it outright or accepting it blindly in the form of a religion or a cult. We can sense divine feelings when we do things for others who need our help; when we go for a stroll in Nature and connect to simple forms of life that surround us; and when masterpieces by other humans mesmerize us. These experiences reveal our radiant spirits within higher spheres of sensation and awareness. Some of us can be in touch with our spirits much better and more often than others can. This capacity evolves thru the power of positive doubts that stir profound thoughts, sacred experiments, and a zeal to delve deeper into these states of divinity. These fine sensations are valid signs about human spirits' existence and their chances to explore spirituality. We cannot find spirituality in churches and mosques merely because people gather in those places for some artificial rituals. Rather, we can find spirituality in our backyards, in our hearts, in the genius of Beethoven, in devoted people like Mother Theresa, in colourful fields, in deep woods, in the flight of a seagull, in magnificent mountains, and in creations of many masters who have enriched our souls and thoughts.

Spirituality is not something to depend on others to explain to us, and it is not restricted to afterlife topics and goals, either. Spirituality also is not far-fetched dogmatic beliefs that religions and cults try to push into our deprived heads. Spirituality is just a basic, sincere, personal experience beyond global description. It starts with a sense of selflessness.

We can exit our physical form occasionally to experience a non-physical existence even if we are not still dead. Our positive doubts and thoughts can lead to such creative visions of existence and our connectivity to it. Within this sphere of spirituality, we grasp a sense of selflessness and responsibility to all other facets of life and their rights for existence in their own ways. These kinds of experiences not only enrich our physical lives, but also support our positive doubts about the possibility of our eventual rise to higher spiritual spheres we have already visited on certain occasions. We can personally create these divine experiences, beliefs, and the ultimate form of transcendence by exploring our positive doubts about spirituality. Appendix C on page 345 shows our physical and spiritual dimensions and their connections to the universe and society in line with our doubts regarding all these relationships.

Doubts' Natural Fusion

This chapter distinguishes five categories of positive doubts for explaining their specific natures. We can train our brains to focus on one or a mix of them when we set out to meditate and explore the nature of our doubts and the means of handling a particular situation. Meanwhile, during our doubtfulness, we eagerly endure the agony of self-exploration in hopes of making better decisions, living more productively, and maybe even finding a peaceful path of life to guide us for the duration of our existence. It would not be prudent for this book to delve into the complexity of our doubts and sorting out a large assortment of demanding doubts and dilemmas crowding our lives almost every day. Rather, a quick mention about the interworking of our personal (positive) doubts seemed warranted as a conclusion. As evident from the public's prevalent erratic moods in society, the burden of many interwoven doubts, even positive ones, to keep our psyches and spirits in sync and happy is huge, especially since our spirits and psyches sense all our doubts simultaneously all the time. Only when we train our brains to distinguish and analyse our doubts separately based on their natures, we give our psyches and spirits a chance to relax and grow as well. It is surely a big challenge and mission to gain a collective perspective about society, self, people, nature, and divinity all in a well-balanced mindset and practise it on a daily basis as well. Appendix C demonstrates the immensity and complexity of philosophical thoughts and positive doubts occupying us at least subconsciously a lifetime.

While this chapter emphasized on the role and burdens of positive doubts and dilemmas in human life, the next chapter will delineate the effects of our negative doubts and the much bigger load of burdens they place on our spirits and psyches every day. Nevertheless, grasping the natures and effects of our doubts, in particular the negative ones, is fruitful for self-awareness in hopes of boosting our spirits and psyches as well.

CHAPTER FIFTEEN
Negative Doubts (Vibes)

Negative doubts (both psychological and logical) can be studied in the same five categories (subjects) listed on page 275 about positive doubts and discussed in the last chapter. 'Positive doubts' encourage us to analyse ourselves, others, and the universe more closely to get a clearer picture about them and come to terms with the mandate of existence. Negative doubts (vibes) obstruct our thinking, decision-making, and acting. They are distinguishable mostly by their natures and effects on our outlooks, moods, and reactions. They stir depression and indecision, contrary to positive doubts that raise our curiosity and awareness. Generally, personal doubts can help us if we delve into our inner self to find a simple lifestyle and philosophy for eluding life's traps. Otherwise, they turn negative and cause self-doubts and cynicism.

Actually, an ongoing, stressful fight continues in our psyches between our positive and negative doubts (vibes) during our daily encounters and anytime we ponder sad social realities. Luckily, positive doubts (vibes) can give us some stamina and optimism to build a balanced life outlook and fight the effects of our negative doubts, pessimism, and helplessness. Still, a big challenge for us is to, i) distinguish the nature of our doubts, and ii) learn how to cultivate positive doubts to curb the burdens of the negative ones.

Negative doubts (including self-doubt) are symptoms of low self-esteem, chronic cynicism, and analytical disability due to a mix of:
- Personal defects (genetic or acquired)
- Bad personal experiences
- Negative outlook on life
- Mental weaknesses
- External factors and forces (seeming facts of life)

Again, for building a better sense, view positive and negative doubts as 'vibes' that we feel during our encounters with odd situations or people, or perhaps even when we look at a person or hear his/her perspective on a topic. We get these vibes regularly, but then we might recall and ponder them more deeply later. In particular, after so much detail about these vibes in this trilogy, we might distinguish and analyse them more consciously during special moments of reflection. In fact, contemplating our positive vibes raises our self-awareness, which helps us do many worthy things for others and ourselves accordingly.

Grasping and defeating our negative doubts (including self-doubt) need a rather magical stimulus to change our mentalities. Naturally, this is a hard mission, since only a long self-awareness process can help us revamp our old mentalities and beloved life values. The process begins when we question our life purposes and routines thoughtfully outside our cynical beliefs with patience and sincerity. This radical attitude in itself erupts as a 'positive thought or doubt,' which initiates the self-awareness process. This sounds like the chicken and egg cliché! How can we concentrate on any type of positive thoughts or doubts when our defects and self-doubt are crippling us? How can we raise our spirits when suffering from depression and negative doubts? We feel helpless, tired, vulnerable, and pressed by volatile, sneaky external forces. Our genetic defects incite and control our judgments and minds, too, and we feel overwhelmed by negative thoughts and vibes. All along, people's regular malice and lies obstruct our efforts for positivism, self-awareness, and discovering the roots, effects, and meanings of our negative doubts to find likely remedies.

Self-doubt's peculiarities noted on pages 283-5 might reveal the sources of our negative doubts, and thus help us make mental adjustments about our distrusts, cynicism, and paranoia—all thru self-awareness and building a solid foundation of thoughts and life philosophy. After all, personal incentive and commitment are the key for turning our negative doubts and thoughts into positive ones without getting carried away by raw positive thinking ideas.

Then again, distinguishing and applying our doubts requires a belief system developed slowly within a simple life philosophy around our inner strengths, including stamina, willpower, logic, objectivity, confidence, morality, analytical ability, and wisdom. Positive thinking per se cannot satisfy these stiff requirements for reforming a person's psyche. We might have lost touch with all these fine traits and become, for example, a ruthless individual incapable of using his/her basic sense of justice, fairness, etc. Yet, self-analysis and awareness can help us rebuild our mindsets and overcome our negative doubts that aggravate the excruciating dilemmas of life. We just need a more authentic value system and lifestyle along with a solid platform and keen interest to gauge our perceptions of life in a more fundamental and honest manner.

In all, grasping and defeating our negative doubts is the only venue to build a peaceful life and successful career, but also boost our spirits with higher wisdom and likely enlightenment.

Our Doubts' Ultimate Wisdom...

Realistically, though, building the incentive and commitment to rebuild our mindsets and resolve our doubts is not straightforward due to varied innate urges manipulating our psyches. We all wish to behave and look assertive, but we cannot push the process until we understand the true nature and roots of our doubts the same way we should know the root of our depression before trying to find a cure for it. We should, especially, realize that our varied positive doubts cannot be fully resolved, considering their nature and crucial role for creative thinking. For example, smart people doubt God's existence forever inherently. This is a wise positive doubt to cherish, since we benefit from envisioning *a kind (of)* God as a pillar of our personal spirituality, while still doubting His nature forever. Even most religious fanatics or atheists have their moments of doubt about God, if not a subtle scepticism regarding their certitude altogether. Resolving this doubt is not necessary or wise, anyway, as it avails a divine venue for building an effective, evolving foundation of thoughts and life philosophy. After all, being atheists or blindly faithful to a religion has been ruining humans and societies' spirits. A group is both when they act like fanatical believers sometimes and then become atheists on some days, all depending on their needs, moods, or doubts. We hate to admit that we can never be sure about so many things, so we keep fooling ourselves by accepting erratic conclusions and circling subconsciously forever within the doubt/no-doubt cycle. Thus, we must cherish the wisdom of our positive doubts to fathom life.

At the same time, we often have many negative doubts that need solutions soon. We might have doubts about our 'dead-end jobs,' 'life priorities,' or 'relationships.' We should not live with negative doubts or tolerate a cyclical process of doubtfulness and certitude forever. The anxiety of not knowing the nature of our niggling doubts hurts, too, as mixing our positive and negative doubts prevents us from building our convictions. For example, when a marital relationship is not working, we go through a long period of doubts about: i) the validity of our reasons for labelling our relationship irreconcilable, ii) the consequences of divorce and having a single life, iii) the chance of finding another person to replace at least some of the simple conveniences of the existing marriage, and many other similar doubts and questions. We live with these doubts and their anxieties for many years, while the direct problems and agonies of such relationships linger as well.

Volume III of this trilogy reveals the enormity of our doubts and dilemmas regarding education, work, organizations, career, marriage, parenthood, life, etc. Sadly, it takes a long time before we can possibly resolve some of our doubts sporadically. The load of doubts and dilemmas we always carry is heavy and they have different levels of significance and priority, too. The amount of thoughts and energy we put into them and the level of anxiety we bear in the process is huge.

Sometimes, we seem to succeed in overcoming our doubts about an issue. We feel relief, confidence, and certitude, but soon somehow lose faith in our judgment as our doubts sneak back into our heads. During these cycles of overcoming and reviving our doubts repeatedly, we deteriorate our self-image and spirit, as we suspect our mental stability to fathom life and make proper judgments. We resent our inability to commit our psyches to a set thought-process and life-path. In particular, during some periods of our lives, e.g., adolescence, we face many peculiar dilemmas and feel besieged by uncertainty. Weighing our options regarding any of those dilemmas during such stressful times is exhausting. Our lingering anxiety makes us feel helpless and possibly even cause mental disorder. In such debilitating condition, we lose our power to focus on each dilemma separately and patiently.

Yet, analysing our doubts is the only way to regain effective control of our minds and lives. Our wisdom and commonsense must somehow help us decide about the nature of our doubts one by one and pinpoint the ones that need a *rather* fast resolution and the ones that can expand our outlook and knack for creative thinking. On the other hand, self-doubt, as a special category of negative doubts, should be handled distinctly and firmly fast as noted on pages 283-5.

We might compare the mental state of a chronic doubtless (dogmatic) person with the situation of a (thoughtful) person who eventually overcomes his legitimate doubts about a special issue. The former's certitude comes from naivety and egoistic pitfalls, as s/he has hardly entertained the likelihood of alternatives and facts beyond what s/he has always pursued naively. In the latter case, however, the person's doubtlessness has evolved only after building certain beliefs and a valid mindset for supporting his/her conclusions after years of reflections and prophesizing around his/her doubts, e.g., regarding God, before his/her mind is finally satisfied with an explanation for his/her questions and dilemmas. Yet, at the end of those exercises comes a meaningful conviction grown slowly in a long process of doubtfulness. Now it becomes a true belief. Therefore, we can say that true beliefs come only at the end of profound doubts. Our doubts make us search for the truths that gradually build up our beliefs.

We can actually detect and associate the bizarre relationships among Ego, doubt, and beliefs in the four stages of aging. During childhood when our mind is not tainted by Ego, we are doubtful about everything and rely on our parents' to answer the questions boggling our minds, while we really do not have any established beliefs or life outlook. During early adulthood, suddenly our Ego soars and we feel the urge to be sure about everything. We think (or like to pretend) that we have all the answers, and thus we rush to develop many strange, raw beliefs starting with the fact that our parents' beliefs and thoughts are outmoded and obsolete.[‡‡]

In our middle ages, we gain some experience and suffer the consequences of our naivety, quirks, and dogmatism in the earlier stages of our lives. We now have some fundamental questions to answer for ourselves and we know that we cannot rely on others to provide the right answers. With our Ego somewhat abating, we become seriously doubtful about life, its meaning, and our role. During these years, we really do not have any set beliefs, because we are doubtful about things and do not build beliefs naively for the sake of having some. Luckily, we have learned some good lessons in life and finally realized the absurdity of our certitude regarding certain beliefs and attitude. Our wisdom demands that we support our beliefs with more solid reasoning and thoughts.

[‡‡] Despite teenagers' tendency to behave egotistically, in fact they are overwhelmed internally by all kinds of doubts that they actively resist to acknowledge (under the influence of their Egos). They disallow their doubts to emerge for contemplation. This mental inconsistency is the cause of further inner conflict and anxiety for them.

In the last stage of our growth, the wiser and luckier elderly finally overcome (or come to terms with) their doubts, or at least some of the major ones. At this time, their Ego stabilizes as they think they have finally found a bit of the truth. Due to their sour experiences with doubtfulness during their middle age, they might succeed in turning their lingering doubts into fundamental beliefs that can carry them during their remaining years.

Settling our doubts brings relief along with a set of beliefs and principles. No more wrestling with so many painful feelings and thoughts after we settle on a plausible resolution for a puzzling dilemma. We reach a set of humble conclusions about main life realities, along with determination and confidence as soon as we balance our clashing thoughts, accept a stoic lifestyle, and prepare ourselves for its possible consequences. At the end of our doubts, we put a stagnant period of our life behind and move on with commitment and a fresher perspective. By settling our *negative* doubts with divine reservation and resignation, we see the need, and find the energy, to act. And by grasping our *positive* doubts, we feel enlightened and peaceful. We have made a decision and a long-term plan. We should indeed feel proud of turning a few of our fundamental doubts into beliefs and philosophies that can stir our life in a positive direction more objectively. Hooray!

Overall, a few conclusions can be reached: First, we can learn to distinguish positive and negative doubts. Second, we can grasp and internalize the messages that come from our positive doubts and the options we choose. Third, we should come to terms with our doubts in a timely manner somehow. For example, we should decide to either leave our nagging, uncompromising spouse, or still try to find ways to improve, or bear, our marriage, or at least determine that we would never find the information we seek to overcome our doubts. Fourth, we could try to learn and rely on our positive doubts to circumvent the inconveniences and pitfalls of decisions or convictions that result from resolving our negative doubts. For example, we might eventually decide that our marital relationship cannot be improved to a desired level. This would be a positive conclusion for a negative doubt that has caused us so much stress a long time. This would end our struggles for making our spouse understand our viewpoints or to adjust her/his attitude in the way we like. Therefore, we can relax and let go of our Ego pushing, or at least hoping, to improve things logically with lots of flexibility. Then again, we must also learn and get ready to live bravely with possible harsh consequences of settling our doubts. Hopefully, we make all the right decisions at the end, instead of changing our position erratically forever.

Naturally, our beliefs and philosophies are mostly unique and personal, as they are built according to our particular logic, needs, doubts, personal attributes and conditioning, intelligence, genetic characteristics, and psychological defects, during the long process of grinding our doubts into beliefs.

Personally, settling my lifelong doubts about the world's basic realities has brought me certain beliefs that I would like to share some of them with you:

1. The deep impurity of human nature is no longer a doubt in my mind. I believe that no human being is even remotely capable of gaining the purity or wisdom that our convoluted imagination of humanity likes to suggest. We surely do good deeds and enjoy many generous and angelic experiences during our lives or at least witness them in others. However, we will never be free from our satanic urges and needs, thus cannot fit the image of piety that we desire to see in human race, let alone gaining the holiness that any wise God can expect from us. We do not like to see our own defects that cause us serious damage. Yet, we are too impatient with other people's flaws that pain us too much. Thus, our inner conflicts and endless personality clashes ruin our spirits, too. The double jeopardy is that we do not know how we hurt ourselves personally and how much we suffer from our desires to rely on others and love such phony, evil people. Certainly, moments of relief also erupt in our lives sometimes when others show mercy or when our selfless love invigorates us.

2. Our relationships can never be as complete and civil as we expect them to be. This can be considered an extension of the previous conclusion about human nature in general, except that, in relationships, the imperfections of two intimate individuals clash much faster and compound the impossibility of reconciliation and teamwork. Our social values and structure support the expansion of Ego, which inhibits spouses' grasp of their real needs and zeal for compassion. We are becoming growingly alienated towards one another, while our perceptions of life's realities and our true needs get more complex. Under these circumstances, the chance for a good marriage is like drawing two pieces of a jigsaw puzzle from amongst millions of pieces and praying that they fit together just by luck. We keep turning these odd pieces around, push their corners, and press them against each other, hoping they would click together. However, all these efforts only bend the corners and destroy the edges, and eventually the pieces get ruined and out of shape. We must be extremely lucky to find even a relative match, and since this is a rarity, we must prepare ourselves for the challenges of companionships on the one hand, and finding other means of compensating for this shortfall in our lives on the other hand. Mostly, we should learn the art of living independently and alone when necessary.

3. The vanity of our socioeconomic systems and the extreme likelihood of our doomed destiny has been a depressing theme throughout this trilogy. Unfortunately, this gloomy destiny seems more certain and unavoidable every day, in my opinion, despite the sadness that my pessimism gives me. Thus, I do not wish to dwell on this matter any more beyond everything I have already said in this trilogy. I am sad enough about this matter already!

4. The universe, God, Nature—or any name we might choose to describe the superpower responsible for human existence—is an inexplicable reality except for its symptoms that we might feel personally only outside religious influences. It flows through us and manifests in our delicate thoughts, inspirations, compassion, passion, perseverance, tolerance, and spirits. Grasping our 'self' gives us a better appreciation of this magical power as if it guides our spirits. Completing many projects successfully, including this trilogy, has been driven by this inspirational source, I believe. It seems to surge inside me as fine thoughts or sensations in timely manners for special purposes. Many of my theories grouped and conversed by certain words and paragraphs have felt like timely inspirations through *my mysterious muse*. In fact, she deserves all the credit! (So, if some or all of this trilogy's discussions sound gibberish to you, just blame her! She did all the editing too!)

Not knowing how destiny, luck, and this supernatural power are interrelated, or are the same, does not deter me from settling (coming to terms with) my doubts about their enigmatic reality. They merely constitute the parameters of our tentative existence for whatever purposes. Ironically, these beliefs have evolved and helped me despite some related, unresolved doubts. For example, I still have major doubts regarding any notions of reincarnation, afterlife, or the existence of any God in the format that we have been conditioned to envision. Still, I do not wish to deny a very remote possibility of some form of non-physical existence for humans, which we are unable to even speculate about its nature.

5. The value of our experiences for our children was a major question and doubt in my mind when I began writing this trilogy many years ago. I sincerely thought that perhaps some of our struggles to understand life, social structure, and opportunities for a fulfilling existence could be documented and proven useful to our children. Now, I have overcome my doubt and believe that my children, like most other humans, are not interested in what others think. They are as much doubtful about our experiences and conclusions as we are all sceptical about the viability of the social structure imposed upon them. They see us as failures and causes of the present mayhem. They think that if we had had any brains, the present world situation would not have been in such a mess. They want to disassociate themselves with our grasp of life as much as we ourselves struggle with our own doubts about the purity of human thoughts, intentions, and nature. I can live with this belief, because I understand my role more clearly now and do not have to doubt it anymore. I do not have to wonder and worry whether I have done enough for my children or not, either. Accordingly, I acknowledge the remote, but still possible, use of this trilogy for expanding children's minds around the globe about life and living. In this regard, Peter Elbow's advice about what we can hope readers learn from our teachings is relevant:

"If your readers have a stake in what you are arguing against, you cannot take straightforward persuasion as your goal. You must resist your impulse to change their beliefs. You have to set your sights much lower. The best you can hope for—and it is hoping for a great deal—is to get your readers just to understand your point of view even while not changing theirs in the slightest. If you can get readers actually to entertain or experience your position for just a moment, you have done a wonder, and your best chance of getting them to do so is not by asking them to believe or adopt your point of view at all." Writing With Power, Peter Elbow, Oxford University Press, New York, 1981, page 203.

Therefore, the best I can hope for is that my children care to read this book patiently and spend enough time to grasp the meanings that I have tried *for years* to convey in my messages. And the best I like to hope for also is that they would overcome their natural urges to contradict any new ideas contrary to the youths' modern values. I hope I have done a *wonder*, according to Peter Elbow's standard at least! Maybe I could also hope that some of you dear readers, who find my points in this trilogy useful, possibly go find and convince my kids or grandchildren to read it as well!

The main point suggested in this chapter is that the wisdom of our doubts rejuvenates our beliefs and raises our resilience, while *boosting our decisions' quality.*

Boosting Our Decisions' Quality

Sadly, most aspects of life, including the birth itself, are imposed upon us and we have little power to elude these constraints—the seeming realities of being! These obscure facts and forces dictate our wellbeing and the framework we can function within, too. In fact, only good decisions and resilience might help us survive and fit within these rough life limitations with some pride and peace. Otherwise, our lives become messier with more disappointments, stress, and sufferings. In particular, our decisions and plans after a long period of analysing our 'doubts' reflect our finer impression of the world and strategy for making important mental changes.

Sometimes, the sacred wisdom of our positive doubts shows in our decisions. The obstacle is that we often ignore our pressing positive doubts, as they seem to be only increasing our stress by demanding deep contemplations about the meaning and purpose of our lives and plans. Therefore, our chronic passivity hinders our self-awareness and learning from our inner voices. We lose our sacred chances to save our souls. We do not give our positive doubts and thoughts enough chance to flourish, to internalize our rare grasps of reality. We suffocate those flares of awakening that sometimes glitter in our cluttered brains in hopes of boosting our spirits. Sometimes, the truth wants to manifest and we ignorantly bypass our chances. For example, we might go to a dear friend's funeral who has passed away unexpectedly due to his physician's misdiagnosis. During the ceremony, we sit and ponder gloomily our precious memories together and then realize how vulnerable we all are and how unpredictable life is. We gauge our values and philosophies, but doubt their meanings or points. We might even feel a need for major fast changes in our lifestyles and mindsets.

This depressing experience appears to open up a window to new life horizons if we can internalize those positive doubts. The moment of 'truth revealing itself' erupts from these experiences to assess who we are and what we are doing. We might decide to adjust our attitude and curb our Egos. Sadly, though, we do not stay with these streams of thoughts and feelings long enough to absorb them fully. In a few days, if not hours, we allow external distractions disrupt our refreshing, dynamic thoughts or forget our pledges gradually in the midst of our daily hustle and bustle. We let our priorities change again and old habits and thoughts take over. We return to our routine problems and pleasures, negative doubts, and forget all about the message of the truth that our friend's death was trying to convey. We let these blissful flickers of positive doubts fade away due to our attachments to the luring social symbols and our demented lifestyles filled with well-rooted negative doubts in our psyches.

Sometimes, we misread and mistreat the message hidden in our positive doubts. For example, we use the sad experience of a friend or family member's death to justify our negative doubts (cynicism) and weaknesses. We question the point of our struggles and pains by a narrow aspect of the message to become more careless and reckless. We misread and mistreat the idea of *curbing our raw ambitions and less worrying* by dismissing our personal responsibilities. Surely, how we read our doubts and thoughts also affects their positive or negative effects for guiding us towards a diviner or darker path of life. Our hasty misinterpretations merely confuse our psyches and obstruct our capacity for clear thinking. They reflect our fears, naivety, and shallow personality.

Accordingly, many of our positive doubts turn into negativity and bad vibes when we do not grasp the right messages in them. We mostly abuse them to fall deeper into our addictions, seek more pleasure, or become lazier and looser, instead of realizing the need for building a viable set of life purposes and actions.

When we face some dilemmas and doubts, we feel helpless and become passive and idle, instead of delving into self-analysis and contemplations. Thus, instead of expanding our life horizon thru some positive doubts, we let our negative vibes and cynicism stir self-imposed depression. We become crippled and indecisive. We bypass the opportunity of turning these debilitating conditions into constructive thoughts that incite more activity and creativity.

Appreciating the messages of our positive doubts can instigate our search for finer ways of living and thinking—and for gauging our negative doubts and thoughts. This hard mental transformation requires some efforts and ingenuity, though. To overcome our self-doubts and elude socioeconomic rules and domination, we should work harder with a positive attitude and expect lesser. For instance, many of us crave self-employment to relieve ourselves from the tyranny of organization work and the negative doubts it adds to our psyches. Still, finding self-employment and earning a decent living need lots of insight, risks, sacrifice, and willingness to be satisfied with less.

Taking passive decisions (by ignoring our inner voices and positive vibes) and hoping the issues or questions fade away on their own reflects our apathy or irresponsibility. We hope to elude a lingering inner conflict by ignoring it, at least for now. We try to live in the now in hopes of suffocating our doubts and their psychological burdens. However, in reality, we continue to carry our doubts, both positive and negative ones, in our subconscious. And they would continue to irritate us now and forever no matter how much we pretend to be living in the now. Any vibe, positive or negative, is overwhelming and stirs anxiety and depression if ignored. Even positive doubts stir deep inner conflict and unrest, although both our doubtfulness and indecision might indeed feel justified. We cannot simply force some thoughts or questions out of our minds forever with the excuse of not having the required information or evidence for a reasonable judgment and decision. Laziness gives our negative vibes lots of nutrition to spread their roots in our psyches and cripple us.

A Chance for Personal Salvation

Most of us feel trapped within life's uncertainties and agonies, while societies' rules and values augment our stress and disability to detect and face our personality limitations. Then, these negative vibes spread deeper in our psyches and deflate our spirits further.

Probably, the only way out of this vicious loop is to digest the points raised in this and last chapters to find a finer life path with lesser stress on raw ambitions and relentless struggles for living. For one thing, we could certainly review our criteria of happiness and focus on finding contentment and tranquility per se. We can try to build 'self' driven goals and 'self' reliance, instead of only imitating the mainstream in our doomed cultures in search of more pleasures and sexuality. Naturally, all doubts (both positive and negative) have psychological effects of their own (including stress and a sense of helplessness) in line with our mindsets at any life stage. Even our positive doubts cause stress until we use them for self-awareness and adjusting our mentalities. Otherwise, they remain as self-imposed limitations crippling us forever.

Although most of our routine decisions are subject to the rules of society, some more potent forces in the universe mandates our spirits and might help us subdue social pressures on us through meditation and self-cleansing. Our spirits can prosper if our 'self' grows slowly during our efforts to become a better being with big humility. Ideally, we might also inject a sense of humour into our lives to enliven the tiny, uptight worlds around and within us. In fact, we might even develop a strong character to laugh life off. A basic sense of humour curbs our arrogance and makes living ten folds easier, after all.

We must go through life and defend ourselves civilly mainly for bearing the growing social and living pains. This mandate is *most likely* an unfortunate consequence of existence as far as our current findings indicate, although maybe someday we humans find a viable means of justifying our being!! For now, however, human existence is as undefined as animals' is. Maybe we know better someday, but have not yet! Still, we can also make specific decisions that focus merely on boosting our spirits and resilience to achieve some personal growth that every human being seeks inherently along with a drive for self-actualization.

Anyhow, our best chance for personal salvation and enduring life's pains and humiliations, nowadays, is to boost our spirits and make our best decisions in a timely manner for managing our needs, ambitions, interactions, and relationships.

Making any major life decision curbs the anxiety of duelling with our doubts for so long. We feel ready to move on with high hopes and perseverance regardless of the likely outcomes, though some flares of uncertainty and anticipation still prick our minds occasionally. We might try to imagine and prepare for peculiar outcomes or situations that could surprise us and ruin our temper, confidence, and faith, especially after doing our homework with due diligence and making seemingly good decisions. The more permanent and deeper the effects of our decisions, and the more sincere our commitment to their success, e.g., in a marriage, the more their failures feel disheartening and painful, of course.

Understanding spiritualism and learning how to build a higher consciousness through self-awareness and positive doubts seem to offer a much better means of managing our frustrating lives and negative doubts that just keep rising in our doomed societies! Then again, so much personal efforts for survival also reignite the old cliché about the role of fate in shaping our lives and how we should envision and handle this historical, lingering dilemma in human life, i.e., the role of fate. Our repeated experiences around some hints about fate cannot be ignored totally, after all!

Most likely our life experiences reveal that our decisions have been ultimately subject to the rules of the universe. Thus, it helps to keep some kind of faith in fate without losing our zeal for good decision-making. After all, the rules of Nature surely supersede the superficial laws of man, which are mainly for protecting and promoting our selfish needs. We seem to have the upper hand by the way we pollute and destroy Nature. However, the inherent laws of Nature and the forces of the universe always dictate the outcomes. We are connected to the laws of Nature more than we are part of our societies and the artificial rules and values of man. The only problem is that we do not appreciate this link truly in line with the amazing inner strengths within humans, nor do we make enough efforts to understand the power of our spirits and insights. If we did, we might come to different conclusions and decisions about our convoluted existence and sad lifestyles.

Of course, deep down, we also mistrust destiny's goodwill on a regular basis, especially when we endure so much agony in life every day after making our conscious and diligent decisions with immense faith. Thus, dealing with this lingering doubt, regardless of our strong beliefs and life philosophies, is another requirement, nonetheless. We often reach some level of pessimism about fate after facing major failures, sour personal experiences, endless social pressures, unfairness, pains, and people's apathy. We ask our spirits, "Why did not God make it happen as we asked or at least show some mercy?" Sometimes, we might simply give up trusting these intangible realities in an alleged 'real world.' This topic has been reviewed in a couple of places in this book. The bottomline is that nobody can ascertain destiny's role or how it operates and affects our lives beyond personal clues that most of us get sometimes. Thus, only we can make just a personal sense about fate and its possible role regarding our beliefs, decisions, and positive doubts!

Ultimately, while it feels essential to believe in a divine power directing our fate, it is more important to always take on a serious responsibility and role as an objective, proactive decision-maker, especially regarding major life decisions, which are stressed in Volume III. This mentality would help us mitigate our deep (and often warranted) cynicism about destiny due to incessant painful experiences and depression. More importantly, we could learn to rely on our ability to control our lives through inner strengths and initiatives along with a moderate faith in fate in the form of a positive doubt. Actually, destiny appears to work so much better in conjunction with our full awareness and constant participation. Maybe our personal high consciousness is actually connected to the universe's consciousness, after all!?

Surely, we all love to speculate on so many possibilities and remain hopeful to soothe our spirits perhaps! Still, these inspiring warning clues do not occur to us at right times or we ignore them, so we often make our decisions emotionally and arrogantly, hurt others, and then face odd outcomes and lifelong disappointments. This fine topic will be elaborated further in the next chapter

Overall, it is still wiser to, i) develop the right decision criteria for running our lives on a finer path of life away from superficial norms, ii) make proactive, timely decisions, iii) modify a decision later if possible and necessary, and, iv) never blame ourselves or others in the hindsight for unexpected results of earlier decisions. We should merely learn some lessons for future. Self-pity for our failures and depression would only waste the mental energy and creativity we need to move forward. Losing our nerves or fussing over bad decisions would not make us wiser for future decisions. Blaming others for our decisions is especially pathetic, although we might wish to blame fate or God a little for fun! If we do not do our due diligence for our decisions (the first three rules noted above) or let other people's undue influence taint our judgment, only we are responsible for the outcome, nevertheless. In fact, all these cautionary points are also for reiterating the importance of staying realistic and proactive with our decisions at the outset.

One major principle always applies, in particular: egotism and domination, as prevalent decision criteria, nowadays, do not raise our wisdom and decision qualities. Only our well-nurtured spirit and sincere desire for a sacred connection with the universe can help us master our doubts and decisions. The phrase "I told you so" is especially prevalent between spouses when they blame each other for the outcomes of decisions a partner makes or for ignoring each other's suggestions. This habit in marriages also reveals the irony of modern societies' jargon about 'freedom!'

All along, we should align two types of conflicting decisions effectively as well: Those that boost our spirits and resilience, and those made for nurturing our needs, ambitions, family affairs, and social interactions. Building our convictions with humility and pondering the existential points raised in this volume best help us live easier if we can align these two basic categories of major life decisions, while always honouring the sanctity of human spirit.

CHAPTER SIXTEEN
Decisions plus Destiny

Probably we like, even more than sex, to be in control of our lives and make sense of it all. Instead, our regular disappointments and failures make us doubt the value of our diligent plans, decisions, analyses, labour, and sacrifices. We blame destiny, bad karma, social unfairness, or people's malice and stupidity, which are all real factors tainting everybody's life, in fact.

SO, REALLY! Why has God created such an imperfect world for humans *specifically* (or inadvertently!) is just mind-boggling! Or has He?! Humans' controversial character, in fact, stirs an odd dilemma when we ponder the amazing precision and harmony gone into the creation and growth of the universe itself, the planet Earth, and even the ingenuity of human body and brain. Thus, why are humans so incompetent to get along and build a peaceful world for themselves? Has possibly God made humans sloppily; or purposely so wicked for His fun?

Even more amazing than this bizarre phenomenon—humans' evil nature—is our innate keenness and dire tenacity to disregard our brains' capacity to design a practical lifestyle that can mitigate our misery, confusion, and devilry. In fact, our resistance to find a more civilized means of existence appears like a well-designed scheme for perpetual human torture, something that other species seem not to bear as much. Their natural serenity and resignation simply makes us look foolish and envy their low intelligence, simplicity, and apparent peace. Our irritating curiosity to fathom the reasons for humans' chronic misery appears like still another major proof about this colossal imperfection of human species.

Why are we so keen intuitively, as if obliged, to prove our foolishness? Why should our thinking ability (disability?) cause us more pains than animals endure? Why cannot we find a means of coexistence like them and spread a lasting tranquility to make even animals jealous? *All these blasphemous questions we ask our spirits regularly to no avail stir added pains and sins, too!!*

But can we ever at least justify our idiocy or only blame God?

A plausible conclusion is that humans' petty existence, amidst the perfect universe, is only a miniscule, irrelevant, and accidental by-product of the creation with no particular design besides their evolution and physical forms. In that sense, human life has no purpose, either—in the big scheme of existence, nor at a personal level as an allegedly thinking species. This gloomy conclusion, however, contradicts this trilogy's discussions about the sanctity of human spirit and mind. Sadly, this conflict is just another life dichotomy we cannot elude, since we have many both positive and negative evidences about humans' role in the universe. We must fight with this big conflict forever, doubt our senses, whine hopelessly and helplessly, and still try to endure our being on a spiritual path of salvation. This and many other dilemmas and dichotomies in our lives have become sources of our misery, no matter how these painful conflicts have been created and why. Whether our mental (dis)abilities or our genetic characteristics make us so incapable of finding peace does not matter at the end, anyway, if we cannot overcome these debilities somehow.

Then again, regardless of humans' place in the universe or their ability to find the purpose of their existence eventually, we cannot dismiss the likely role of some supernatural forces that rule our destiny rather randomly. These instinctive, forceful sentiments (plus our nagging existential questions) keep us bewildered and unhappy. Thus, we just accept our inability to grasp these alleged supernatural forces even less than we can ever understand human nature. Dwelling over God's wisdom and plans about human life would also only stir depression and tension. The ongoing quarrels amongst philosophers, spiritualists, and scientists would also only raise our confusion, since we are such an imperfect, but curious, species. The book, *War of the Worldviews*, by Deepak Chopra and Leonard Mlodinow, reveals humans' struggles for answers that do not seem to be forthcoming anytime soon.

This author's life experiences discussed in Chapter Ten offer some good examples of destiny and decisions working together mysteriously. They demonstrate how proactive decision-making had been necessary to implement risky and adventurous plans, but more importantly the fact that without some divine interventions those plans would not have materialized. At the same time, the overall tally of the author's life, as given at the end of Chapter Ten, shows the unreliability of both our decisions and destiny. On the one hand, we do not want to fight our fate or lose faith in its divine purpose. On the other hand, trusting fate is hard without any chance of ever knowing the reasons behind our erratic luck, or wondering why God has destined a gloomy fate on us, despite our divine beliefs and sincere efforts.

Considering our seeming helplessness within this mysterious universe, *just* trusting fate *somewhat* patiently often feels easier to us. Our lifetime hardship and quarrels to realize our decisions and desires is stressful and frustrating, after all. Then again, we notice that our bad decisions, vacillations, doubts, or faiths in fate per se, have all contributed to our doomed destiny, too. We realize our past major mistakes when we are a bit more objective and less fatalistic. We acknowledge that our regrets or misfortunes are normally the result of bad decisions or indecisions in the past.

Thus, we feel obliged to make our best decisions rationally regardless of our beliefs. After all, our instinctual need to control our lives makes us act no matter how much we trust fate. Heck, we crave to control other people's lives, too, if we could. We all like to be big leaders and proactive. Thus, we try to make good judgments and assess our options and choices. Few of us have the patience and courage to rely on destiny alone, not to mention the impression of naivety that such attitude gives to others. Usually, we strive to strike a balance without knowing how best to achieve it. We merely do our best and hope that the right mix of 'destiny' and 'decisions' would afford us a better chance for survival and happiness than depending merely on fate or ignoring it outright. Few of us have the courage and arrogance to deny fate fully and show our shortsightedness. What other rational choice have we? Relying fully on fate or trusting only our wisdom merely reflects our gullibility, rigidity, and arrogance. Still, discovering the right balance remains tough and personal. All along, our lasting qualm for trusting fate at least a bit or making more decisions and plans proactively drains our minds and spirits, often in vain. *The quality and sincerity of a person's relationship with his/her God affect the level of trust s/he develops in fate as well! But not vice-versa, as some scholars and religions have proposed!!*

Ultimately, our lifetime routine doubts and disappointments besiege our brains no matter how much we trust destiny and our decision-making ability. Still, as reiterated in several places in this trilogy, we must always remember that one simple (maybe innocent) mistake, or a wrong turn, could ruin our lives forever.

Decision-making Options

We often blame ourselves for not thinking properly and making the right decisions when we had had a chance. We also regret our emotional and hasty decisions. We often gain this wisdom when our errors seem irreparable. In all, our regrets for making wrong decisions or acting sloppily in the past often exceed the pleasures of making proper, timely decisions.

Usually, we make our decisions by i) playing an active role, ii) letting someone else make them for us, or iii) leaving them to fate (to live in the now ourselves!) One of these choices prevails either through our conscious decision or by the force of nature. Yet, commonsense dictates that playing an active role is more sensible than letting someone else control our lives or waiting for things to happen to us without adequate control and preparation. At the same time, active decision-making takes a lot of energy and brains. It needs solid decision criteria, a reliable information base, valid values, time, patience to gauge all the relevant factors, and ability to choose and analyse *real* facts. To get a full picture about any vital decision, we must really take our time patiently to ponder many angles, elements and situations surrounding it.

We all recognize and study decision variables subconsciously, since we believe our success and happiness depend on the quality of our decisions and their timeliness. Our egological tendencies[§§] and emotions also goad us to make fast judgments and decisions. Yet, procrastinating feels easier, as making decisions brings more responsibility and higher risks of failure. Our chronic doubts and laziness also deter our decision-making chore.

Meanwhile, most of us learn that, in the large scheme of things, no absolute answers exist for life dilemmas, considering people's wide misperceptions of reality. Everything is relative in terms of time and circumstance, including people's attitudes and decisions based on their peculiar tastes, perceptions, Egos, greed, personal interests, outlooks, and the prevailing socioeconomic pressures. Thus, in fact, our doubts and reasons about humans' dire disability to fathom life appear quite valid, which then justify their difficulties for making decisions, especially the right ones.

Thus, in this chapter, decision factors, conditions, elements, and criteria are discussed in some detail along with our habits and motives for making, or eluding, decisions. Surely, observing all this diligence, especially when pressed for a fast decision, is hard due to the enormity of variables and risks involved. Still, recalling or studying the following decision variables is especially vital for tackling life's major decisions discussed in Vol. III of this trilogy.

[§§] Egological tendency is explained in Appendix A at the end of the book.

For one thing, making decisions does not always mean taking actions or risks. Rather, even a measured decision not to proceed with an action is indeed a sign of wisdom and firm commitment. Decision-making is merely for taking charge of a critical question or situation and acting upon it in a timely manner with a plan rather than procrastinating with crude excuses. Of course, we are trained to give a higher significance to active decisions, because passive decisions usually come across as one's inability to take action or risks. This mentality sometimes even forces us into bad decisions just to feel proactive and decisive.

An active decision leads to a specific action that normally brings challenge, risk, change, and vitality. For example, we may be pondering for some time to buy a house. All the information about the market condition and personal income are available, yet uncertainties about future always exist. Perhaps mortgage rates are low, so we favour the decision of buying a house seriously. In this situation, a decision to buy is 'active,' because some actions and risks are necessary. A decision not to buy is 'passive,' simply because we do nothing, maybe in fears of losing our employment or interest rates going up after we took on a large mortgage.

Still, a passive decision is preferred over *indecision* that only reflect our inability to commit ourselves one way or other, until it is too late; e.g., market conditions change adversely, or we use our down-payment on some other project. A passive decision shows individual's ability to assess the situation, chose an option, get mentally ready for the worst outcome, and move on.

The advantages of active over passive decisions depend also on the type, risks, and timing of a decision. Major life decisions, in particular, have much higher consequences, either positively or negatively, depending on the timeliness and effectiveness of our decisions. For example, we appreciate the gravity and difficulty of a decision about marriage, compared with a simpler one, such as a decision on the kind of automobile to buy. Overall, however, the significance of an active or passive decision lies in our ability to gauge the value of potential rewards, risks, and the advantages of avoiding unnecessary headaches, compared with the possible loss of opportunities (especially in relation to major decisions).

Our outlooks, perceptions of our real needs, priorities in life at certain points, personalities, and risk orientation goad us to be an active or passive decision-maker overall. For active decisions, we assess the chances of rewards in line with the level of risk. We try to project the expected outcome by using available information and insight about future possible events. However, we should still prepare ourselves for a totally different outcome as well. Passive decisions eliminate the stress and hassles of active decisions at the cost of bypassing potential opportunities and rewards. Still, passive decisions might also reflect our wisdom for choosing a simpler, natural lifestyle, instead of wasting our brains and lives in pursuit of our endless crude ambitions.

Similar analyses of opportunities and risks can also be made for our indecision. However, the main drawback of indecision lies in the frustration of not knowing what we really want or must do. The problem of indecision stems mainly from our inabilities to take charge of our life direction. We may pretend or presume that our indecision implies our complete faith in destiny and letting things happen naturally. However, trusting fate is different from allowing all kinds of external sources and forces interfere and affect the direction of our lives. Our *commonsense* often insists that it is unwise to remain passive and let our future be severely affected by outside forces when we have enough intelligence and willpower to play a role. The minimum merit of our decisions is that they often offset the effects of adverse external forces (mainly other people) that keep interfering with our lives for their own benefits. Taking such malicious interferences and influences as a logical and inherent part of destiny is not *usually* wise, though we cannot dismiss fate fully, either. An extreme case is our inability to decide about our careers or our real interests in life.

Indecision is attributed to chronic doubtfulness, laziness, low self-image and confidence. Then again, making good decisions is surely too tricky about so many uncertainties besieging us!

Actually, we can be sure only about two things in this world: We are granted a physical existence at a special time accidentally, and this journey ends at another specific moment usually with lots of despair, anguish, and regrets. Beyond these two certainties, everything else occurs to people in the context of perceptions, questions, uncertainties, hopes, and doubts, while we feel obliged to understand the value of our lives, find the right answers, and make the right decisions.

Decision-making Factors (shown in bold italics in this section)

Naturally, a major factor for decision-making is access to right *information*. Still, we are usually deceived or tempted by corrupt information that is spread maliciously or carelessly. It is hard to detect misinformation in greed-driven societies. We may learn to doubt the information that some so-called professionals, such as investment advisors, car dealers, real estate and insurance agents, mechanics, lawyers, and incompetent or greedy physicians often provide. These bad experiences and mistrusts raise our chronic doubts regarding the state of our societies and human nature.

Uncertainty is another big factor affecting our decisions, since we abhor *risks* and *disappointments*, which are, in fact, two other decision-making factors by themselves. ***Outlook, personality, logic, and indecision angst*** are other factors affecting us during the decision-making process. For example, some people usually feel less worried, consciously or ignorantly, about future—for 'living in the now,' perhaps. However, most of us are usually concerned regarding the long-term implications of our decisions and their impacts on our future. We prefer to work harder, and forego the luxury of living in the now, to secure a longer-lasting peace of mind and a more stable future. There is always going to be a trade off: We can work hard and accept some inconvenience now for enjoying a less stressful life in the long run, compared with situations where people prefer to 'live in the now' fully or somewhat. The latter group is either nonchalant or ignorant about the risks of their lax personality and facing more uncertainties all their lives. Again, it is hard to say which group is right or luckier in terms of their life philosophy. A major issue, nowadays, is that society and merchants encourage people to spend more money, be carefree, and focus on today, which are all recipes for wrong decisions and losing track of one's life.

Our ***approach, mentality, and diligence*** are other important factors that influence the outcomes of our decisions. Our brains' constant effort to predict and assess our choices is for weighing risks versus the value of success, and then using this information to adjust the criteria for future decisions or correct bad decisions if possible. Deep in our unconscious, we usually seek consistency and harmony in our lives regardless of our personalities, even if we are an easygoing person wishing to live only in the now. After all, everybody feels elation or defeat by the levels of turmoil and tension in his/her life. Ironically, we also often feel the vanity of our lifetime efforts for some pointless goals or affection around some lousy, confused humans! Another big dichotomy!

On the one hand, we mostly *prefer* intuitively to use uniform and reliable criteria for our decisions based on our intelligence, beliefs, and life philosophy. On the other hand, most people make their decisions quickly (often hastily) just to move on, because indecision feels unattractive or a sign of self-doubt. Besides, our impatience and arrogance prevent long reflections before making our decisions. This dire human habit is explained in Appendices A and B at the end of the book. We abhor the stress of analysing our options and wrestling with the ***unknown*** too long. We also like to mitigate the likelihood of feeling ***guilt*** later for choosing wrong options, especially after long contemplation. The more we fuss over a decision now, the more pains of guilt and failure we might face later as well. Thus, we prefer to suppress our doubts, move on fast, and feel less guilt if the outcomes do not turn out as expected. Instead, we always like to blame our destiny, bad luck, or other people for our agony of defeat after our hasty decisions. That is both easier and less stressful than handling our doubts and options more seriously with patience. After all, quick decision-making makes us look decisive and feels less stressful in the short run; no responsibility and no pains of thinking and exhausting our brains. Right? Wrong? Now, which option is wiser is hard to say, as people have different personalities, priorities, and preferences. Human logic does not follow a special strategy or standard.

Still, we should remember: The outcome of many decisions made today become apparent only several (or many) years later, often when correction is impossible and our lives feel stressful or at least unfulfilling. Especially, from millions of decisions we make in our lives, about a dozen have the greatest impact on our health and happiness. We make these 'major life decisions' to prosper within the routine life structure, as discussed in Vol. III of this trilogy. At the same time, making the right decisions about these handful major life issues is getting harder every day due to the rising social complexities and our eagerness (and frustration) to prove our abilities and individualism. All these factors add up and make decision-making a tough challenge, nowadays.

Besides all these hurdles, most of our major decisions must be made at an early age, prior to 30 or so, when unfortunately, as a young person, we are driven by passion and sexuality, have the least experience about life, and are quite careless in our views of life beyond those youthful aspirations. As a young person, we also feel both invincible and wise, so make more hasty and risky decisions. For example, we may get trapped in a lifelong boring profession due to our shoddy decisions about education or career. Most of us find it easier to just follow social norms and values, e.g., get a degree, anyway. Then again, many people with limited education and ambitions succeed in pursuing a less stressful life that feels fulfilling or at least not boring. The point is that making the right choices is getting harder, especially in modern societies driven by superficial values and mechanisms. Instead of thinking independently and building our lifestyles and beliefs, we naively trust the social order, although we often notice how our modern lifestyles are causing us only more stress, disappointments, and confusion. We ignore that our societies are running out of both economic and moral resources.

Especially, socioeconomic's rising complexities demand extra attention to the accuracy of our decisions, while our social needs set the path of our lives. Our choices show the authenticity of our needs and personalities or our naiveté. The outcomes of many decisions made mechanically by imitating people often damage our lives significantly, if not entirely, e.g., a bad marriage. We learn only years later how naïve and idealistic we had been. In particular, the mentality of 'taking life in our strides and living in the now'—to mitigate our disappointments and stress supposedly—might ruin our future. This liberal philosophical slogan goads people to undermine the complexity of life decisions (in order to 'live in the now' most actively). This mentality causes only more frustration and suffering later.

Without making objective judgments and decisions today, we would usually face dead-ends and desperation eventually. We would get trapped in life's processes and pay a high price for our negligence all our lives. Especially, downplaying the criticality of *major life decisions* or our doubts about the right course of action might lead to self-destruction and suicidal thoughts. Yet, at this juncture, even suicide would not stand the basic test of logic, let alone offering a valid justification. At best, it reflects the frailty of any life philosophy that might support suicide as an option for a healthy person. It often shows our failure to think straight around the decisions factors listed in this chapter to make good decisions, follow a simple lifestyle, and learn to live with the outcomes.

Our decision criteria are often built around misleading social values, too. Blindly following social teachings and routines might mislead us completely, because they are built, nowadays, only for serving the interests of certain groups and businesses and not the public. This means we need sounder decision criteria based on a proper personal life philosophy and altruistic convictions.

Naturally, making the right decisions thoughtfully in a timely manner is vital for our own welfare and long-term sanity. They must be effective, since predicting the implications of our shoddy lifestyles and dreams are getting harder, nowadays. Furthermore, with so much emphasis on individualism, a general formula or philosophy cannot suit or satisfy everybody anymore. Only our personal philosophies and life path can serve our unique needs, especially the psychological and spiritual ones. All these decision factors and conditions demand our lifetime scrutiny.

Decision-making Conditions

Two sets of conditions contribute to the decision-making process:

A. We **feel ready** to make a decision, as:
1. We believe to have all the necessary information,
2. We are too emotionally attached to a situation or person and do not care about the accuracy of information or the validity of our reasons,
3. A decision is required quickly (forced) despite the absence of all information,
4. Enough information would never become available, so we prefer to accept the risks and consequences, or
5. We feel a combination of the above four.

B. We **delay** making a decision, since we have doubts about:
6. The quality or validity of the information,
7. The timing or urgency,
8. The level of risks and consequences of the decision,
9. Taking risks in general and facing the unknown, or
10. A combination of the above four.

It is hard to generalize whether our doubts normally hinder our decision-making ability or actually help us by delaying our decisions until we are satisfied about all the required conditions and information. Besides its type, a decision also depends on a person's level of intelligence, personality, awareness about the nature or rationality of his/her doubts. These conclusions sound useless for enhancing our decision-making abilities; it makes us wonder when doubts are warranted or only nuisance—back to square one! One might even argue that considering our doubts a positive factor is absurd, as they impair our judgment and action about a decision at hand. As explained in the previous chapters, however, exploring the sources and meanings of our doubts can sharpen our judgments and awareness. Those discussions might be also useful for distinguishing positive and negative doubts (vibes) and using them properly for decision-making.

Sadly, most of us are often poor decision makers, since we do not realize, 1) the right decision conditions and timing, and 2) the nature and roots of our doubts. This general awareness (and the ten conditions of decision-making noted above) offers a platform for analysis when a decision is needed. It also helps to gauge the causes of our hasty decisions or procrastination. Obviously, a calculated decision to 'not make a decision' is better than our procrastination, which looks like ignoring the need for a decision and our inability to grasp our options and solutions. Our goal is to bring all the relevant data to a conscious level and process them together. If we decide to 'do nothing' after a careful processing of data, that would be a worthy 'decision,' though possibly not an effective one. It might only help us overcome our doubtfulness, but most likely does not eliminate our doubts.

Decision-making Elements

The following main elements of decision-making appear rather obvious to all of us, yet we do not consider them consciously and patiently to raise the quality and integrity of our decisions:

a) The evidence and criteria for measuring it.
b) The validity of decision objectives.
c) The strengths of our incentives.
d) Personal commitment and motivation.
e) Timing.

The evidence and criteria: Besides strong evidence to support our decision, we need solid and objective criteria to validate the soundness of the evidence, but also control our soft emotions. Yet, we often invent some superficial evidences only for justifying our predispositions, misperceptions, crude logic, and temptations. For example, when we think our marriage is doomed, we choose any evidence to support our decision and use biased criteria to assess and present only certain kinds of evidences. Thus, we often end up making a bad decision, while the outcome only reiterates our egoistic attitude to ourselves and others. Naturally, the means of validating the criteria and assessing the evidence through both analysis and commonsense are also extremely important, thus decision criteria are analysed further on page 332.

The purpose: Every decision must have one or more objectives, but usually, we ignore or undermine the right ones or adopt false purposes that change the whole scope of the decision. We do this often due to our emotional and hasty reaction to a situation, event, or person. For example, when we are angry with our children or spouse, we may conclude that they are intentionally hurting us or ignoring our individuality or authority. Therefore, we decide to retaliate in our own ways, and thus create a tenser relationship with lesser chances of understanding the real issues concerning everybody. In fact, in situations like these, we may be in fault for two things. First, we might have misunderstood our spouse or children's comments, or have been agitated by the way they have presented their points. Second, we adopt a false objective (e.g., retaliation) to make a decision (which we think is necessary fast). In such situations, especially when we are emotionally pressed or depressed, it is wiser to avoid making judgments and decisions until we get a chance to cool down and understand the objectives of the parties involved, but more crucially validate the purpose or timing of our decision (reaction).

Not making a decision would definitely be to our advantage if it were not supported by legitimate and constructive intentions. In the end, we would maintain our physical and mental health better by not wasting our lives on decisions with malicious, unrealistic, or irrelevant purposes. Also, we get a better chance to boost our relationships by ignoring people's vindictive challenges unless they get out of control.

Sometimes, problems arise from our unrealistic or irrelevant objectives. For example, we might decide to do higher education for getting rich. This objective is both unrealistic and irrelevant for the decision of pursuing higher education. It is unrealistic, since higher education is no guarantee for finding opportunities to get rich. And it is irrelevant, because higher education is mainly for applying our potentialities in the service of humanity, and for self-actualization, etc. As another example, a marriage decision is not for making a change in our lives or satisfying some egoistic personal needs, including our financial or mental deficiencies. It probably is not for having children per se, either, never mind for the purpose of sex. All these demented objectives create a wrong mental vision of our purpose and criteria for making decisions, thus failure becomes inevitable.

The incentives: Every decision has its potential consequences, which we must predict as best we can. We should be willing to take the risks of being wrong, while looking forward to some kind of a positive outcome. Thus, an incentive usually drives our decision, although sometimes we make a decision without any tangible incentive attached to it. We do it only out of pride, fear, or egoism.

The incentives and objectives of a decision imply different things, although they are closely related and sometimes the same. The purpose of a decision is to accomplish a goal, but incentive is the reason substantiating that target. Our incentive determines why we pursue this objective and what happens when we get there. Another way to distinguish the objective and the incentive is to think of them as 'what' and 'why' of a decision respectively. The objective is *what* we aim for. The incentive is *why* we do it.

Both 'what' and 'why' of making a decision should be valuable and unselfish. Distinguishing what and why is also important.

Both the objectives and incentives of any decision should be legitimate and relevant, too. The incentive of 'seeing somebody suffer' as a result of our decision is not legitimate or relevant. The incentive of making a lot of money in a certain investment is not directly relevant and valid for finding the ultimate purpose of life, i.e., peace of mind, either. Maybe what we do with the money creates a better vision of an incentive for our decision. We might, for example, imagine a relaxing vacation with the money we earn for the extra work we do. The value and vision of an incentive reduces the level of stress that a decision and subsequent efforts cause. Our decisions lacking a legitimate, relevant purpose cause stress. We often have many false incentives like making 'more money than we ever need,' or 'taking revenge.' However, these types of criteria cannot be legitimate *purposes* or *incentives* for planning and working too hard or bearing immense emotional burdens.

Often, even our major decisions may have to be made with inadequate information or options, which means the predictable outcomes (and maybe even our incentives) are often tenuous and speculative. For example, with limited opportunities or financial resources to get a desired education, we are forced to compromise and pursue an education and career that may prove a waste of our lives, or conversely result in a successfully quiet life, though our incentives had not been quite clear or valid initially. Nevertheless, a vision of some tangible incentives increases our motivation for accepting the risks and hardships that are usually required for accomplishing the tough objectives of our decisions.

We get our life energy from our achievements. We need to achieve something in order to fuel our life journey forward. This inherent, strong need makes us seek all kinds of adventures and take risks. Sometimes, we even adhere to negative activities and thoughts (with no legitimate purpose and incentive) in hopes of feeling successful and getting enough energy to endure life. We adopt artificial and perhaps illegitimate incentives for ourselves to make decisions that have no value for enriching our lives.

The commitment: The overall commitment and motivation for our decisions and subsequent implementation of their details are naturally important for achieving good results. Commitment and motivation result directly from the three decision elements noted above: evidence, purpose, and incentive. Usually when we use these elements properly in decision-making, we gain adequate momentum and motivation to make decisions and pursue them methodically—unless a person is lazy or too passive by nature. Enthusiasm and ownership of a decision are other elements that make our decisions successful. Sometimes, we might seem to be involved with a decision, whereas in reality we are participating only because we have to, or only like to pretend being interested. Sometimes, we are in fact interested in the success of a decision, but do not have the time or patience to spend on the required work. Thus, we delegate it to somebody else and hope that we get the exact results. Sometimes, we do not have the right criteria for making important decisions, thus rely on the judgment of others often recklessly, e.g., about a person we want to marry.

On the other hand, we sometimes impose our decisions upon others, or do not create the right atmosphere for teamwork and involvement of people who have, or should have, some say or interests in the decision. Again, like the example of choosing a companion, we might dominant the situation and prevent the full participation of our partner in discussions and decisions that would affect the crucial decision of marriage. Thus, we face sad consequences when both parties have not been fully involved and committed to the decision for the right reasons. They are there for the wrong incentives; and we do not realize it until it is too late. In fact, if the persons directly affected by a major decision show reluctance to express their viewpoints openly, or merely submit to our whims casually, we must be alarmed about the imminent failure of that decision if we proceed. This lack of commitment would taint the process. Sooner or later, the signs of opposition or apathy would surface and ruin the outcome.

Normally, we associate decision-making with freewill, though in reality many decisions are a form of compromise or coercion —often in inconspicuous manners. Accordingly, when people are not responsible for their decisions, they are less inclined to take ownership of them and implement them. People's commitment to any decision, and its success, is necessarily a function of how much they have contributed in making and developing it. In all, the chances of success of any decision depend on the level of initial analysis, including our doubts, that has gone into it.

The timing: The lengthy discussions about 'timing limitation' in Chapter Nine demonstrate the importance of timing as a vital decision-making element.

Decision-making Criteria

All our decisions, e.g., what to eat, where to go, what kind of education to get, whom to marry, etc., should make sense. Thus, we set certain criteria based on our personal tastes, preferences, and lifestyles, which give different emphasis to material things, physical pleasures, and soul-searching objectives. We build our decision criteria consciously or subconsciously to evaluate our decisions prudently and pursue our primary goals consistently in line with a personal life philosophy. Our decision criteria also depend on the nature of decision, including its importance, risks, timing, plus all the decision factors, conditions, and elements noted in this chapter. Every decision must have a main objective and a huge incentive, yet all our decisions have a few common, ultimate goals, e.g., our lifelong health, success, and happiness. We make our decisions based on the values (criteria) that make sense within our life philosophy to fulfil our long-term needs.

Intuitively, we seek a life path that can bring us a manageable routine and peace of mind. We imagine that our choice is correct and is the best option for reaching our ultimate goals. However, all prevalent life paths in human history have failed to bring us a real sense of success or lasting happiness. Our lousy lifestyles and sloppy decision criteria supporting them have not given us even some solace. In fact, our value systems and cultures have been preventing us from finding even some basic peace of mind, let alone ultimate happiness. Meanwhile, our raw positive thinking mottos and obsession to find happiness have caused us all more confusions. They have only made us raise our expectations from life, instead of learning the reality of living in our complex and callous societies with all sorts of hardships we must overcome.

Contrary to what we like to believe, happiness and success are not absolute states to reach on a permanent basis. We cannot grasp even their meanings and offer a path towards them. Instead, we have invented some raw decision criteria for various issues in life, like getting good grades at school or accumulating wealth as measures of success and eventual happiness. We teach children to work and compete hard. However, outside these elementary definitions of success and happiness, we have failed to formulate good ideas to share with others about real success and happiness. Actually, it is both depressing and surprising that we have not, as human beings, been able to come up with a more practical way of sharing peace and contentment among us. Our philosophers and prophets in the last millenniums have failed to come up with guidelines that could help us be better humans and suffer less. We have all failed collectively as humans to defeat superstitions, religious fanaticism, greed, and superficialities, too, in order to find a more meaningful and peaceful life for all.

Theoretically, at least, we imagine that a general structured process of thinking could help the public find a suitable life path and the right decision criteria for a practical sense of success and happiness. The objective is not to restrict personal intuition and creativity, but rather increase all of those by providing a good framework and philosophical background to guide people think outside the box and get a better sense of reality. We need tools to develop useful decision criteria that can support our major life decisions at least and prevent the extra pains of living, nowadays.

As a first step, maybe we should change our mentalities about 'happiness,' in order to make our life decisions easier and more realistic. Maybe choosing simpler goals such as 'coexistence' and 'peace of mind,' as main criteria for making major life decisions, is more sensible. That is, regardless of our criteria of success, our ultimate objective (incentive) must be 'to achieve peace of mind' —contentment—and not necessarily happiness. Whether and how either happiness or peace of mind can be found depends still on an individual's perception of these concepts, and his/her point of reference in life. Many people, in fact, think of 'pleasure' when imagining happiness. On the other hand, 'peace of mind' only needs a simple lifestyle to increase one's independence and chances of living with minimal stress and worries in the long run, which means merely contentment, instead of pleasures, wealth, and power. Still, 'peace of mind' would be an easier and more realistic incentive (and criterion) to define and pursue, compared to 'happiness,' which is only a myth. The obstacle for pursuing 'peace of mind' is that one should develop a solid foundation of thoughts that can keep one's spirit high in a simple lifestyle.

Another Warning for the Youths

Probably the warning for the youths printed at the beginning of the book makes even more sense now. Thus, the author suggests another review of that short section, especially to the youths.

Reading Appendix A at the end of the book about humans' egological harmful tendency is highly recommended to the youth as well. In fact, this egological shortfall harms youths the most.

Appendices B and C, especially the former, are also highly useful for the youths.

Epilogue

People's sense of emptiness and confusion are largely due to their spirituality needs being muddled in our phony societies. We are mostly unaware of this mental deprivation souring our spirits, as we are too distracted by our efforts for survival, life's hardships, and religions. Nor do we get an incentive to think outside the box and learn personally about our innate need for spirituality mostly for coping with life's pains within a rather stoic, sacred lifestyle.

On the one hand, spirituality is humans' basic need that must be satisfied in order to stop hurting one another so much. On the other hand, religions have been misguiding us about both divinity and social living. Merely a large amount of fanciful stories and promises about God has been dumped on people. Teaching such archaic religious routines or atheism to our kids, as two handy alternatives, nowadays, is also harmful for them and humanity.

This book's crude ideas about finding spiritualism personally through lots of reflections and devotion merely for 'self'-growth and mere mortal salvation must have also sounded weird to many readers. Even sounding more far-fetched is the author's ideal of a truer spiritualism replacing fanaticism, ignorance, and violence that religions have advocated through so much nonsense about God. Still, a rational knowledge of spirituality also seems urgent to clarify its practical purposes, processes, and principles at least. After all, is not yet time for us to say, 'Enough is enough…??!!'

Clearly, expecting people define and develop their spirituality rituals just in hopes of living easier without expecting any rewards, such as a promise of afterlife, is too much. Trusting the sanctity of our spirit per se to stir our innate divinity is also excessive for us lazy humans with mediocre patience, intelligence, and ethics. Instead, sticking to our religious rituals superficially feels simpler and more fun now that the modern world lets us mix religion with our whimsical lifestyles and obsessions for wealth, love, and happiness so liberally. Giving up our conveniently mixed phony lifestyles and religions needs an incredibly (magical) incentive.

A big hurdle is that we have never been taught the discipline and wisdom to fathom a simpler path of life for self-awareness and self-realization by curbing our obsession for pleasure and investing some time and efforts on pure spiritualism. Our modern jargons and teachings lure our ambitious minds and our religions promise us a chance for immortality. In all, humans are now too self-absorbed with no mindset and patience to seek spirituality just for boosting their spirits or finding peace and enlightenment. Any suggestion to control our materialistic mentalities and thirst for pleasures to find peace and happiness through self-developed spirituality simply feels foolish to us spoiled humans now.

Thus, a big question is whether and how any other device, if not our fortified spirits, might ever help us curb our egotistical and lustful atrocities worldwide. Or could people ever realize the sanctity of a moralistic lifestyle just for self-realization contrary to what they are used to so much. This radical mentality must bring them tangible results worth their sacrifices. Still, some people's inherent urges for health, self-esteem, and peace could eventually give them enough incentive to strive for 'self'-growth and a finer lifestyle as an ultimate personal victory in life along with likely enlightenment. A self-awareness ritual stresses on these objectives to trigger people's natural drive (incentive) for spiritualism in hopes of accessing and boosting their deprived spirits.

As noted in other parts of this trilogy, this author believes that some of humans' higher needs on Maslow's 'personal needs tree' must indeed be viewed and treated as basic psychological needs. For example, our need for a companion is so strong it should be considered a basic need in modern societies; at least in hopes of adjusting people's mentality about this matter, which might then mitigate the rising level of failures in marriages and societies. The same thing can also be said for our deprived need for spirituality. While it sits at the highest level of Maslow's needs hierarchy in line with self-actualization, treating spirituality as a basic need can surely boost both humans' personal welfare and humanity in general—mostly in hopes avoiding our looming demise as well.

Eventually, if we succeed, a comprehensive presentation of spirituality can offer simple rituals to reach our souls and raise our consciousness based on our divine reflections and efforts to find our personal connections with the universe. We might also invent a uniform means of divine self-realization, which is built around plausible ideologies and goals through ongoing research, very much the same way science emerges, grows, and assists us.

Any spirituality teaching must somehow consider and respect people's general weakness to contemplate regularly for boosting their self-awareness and spirits. Thus, perhaps the main objective should be to provide incentives and means of reducing people's naiveté and egotism through simple guidelines and disciplines. Maybe they could just help people grasp the purposes of personal spirituality to feed their spirits and curb their sufferings, although we should still cherish our positive doubts about humanity, since no ultimate truth exists for us despite the sanctity of human spirit.

To grasp 'the truths' of existence and spiritualism, we should first speak only the truth to the public and still caution them about some level of doubtfulness that is always needed even for our most *seemingly trustworthy* truths, including our spirits' sanctity.

Let us face the truth honestly!

List of Appendices

Appendix A: Humans' Egological Conditions. 339
Appendix B: Logic Aversion Drive 342
Appendix C: Humans in the Universe 345

Appendix A
Humans' Egological Conditions

Besides its extreme vulnerability discussed in Chapter 2, humans' logic makes us think too highly of ourselves, cherish our naive personalities and outlooks, and boost our egos constantly. Then, our egos return the favour by making every one of us think that our peculiar logic is not only perfect about everything, but also superior to everybody else's. Accordingly, social interactions and sense of cooperation among people deteriorate further when the effects of humans' lousy logic and fat egos combine constantly. This horrendous concerted force, called 'egologic' in this book, causes personality quirks or even psychosis for most people.

Therefore, together, our ego and logic are constantly boosting each other and making a complete fool of us—our poor Self! The effects of egologic can be studied in five major groups of people shown in Diagram A.1.

Diagram A.1: Humans' Egological Conditions

Effects of Human **Ego + Logic** ↘		**Logic**	
		Opinionated	Average
Ego	Extreme	I **Dogmatic** 10%	II **Arrogant** 10%
		V **Narcissist Eccentric** 70%	
	Average	III **Cynical** 5%	IV **Dumb** 5%

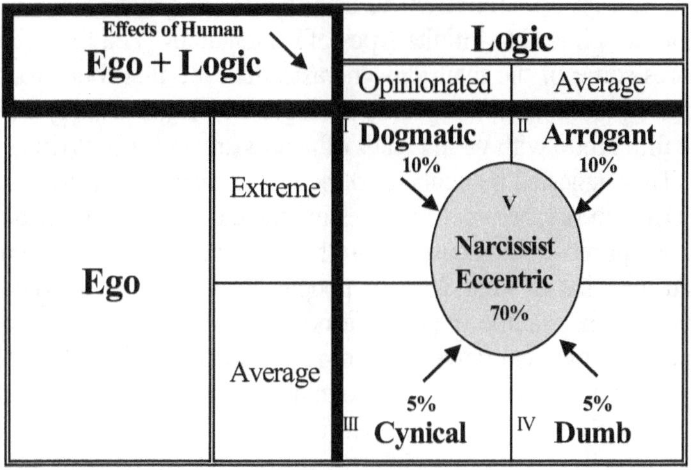

Everybody holds some levels of all the typical idiosyncrasies noted for four oddest groups in the above diagram. Nevertheless, five general classes can be identified according to the following highly detectable symptoms:

I. Extreme Ego in opinionated people makes them dogmatic.
II. Extreme Ego and average Logic make a person arrogant.
III. Average Ego in opinionated people makes them cynical.
IV. Average Ego and average Logic make a person dumb.
V. Varied levels of Ego and Logic create the majority (about 70%) with unique minds, personalities, idiosyncrasies, and qualities. These vast combinations infuse different mixes of narcissism and eccentricity in people, along with traces of dogmatism, arrogance, cynicism, and dumbness that other four groups show too deeply and directly more often. Note that conceit (ego) is usually rooted in humans, especially nowadays, and human logic is very poor overall, anyway.

The first four groups are the outcomes of extreme interactions of ego and logic and contain about 30% of the world population. The fifth group, around 70%, have various degrees of ego and logic, which lead to infinite types of personalities. Yet, this group shares some of the fatal idiosyncrasies that the first four groups have, in addition to the specific egologic effects that usually build the fifth group with varied loads of narcissism and eccentricity.

The suggested percentages of people in each group, as shown in Diagram A.1, are very rough estimates and merely hypothetical for the purpose of discussions in this section. However, it seems plausible that at least 30% of people have extreme egological defects, whereas the majority (around 70%) suffers from some types of egological flaws, plus some lesser degrees of other kinds of idiosyncrasies, including dogmatism, arrogance, cynicism, dumbness, narcissism, and eccentricity.

Naturally, our logic and ego have some useful properties that help us manage our lives and deal with people. Yet, the negative effects of egologic on our personalities are much more severe and noticeable, especially in terms of encountering and humouring people. Humans are controversial mostly due to the effects of their innate egological tendencies.

Human ego and logic enforce each other's potency and cause further deterioration of personality within one of the five noted categories above. Egologic raises humans' vanity exponentially as well, beyond what our ego and logic would usually do on their own already. In effect, egologic makes us a bad person since our demented logic makes us feel so important and our ego makes us trust our logic and self-image wholeheartedly. It makes us lose our objectivity and it kills our incentive for exploring the path of goodness for becoming a better being. **The only way to reduce the egologic effects is to learn some humility.**

Furthermore, egologic effects are many folds more critical in younger people in terms of causing wrong viewpoints and flawed personalities. The younger a person, the more s/he is susceptible to his/her egological tendency for three reasons: 1) a person's logic and objectivity are substantially undeveloped due to limited life experiences, while s/he is also threatened by high emotional tendencies, 2) his/her ego is much more inflated and he/she feels smart, wise, and invincible, and 3) decisions at this stage of one's life are potentially too destructive and most potent for derailing one's destiny. When these three reasons combine, the effects of egologic during a person's early ages are much riskier with high potentials for catastrophe. Therefore, it is even more important for younger people to realize and beware of the repercussions of egologic as explained in this section.

Accordingly, the youths' apathy for the elderly's wisdom—as a tool to mitigate the effects of egologic—is a big disservice to themselves and a major cause of cultural and social demise. They think they are smart, but are really setting the grounds for ruining their own kids' lives with their low senses of reality.

Appendix B
More about Human Logic
Logic Aversion Drive

The following discussions and suggested statistics are theoretical. They are included in this appendix merely as an additional insight about human logic to complement the discussions in Chapter Two and Appendix A. They are mostly hypotheses requiring further studies and speculations. These topics are placed in these two appendices in order to reduce the complication of discussions about logic in the main body of the book.

****

Factors of Human Logical Defects

In addition to humans' emotions, logic limitations, and egological symptoms (as explained in Appendix A and Chapter Two), our decision-making capacity suffers from an even more disturbing condition, which we might call Logic Aversion Drive (LAD). This occurs when we defy our logic adamantly with odd tenacity. That is, even when our logic offers a solid ground for judgment and decision-making, and we can manage both our emotional and egological tendencies, we consciously ignore all the facts and our sensible options due to our preconditioned mindsets, habits, pride, idiosyncrasies, sickness, obsessions, dogmatism, raw ambitions, prejudices, spite, and many other psychological defects. A good example for this pervasive condition—humans' logic aversion drive—is our wealth-gathering obsession. After we accumulate enough wealth to guarantee a rich life even for our grand-grand children, most of us still cannot use our sound logic that screams at us to stop worrying about, or hustling for, more, even at the expense of damaging our body, mind, and spirit even further. Any kind of addiction is another example of our aversion to use logic, or even fighting it doggedly. Even artistic and scientific endeavours, when a person devotes his/her whole life to them, often feel against our logic, because we seem to be wasting our precious lives away. Yet, we, the artists or scientists, writers and philosophers, cannot stop ourselves at the cost of missing many other privileges of existence.

Many reasons exist for our inability to abide by even our own sound logic, but the outcomes and our pains for this shortfall are simply bizarre and educational, especially for self-awareness. For one thing, spite and arrogance often stop our brains from working altogether, let alone using logic. We often even feel our stupidity and loathe ourselves for sabotaging our long-term interests on top of killing our spirits, yet cannot elude our spite and pride. Then, some of us wonder why and suffer even more!

Thus, the following four types of logic-related defects cause a great deal of problems in our lives all by themselves:

- Logic limitations (as discussed on pages 50-60)
- Emotional tendencies (e.g. love) overwhelming our logic.
- Egological symptoms (as discussed in Appendix A)
- Logic aversion drive (discussed in this appendix)

It might be interesting to guess the effects of each of the above factors on the overall degree of humans' decision inaccuracies or insensibilities merely due to our inabilities to i) appreciate the role of logic and related decision factors, and ii) look for possible means of handling each factor *logically*. The author has taken the risk of proposing some rough estimates about people's decision inaccuracy in general due to the effects of the above four human tendencies related to logic. He estimates that at best only 10-40% of humans' decisions are sensible in the overall scheme of things for their ultimate, lasting welfare as shown in Table B.1 on next page. The insensibility of humans' decisions can be measured in the context of the two worlds we live in, i.e., the perceived versus real realities as noted in Chapter Two. (Also, see next page's footnote.)

Table B.1: Decision Inaccuracy Ratings

Factors of Logical Defects (Causes of Bad Decisions)	Within the rules and values of:	
	Perceived[***] Reality World	Real Reality World[***]
1. Logic limitations	10%	15%
2. Emotional tendencies	15%	25%
3. Egological conditions	15%	15%
4. Logic aversion drive	20%	35%
Total tainted decisions	**60%**	**90%**
Fully sensible decisions	**40%**	**10%**

As one or a mix of the above four logic-related deficiencies interfere with our decision-making ability, our daily lives and psychological welfare are compromised, just because we cannot think straight. The author estimates that 60-90% of our decisions are tainted by at least one of these four factors. Any of these four areas of logic-related flaws causes severe imbalance and damages our routines and decisions, yet the fourth one, i.e. Logic Aversion Drive (LAD), interferes with our thought process most often and affects our way of acting and behaving most directly even against our own welfare and logical senses. We keep doing things that we do (or must) suspect to be useless, harmful, and wrong, thus ruin our spirits and a chance for redemption.

If we could invent a process to help people overcome their LAD at least, their miseries would be reduced substantially, the whole social structure would improve drastically, and our chances of becoming better beings would increase substantially as well. For example, just imagine humans realizing that their greed is merely ruining their lives as well as the foundation of human thoughts and social structure.

In fact, if somebody could invent a process to help people overcome their LAD, s/he would become a billionaire!

[***] Real and Perceived Worlds are explained in Vol. I of this trilogy in Chapter Three.

Appendix C
Humans in the Universe
(and in society)

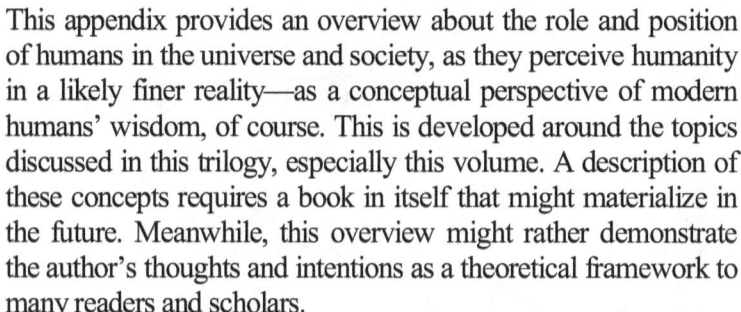

This appendix provides an overview about the role and position of humans in the universe and society, as they perceive humanity in a likely finer reality—as a conceptual perspective of modern humans' wisdom, of course. This is developed around the topics discussed in this trilogy, especially this volume. A description of these concepts requires a book in itself that might materialize in the future. Meanwhile, this overview might rather demonstrate the author's thoughts and intentions as a theoretical framework to many readers and scholars.

The main goal here is to highlight human dimensions briefly within the contexts of i) the universe, and ii) society. **First,** it is suggested that psyche and spirituality are also intrinsic human dimensions besides body, mind, and spirit that were emphasized in this volume. While brain is the engine running human affairs and thoughts, psyche denotes our mental state and nurtures our critical experiences and plans. In the same manner, spirituality reflects our divine wisdom and capacity through our spirit's evolvement in line with our psyche's power and approval.

Second, these five dimensions construct humans' physical and mental capacity for both social living and personal growth into metaphysical spheres. **Third,** besides the idea of body-mind connection, this theorem suggests that all five intrinsic human dimensions interact in the manners shown in Diagram C.1 during at least ten main connections. **Fourth,** these connections develop at least ten main auxiliary human dimensions that we also apply regularly to facilitate our behaviour and personal growth.

Fifth, humans' interfaces with the universe and society create their visions as well as mental (dis)abilities, as demonstrated in Diagrams C.2 and C.3, for the universe and society respectively. **Sixth,** grasping these human dimensions can enrich our lives.

346 Appendix C

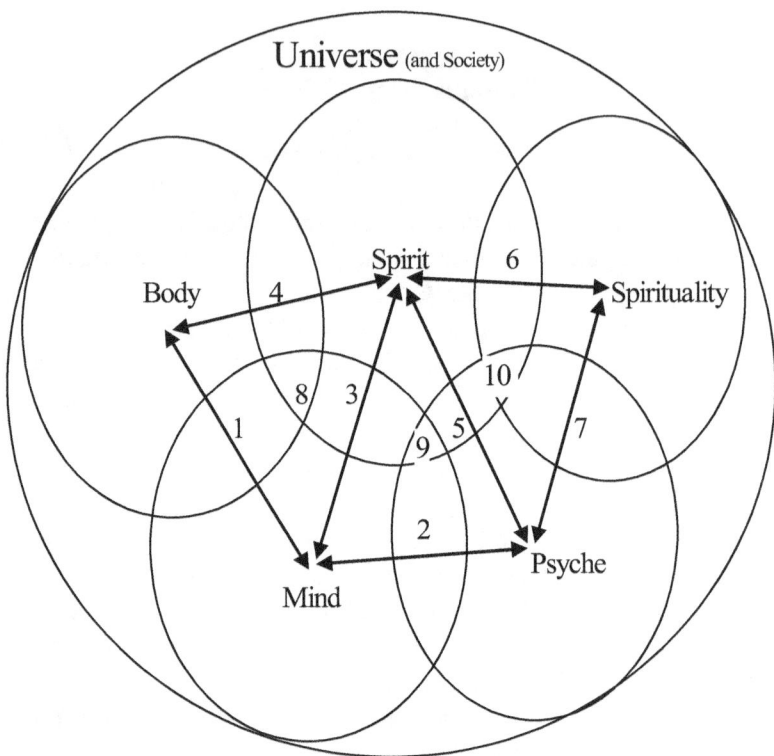

Diagram C.1: Humans' Inner Connections (Front Hemisphere)

Human Inner Connections (Intrinsic Dimensions)	Ref. #	Developed (auxiliary) Human Dimensions* (Outcomes/Symptoms)	Human Drives (Attributes & Processes)
Mind-Body	1	Personality	Actions, needs, decisions, doubts
Mind-Psyche	2	Cognition	Logic, thoughts, intelligence
Mind-Spirit	3	Insight	Feelings, instincts, passion
Spirit-Body	4	Identity	Authenticity, ideals, inner strength
Spirit-Psyche	5	Foresight	Imaginations, curiosity, compassion
Spirit-Spirituality	6	Conscience	Premonition, enlightenment, peace
Psyche-Spirituality	7	Potentialities	Self-actualization, divinity, values
Mind-Body-Spirit	8	Self-awareness	Urges, reflection, resignation
Mind-Spirit-Psyche	9	Self	Self-analysis, self-cleansing, freedom
Psyche-Spirit-Spirituality	10	Consciousness	Wisdom, vision, vivacity

* The relationships among the main ten 'inner connections' and 'developed dimensions' are not absolute, but they all rather overlap with their neighbouring dimensions, e.g., in the case of Personality and Cognition.

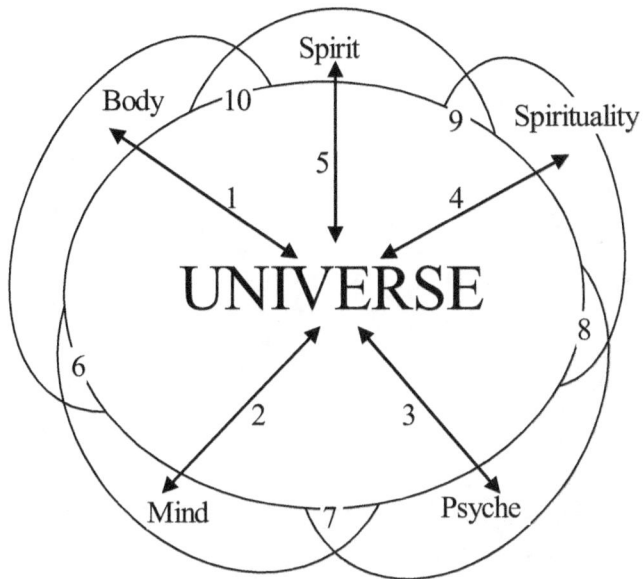

Diagram C.2: Humans' (Main) Outer Connections with the Universe*
(Back Hemisphere)

Universe's Main Connections with:	Ref. #	Principles** Symptoms	Main Outcomes
Body	1	Existence	Life, death, growth
Mind	2	Science	Knowledge, renovation, survival
Psyche	3	Philosophy	Perceived reality, controversy, despair
Spirituality	4	Supernatural	Real reality, truth, awe
Spirit	5	Afterlife	Refuge, salvation, delusion
Body-Mind	6	Nature	Beauty, majesty, mystery, authenticity
Mind-Psyche	7	Facts	Dilemmas, pride, sufferings
Psyche-Spirituality	8	Myths	Ideas, confusion, relief
Spirituality-Spirit	9	Faith	Confidence, Trust, dogmatism
Spirit-Body	10	Beliefs	Experience, hope, conviction

* There are another 16 secondary human connections with the universe that are not shown here, including the combined connection of all five human dimensions with the universe.
** The relationships among the ten 'principles' and ten 'universe connections' are not absolute, but rather they overlap with their neighbouring principles, e.g., in the case of Existence and Science.

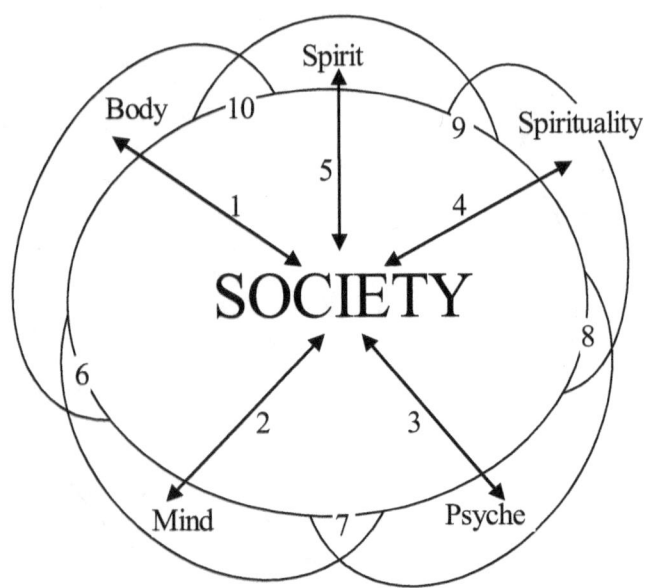

Diagram C.3: Humans' (Main) Outer Connections with Society*

Connections Society with:	Ref. #	Symptoms**	Main Outcomes
Body	1	Slavery	Deprivations, pressures, uncertainty
Mind	2	Limitations	Economy, insecurity, wars
Psyche	3	Manipulations	Greed, egoism, control
Spirituality	4	Speculations	Religions, hostility, hypocrisy
Spirit	5	Fantasy	Love, happiness, success
Body-Mind	6	Superficialities	Artificial needs, consumerism, chaos
Mind-Psyche	7	Obsessions	Neediness, sexuality, psychosis
Psyche-Spirituality	8	Gullibility	Conceit, cruelty, exploitation
Spirituality-Spirit	9	Superstitions	Witchcraft, deceit, credulity
Spirit-Body	10	Anticipation	Stress, competition, disappointments

* There are another 16 secondary human connections with society not shown here, including the combined connection of all five human dimensions with society.
** The relationships among the ten 'symptoms' and ten 'society connections' are not absolute, but rather they overlap with their neighbouring symptoms, e.g., in the case of Slavery and Manipulations.

Thank god, the rules of the universe would always supersede the superficial laws of humans and society!

www.ingramcontent.com/pod-product-compliance
Lightning Source LLC
Chambersburg PA
CBHW020348170426
43200CB00005B/92